Jesuit Education
and Social Change
in El Salvador

GARLAND STUDIES IN HIGHER EDUCATION
VOLUME 5
GARLAND REFERENCE LIBRARY OF SOCIAL SCIENCE
VOLUME 1055

GARLAND STUDIES IN HIGHER EDUCATION

This series is published in cooperation with the Program in Higher Education, School of Education, Boston College, Chestnut Hill, Massachusetts.

PHILIP G. ALTBACH, *Series Editor*

Jesuit Education and Social Change in El Salvador

Charles J. Beirne, S.J.

Garland Publishing, Inc.
New York and London
1996

Library of Congress Cataloging-in-Publication Data

Beirne, S.J., Charles Joseph.
    Jesuit education and social change in El Salvador / Charles J. Beirne, S.J.
        p.   cm. — (Garland reference library of social science ; v. 1055.
Garland studies in higher education ; v. 5)
        Includes bibliographical references (p.   ) and index.
        ISBN 0-8153-2121-X (alk. paper)
        1. Universidad Centroamericana José Simeón Cañas—History.   2. Edu-
cation, Higher—Social aspects—El Salvador.   3. Jesuits—El Salvador.   4.
Social change—El Salvador.   I. Title.   II. Series: Garland reference library
of social science ; v. 1055.   III. Series: Garland reference library of social
science. Garland studies in higher education ; vol. 5.
LE11.S35B45   1996
378.7284—dc20   96–4173
                                                                            CIP

Printed on acid-free, 250-year-life paper
Manufactured in the United States of America

DEDICATION
JOHN JOSEPH MOAKLEY
MEMBER OF CONGRESS
STATESMAN
FRIEND OF THE UNIVERSITY OF CENTRAL AMERICA
FRIEND OF THE PEOPLE OF EL SALVADOR

CONTENTS

SERIES EDITOR'S PREFACE

Higher education is a multifaceted phenomenon in modern society, combining a variety of institutions and an increasing diversity of students, a range of purposes and functions, and different orientations. The series combines research-based monographs, analyses, and discussions of broader issues and reference books related to all aspects of higher education. It is concerned with policy as well as practice from a global perspective. The series is dedicated to illuminating the reality of higher and postsecondary education in contemporary society.

Philip G. Altbach
Boston College

Series Editor's Introduction

I am especially pleased to include *Jesuit Education and Social Change in El Salvador* in the Garland Studies in Higher Education series and to have it associated with the Boston College Center for International Higher Education. This volume is an important book in several respects, and it reflects some of the foci of our center. It tells at least two important stories and provides unusually powerful insights into the challenges faced by universities in developing countries.

Father Charles J. Beirne weaves the tragic story of the murders of the Jesuit priests and others by the El Salvador military with a broader discussion of the development of the Universidad Centroamericana in El Salvador. The two stories are directly related. The priests were killed precisely because they were building a university committed to democratic values and social change. In the midst of El Salvador's bloody civil war, this was a truly subversive activity, and the Jesuits paid a high price for their commitment.

This tragic event is placed in the broader context of higher education development in the Third World. Father Beirne shows not only that the Universidad Centroamericana was trying to build an effective academic institution in a very hostile environment, but also that this particular institution had an added sense of commitment to social change. All of this is very much in keeping with the Jesuit tradition.

Building a university with a conscience is not easy in any environment. It turned out to be a lethal combination in El Salvador. Father Beirne analyzes, from the inside, how such a university is developed. He points out that the challenges not only are from a hostile external environment but also relate to internal difficulties. Some at the university and in the Church hierarchy were not in favor of the university's mission. Further, since a university with a social commitment is unusual, if not unprecedented, it had to be invented as it was developed, and this too proved especially difficult in the context of El Salvador. It would not, however, have been easy anywhere.

The Universidad Centroamericana triumphed over its many difficulties and in this way vindicated the slain Jesuits. The saga is by no means finished. The university faces additional challenges as it seeks to institutionalize its social justice mission. It tells us that social change is not easy but that convictions and commitment count for much even in a very hostile environment.

Philip G. Altbach
Boston College

ACKNOWLEDGMENTS

The research reported in this book was assisted in part by a grant from the Spencer Foundation.

Since this study began in 1987 at Santa Clara University, many debts of gratitude have been incurred that the author gladly recognizes, even though, unfortunately, no blame for its limitations can be spread around.

First of all, I want to thank the Central American Province of the Society of Jesus and the University of Central America (UCA) for making the archives available to me, and the Jesuit communities in El Salvador that encouraged my labors and allowed me to share in their work for the people of El Salvador over the past decade.

A note of special thanks goes to Juan Hernández Pico, S.J., who read the whole manuscript twice and gave inestimable assistance, and other colleagues who plowed through earlier versions of part or all of the text: J. Dean Brackley, S.J., Rodolfo Cardenal, S.J., Joaquín Samayoa, Jon Sobrino, S.J., Knut Walter, Michael Czerny, S.J., Luis Calero, S.J., Terry Karl, Román Mayorga, Luis de Sebastián, and Philip G. Altbach. Their valuable suggestions kept me from straying too far from the truth.

While enjoying the hospitality of the Jesuit community at Boston College, thanks especially to Joseph Appleyard, S.J., and James Collins, S.J., I began to write this book and to organize a capital campaign for the UCA. The personal encouragement and support from J. Donald Monan, S.J., president of Boston College, not only helped my writing, it made possible my fund-raising on behalf of the UCA. William J. Neenan, S.J., academic vice president of Boston College, named me a visiting scholar, and the Office of Research Administration helped process funding. A special word of thanks goes to the late Paul Le Conte and his successor, Mary Lou De Long, both in the position of vice president of university relations, and their generous and fun-loving staff, who offered professional advice and assistance to a fund-raising neophyte.

Thanks also to the Lawlor, Herencia, and Riera families, who allowed me to relax at their beach houses while I was chipping away at the documentation. Much of the early reading was made more pleasant at the home of my sister, Maureen Beirne Streff, her husband, Charles Streff, and my nephew Jon and niece Meghan. A special word of thanks to my mother, Catherine Beirne, great enthusiast for all the projects of her four children, and secretary extraordinaire.

I also want to thank the Santa Clara University community, the Woodstock Jesuit community in Washington, the Loyola Jesuit community and the Jesuit Seminary and Mission Bureau in New York, the Colegio San Ignacio Jesuit community in Puerto Rico, the Jesuit conference staff and the Neale House Jesuit community in Washington, and the staff at the Tulane University Latin American Library.

Paul S. Tipton, S.J., president of the Association of Jesuit Colleges and Universities, and his generous executive assistant, Barbara Potter, have helped the UCA and my work on its behalf for many years, and deserve great thanks.

The invitation from Dr. Terry Lynn Karl, director of the Center for Latin American Studies, for me to be a visiting scholar at Stanford University provided the ideal atmosphere to complete research and finish the text. To her, the staff of the center, and the Stanford librarians, I am grateful. The gracious assistance of the Stanford staff was complemented by my colleagues at the Newman Center and the St. Thomas Aquinas parish in Palo Alto.

I am particularly grateful to Joseph P. Parkes, S.J., the New York Jesuit provincial superior who agreed to my sabbatical in the 1993–1994 academic year to complete this book.

The book is dedicated to Congressman Joe Moakley, who gave valuable time from his own district and has labored for many years to serve the people of El Salvador—gaining asylum for refugees, tracking down killers, putting pressure on reluctant bureaucrats in Washington and San Salvador to tell the truth, and playing a major role in bringing inklings of peace to that embattled little country.

For many years, Congressman Moakley has had the extraordinary assistance of Jim McGovern, who incurred both the wrath of the Salvadoran military by his persistent questioning on the Jesuit case, and also, more importantly, the deep gratitude of the people of El Salvador.

Charles J. Beirne, S.J.
University of Central America, José Simeón Cañas
San Salvador, El Salvador

Jesuit Education and Social Change in El Salvador

1 SETTING THE SCENE

This book examines a unique model—the university for social change—the University of Central America, José Simeón Cañas (UCA) in El Salvador.

The faculty teach classes and engage in research, students attend the classes and complete degrees, and administrators worry about whether they will be able to pay the bills; yet this is a different kind of university. For even if all the aforementioned "actors" play their traditional roles adequately, they still will not achieve the central goals of the university itself; namely, to effect social change and help create a just society. Other universities may include citizenship and community service in their mission statements, and many excel in these areas, but few take social change as their primary aim.

As six Jesuit priests and their two associates at the UCA discovered early on the morning of November 16, 1989, implementing such a university model can be costly. It upsets the powers that be, and they react decisively. Salvadoran soldiers sent by the minister of defense and his colleagues in the high command murdered these priests and the two women who had taken refuge for the night in a guest parlor of the Jesuit residence as insurrection shook the capital city of San Salvador.

The UCA story is fascinating in itself, but far more significant is a study of the university "model" that has emerged over these past three decades. The assassination did not make this model worth studying; instead, it called attention to a phenomenon that merited attention even before that tragic event.

From the UCA story much can be learned about the role of a university in a developing country, especially in a time of significant national change, such as a gradual easing toward democracy after years of military domination. Because of its relevance in El Salvador, the UCA model might also have much to say to other universities around the world.

Therefore this book hopes to suggest answers to a number of important questions such as the following:

1. What is the proper role of a university in a developing country?
    Is it to train professionals who manage the political, economic, and social status quo, or to prepare graduates who will help create a new society?
    Is it to be an oasis in which scholars separate themselves from turmoil in order to research topics of personal interest, or a center for research on central problems of that society the university seeks to serve?

2. What has been the specific role of the University of Central America, directed by the Jesuits in El Salvador?
    What have been the UCA's mission and special characteristics over its three-decade history?
    Who founded the UCA and why?
    How and why did the UCA change?
    What factors assisted or hindered change?
    What types of internal and external opposition did these changes provoke?

3. What does this university model have to say to other institutions?
    What are the strengths, weaknesses, and yet-to-be-developed elements in the model?
    Are key elements of the model transferable to other parts of the world?
    Does the model raise questions about the very mission and approach of any university and its relationships to the wider communities beyond its campus?
    Who are the model's ultimate beneficiaries?

An Overview of the Text

The book begins with the historical, social, economic, and political context of El Salvador: centuries of poverty and oppression, with power and privileges for a few, and misery for the vast majority. It covers major historical events, the effects of various economic models, and the role of the military in the country. This brief history sets the stage for the story of the UCA itself and explains the desperate needs of the Salvadoran people that the university has tried to address through its teaching, research, and social outreach.

Next comes a quick glimpse of views on the nature of a university, from John Henry Newman to A. Bartlett Giamatti and Pope John Paul II, to help the reader compare and contrast these approaches with the UCA model. Some universities stress knowledge as an end in itself, others see teaching as paramount, and still others put their major emphasis on research. What does the UCA emphasize, and why?

Important factors contributed to the focus at the university: the Catholic Church's Second Vatican Council, the 1968 declarations of the Latin American bishops' meeting at Medellín, Colombia, the Jesuit provincial superiors in Río de Janeiro, and the General Congregation of the Jesuits in 1974–1975. We also look at liberation theology, which embodies so much of the UCA educational philosophy, and finally, closely examine seminal documents that express the new vision of the UCA as a university for social change.

Exploring these seminal documents is very important because of the centralized governmental structures in both the Catholic Church and the Jesuit order. Even though receiving an official document from Rome or Río does not guarantee a new way of thinking and acting, nevertheless, this international dimension can spur local educators to consider questions that they might otherwise ignore because of pressing local problems like survival.

Then the historical narrative begins, with the early years of a university founded to protect students from "communism" and "secularism," evils seen as rampant in the University of El Salvador. The original benefactors' list reads like the social register of San Salvador; indeed, the president of the republic, Colonel Julio Rivera, presided over the inauguration ceremonies. The bishops of El Salvador wanted a "Catholic" university, strictly defined by Vatican officials; the Jesuits in Central America and their lay colleagues established an institution of Christian inspiration, free from ecclesiastical entanglements.

Local Jesuit superiors considered closing the UCA before it really got off the ground, and they debated with Rome on whether there were enough Jesuits to staff the three universities in Central America—a question still unsettled.

One begins to see a new vision emerging as a key Jesuit, Ignacio Ellacuría, joined the UCA board of directors in 1967, and the Central American Province participated in the international sociological survey of Jesuit institutions, and then gathered together for an important retreat and week of reflection in 1969 to spell out the implications of this new vision. This retreat also revealed deep divisions within the Jesuit order.

The rectorate of Luis Achaerandio, S.J. (1969–1975), saw the beginnings of a changing university: new academic programs, stirrings of research, and social outreach. The UCA took over the journal *Estudios Centroamericanos,* which became an important source of social analysis on issues such as the 1969 war with Honduras, appropriate technology, agrarian reform, and the fraudulent elections of 1972. During this period, the UCA began serious planning with an initial loan from the Inter-American Development Bank (IDB) for construction and faculty development. Achaerandio encouraged the incorporation of lay colleagues into the process of redefining the university mission, and they were to play a major role.

Román Mayorga's term of office included serious academic and financial planning, a major loan from the IDB for almost $10 million, and a sharper focus on crucial national issues, with the result that bombs began to explode on the university campus and threats to mount against key lay and Jesuit personnel. In 1977, death squads gave the Jesuits a month to leave the country or they would be killed. Although the Jesuits refused to go, they slept in private homes every night, and then returned to their offices and classrooms during the day.

The remaining chapters cover the Ellacuría decade: 1979–1989. This remarkable Basque priest took over when Román Mayorga, the lay rector, and Guillermo Ungo, the director of research, joined the five-man reformist junta that seized control of the Salvadoran government on October 15, 1979. In November, 1980, Ellacuría narrowly escaped into exile and guided the UCA from abroad for over a year.

Despite continued bombings and attacks in the press the UCA expanded its academic programs (law), its centers for social outreach (human rights and opinion polling), and its publications *(Proceso, Carta a Las Iglesias,* and *Revista Latinoamericana de Teología)*. The UCA played a major role in calling for negotiations to end the civil war that had erupted in the early 1980s.

Behind the scenes, Ellacuría met with major players from all sides, and appeared in public as a symbol of opposition to oppression and an unofficial standard-bearer of the martyred Archbishop Romero's legacy. He clashed with President Duarte on policy and practice, but he also helped mediate the release of the president's kidnapped daughter. He defined the UCA with clarity and forcefulness, and in some ways, he became the UCA's presence in the Salvadoran community along with his internationally known colleagues Jon Sobrino, Luis de Sebastián, Segundo Montes, and Ignacio Martín-Baró. They helped create and develop liberation theology, and encouraged efforts to forge a just society. They opposed what they called "reforms with repression." They got at the core of Salvadoran reality with clarity but their work also had shortcomings.

Some will point out that during the war the university neglected teaching and research in significant ways. But through both their vision and their limitations, the UCA faculty and staff helped create a unique model of a university committed to the Salvadoran community.

Efforts to keep the university together after the assassination are covered briefly toward the end of the book. New Jesuit team members from Spain, Mexico, Canada, and the United States came to help the survivors continue the work of the martyrs and their colleagues. Controversy smoldered over whether the university mission would change; some thought the UCA had lost its soul, and that it would now shrink and seek cover. Others pointed out the devastating effects of so much power and influence in the hands of just a few Jesuits. But the two survivors of the five-member board of directors had met before the martyrs were interred in the Romero Chapel, and began the process of reconstruction.

This survival process, its ups and downs, forms an important part of the model itself and tests its vitality, and, therefore, our analysis will take this experience into consideration. But these events are still too close to do them justice. And so, a fuller story of the UCA post-assassination period will be left to others.

As the UCA recovery progressed, President Alfredo Cristiani and the insurgent leaders signed a United Nations–sponsored peace agreement in Mexico City on January 16, 1992, that catapulted El Salvador into a hopeful yet stormy new era that may lead to real democracy and bring fresh challenges for the university.

In response to these emerging challenges, the UCA started departments of public health and education, and a radio station to extend the UCA's presence in the Salvadoran community. The UCA played a major role in early democratization attempts by helping the United Nations Truth Commission and Ad Hoc Commission, as well as other agencies, implement the peace process.

The final chapter of this book distills major ingredients of the model, its strengths and weaknesses, and its yet-to-be-developed elements. It attempts to answer the questions raised earlier about the role of a university in the process of social change in a developing country.

THE ASSASSINATION

Early on the morning of Thursday, November 16, 1989, almost 300 soldiers surrounded the University of Central America, José Simeón Cañas, better known as the UCA, while forty-seven others strode onto the campus through the pedestrians' entrance.[1] They milled around for some time before making their way up to the residence of the Jesuit priests and the Archbishop Romero Pastoral Center. A special task team then began to pound against the gates at each side of the house.

Awakened by the noise, the president, Ignacio Ellacuría, S.J., and a dean, Segundo Montes, S.J., let the soldiers in on one side, while the academic vice president, Ignacio Martín-Baró, S.J., did the same at the other end. The soldiers knew where to go because they had searched the house just two nights earlier. Nonetheless, in the guest parlor they were surprised to find two women who had taken refuge for the night; one soldier trained his gun on them. In a booming voice Father Martín-Baró castigated the invading soldiers: "This is an injustice; you are just rotting flesh."

The soldiers rounded up these three priests and two others who had come out of their rooms, Amando López, S.J., and Juan Ramón Moreno, S.J., philosophy and theology professors. They made them lie face down on the patch of grass outside the back door. Then, Lieutenant José Ricardo Espinosa Guerra, a graduate of the Jesuit high school in San Salvador when Segundo Montes was rector, gave the execution order. Oscar Mariano Amaya Grimaldi, known as Pilijay, opened fire against Ellacuría and Montes, while Antonio Ramiro Avalos Vargas, known as Satan or Frog killed Amando López and Juan Moreno. The firing of automatic weapons at close range sent blood and brains flying in all directions, spattering the garden and the wall of the house.

Meanwhile, according to one version, Ignacio Martín-Baró continued to lie face down on the ground with his feet resting comfortably one on top of the other, still alive. Then one of the soldiers went from body to body, delivering a coup de grace; this single bullet pierced the skull of Martín-Baró, and now all five were dead. Some say Martín-Baró was shot first, and then the others.

A short time later, Tomás Zarpate, guarding the two women in the guest parlor, shot them both.

Joaquín López y López, S.J., a seventy-year-old Salvadoran Jesuit, a UCA founder in 1965, and director of Fe y Alegría, an educational program for poor students, then appeared in the doorway right next to the execution site. He muttered, "You are not going to kill me; I don't belong to any organizations." He then turned and walked back to his room. A soldier followed him inside and shot him.

Lieutenant Espinosa ordered Corporal Cotta Hernández to drag the bodies of Ellacuría, Montes, Martín-Baró, Moreno, and Amando López into the house. When the corporal dumped Juan Moreno's body into the second room to the right, that of Jon Sobrino, S.J., who was out of the country at the time, he knocked a book off the shelf and it landed in Moreno's blood. The book was Jurgen Moltmann's *The Crucified God*.

Pilijay, the executioner of Ellacuría and Montes, strolled past the bodies to a side wall where he sat down and drank a beer.

A soldier set off one flare, and then a second one, as a signal to the surrounding troops that the deed was done. Avalos Vargas, who had killed Amando López and Juan Moreno, heard noises as he passed the guest parlor where the women had been shot. He struck a match, peered inside, and then fired a round to make sure they were dead.

Before leaving, the soldiers set fire to parts of the Romero Pastoral Center, shot at a picture of the archbishop, right through the heart, and left computers in smoking ruins. They fired at the glass doors of the chapel; one bullet hit the wall in back of the altar right at the foot of the cross. The assassins scribbled crudely painted messages on the walls and the door of the center to suggest that insurgents from the militant antigovernment group Frente Farabundo Martí para la Liberación Nacional (FMLN) had been the real killers. And then they left without interference from the several hundred soldiers surrounding the UCA campus.

On September 28, 1991, almost two years later, a jury convicted Colonel Guillermo Alfredo Benavides Moreno, head of the military school and commander of the assassination zone, and Lieutenant Yusshy René Mendoza Vallecillos, but they found another two lieutenants and the execution team not guilty, even though all of them had confessed to their crimes.

On November 17, 1991, just two years and a day after the assassination, in his final report to the United States Congress on the Jesuit case, Representative J. Joseph Moakley accused four important military officials of complicity as intellectual authors of the crime: General René Emilio Ponce, minister of defense; General Juan Orlando Zepeda, vice minister of defense; General Juan Rafael Bustillo, onetime head of the Air Force; and Colonel Francisco Elena Fuentes, commander of the First Brigade.

The March 15, 1993, Report of the United Nations Truth Commission added General Inocente Orlando Montano to the list, and accused General Ponce of actually giving the order to Colonel Benavides Moreno to arrange the assassination of Ignacio Ellacuría and to "leave no witnesses." The report cited many military personnel for covering up the crime, including Colonel Oscar León Linares, head of the Atlacatl battalion, whose soldiers had pulled the triggers, and Colonel Antonio Rivas Mejía, who had been in charge of the "investigation."

WHO WERE THE MARTYRS?

The six Jesuits had dedicated many years of service to Central America and to El Salvador in particular.[2] Only one was a Salvadoran by birth, Joaquín López y López, but the other five were Spaniards who had come to the region for their second year of noviceship at about eighteen or nineteen years of age. Three of the Spaniards (Ellacuría, Montes, and Martín-Baró) were Salvadoran citizens.

The oldest of the group, Joaquín López y López, known affectionately as Lolo, entered the Jesuits in El Paso, Texas, in 1938 at the age of twenty. His early training took place in the United States. Then he returned to teach at the Jesuit high school in San Salvador, the Externado de San José, before going back to the United States and then on to Spain to complete theological studies. After ordination to the priesthood in 1952, he returned to his native El Salvador to teach once again at the Jesuit high school, where he organized massive catechetical programs in which 800 Catholic high school students taught 20,000 students in poor barrios. In 1961, he supervised the construction of the high school chapel and then formed part of the team that founded the UCA. He lobbied for passage of the private schools law in 1965, gathered parent signatures on petitions to start the university, and helped with early fund-raising.

In 1969, he founded the Fe y Alegría schools, which serve 48,000 poor adults and children with thirty centers in eight departments (states) of El Salvador. His famous annual lottery helped pay the bills, but he skirted the edge of bankruptcy, running the schools on a shoestring budget. He was still directing these programs when the assassins ended his life, just months before prostate cancer would have done so.

He was a quiet, self-effacing man who enjoyed living in the Jesuit community of the university he had helped to get started. Although sometimes uncomfortable with changes taking place in the order and the church, nevertheless he kept himself informed by reading UCA publications, and he encouraged the work of his companions.

Next in age comes Ignacio Ellacuría, a Basque born in 1930.[3] He formed part of the first group of novices who came from Spain with their director, Miguel Elizondo, to start the novitiate in El Salvador at Santa Tecla. After his first vows as a Jesuit, he was sent to Ecuador for humanities and philosophy studies. One of his Jesuit professors, Aurelio Espinoza Polit, encouraged a love for the intellectual life in Ellacuría during those years. As is the custom in Jesuit seminary training, between his periods of study of philosophy and theology, Ellacuría returned to teach in a Jesuit institution, the diocesan seminary at San José de la Montaña.

Theological studies at Innsbruck brought Ellacuría into contact with another very important teacher, and one of the principal Catholic theologians of the twentieth century, Karl Rahner, S.J. Next he began doctoral studies in philosophy under the man who was to be such an important influence in his life, the Spanish philosopher Xavier Zubiri.[4] Eventually Ellacuría became Zubiri's principal colleague and interpreter. He returned to the recently founded UCA in 1967, and there he spent the next twenty-two years as a teacher, writer, and administrator.

Ellacuría was brilliant, shy, reflective, and, at times, overpowering. His creative imagination fashioned much of what was to be the UCA's role as agent for social change. He inspired awe and respect, and yet his Jesuit companions could also enjoy his enthusiasm for Spanish soccer and his Wednesday *frontón* (paddleball) games back at Santa Tecla. As we will see later, he was a complicated, extraordinary individual who became one of the major figures in late-twentieth-century Salvadoran history.[5]

Segundo Montes, with his imposing reddish beard and flashing blue eyes, earned the nickname Zeus from his UCA students. He was born in Valladolid and came to the Santa Tecla novitiate in 1951 at the age of eighteen. He followed the same basic program in Ecuador as Ellacuría, and then came back to the Jesuit high school in El Salvador to teach physics. Theological studies in Spain and Innsbruck were followed by ordination to the priesthood in 1963. Then he returned to El Salvador for a decade at the Jesuit high school, the Externado, including a term as rector.

From the early 1970s, he also taught social studies at the UCA and then completed a doctorate in social anthropology at the Universidad Complutense of Madrid before returning full time to the UCA. From 1980 until his death, he served as chair of the sociology/political science department, wrote for and helped manage the journal *Estudios Centroamericanos (ECA),* and encouraged the organization of the university's law program. But from 1984 on, he found his real calling—working with the growing number of Salvadoran refugees. He traveled the country under harsh conditions to study their plight and he told their story in El Salvador, the United States, and Europe. This work was a centerpiece of the UCA Human Rights Institute (IDHUCA), of which he served as first director.

When he was not writing one of his many books, he puttered around the house, making good use of his physics background to reconnect telephone wires and repair aging appliances. On weekends he served as pastor in a poor parish on the outskirts of Santa Tecla. The author concelebrated mass with him one Sunday and had a chance to see the great affection the poor people had for "Zeus."

Juan Ramón Moreno was born in Navarre just a few months after Segundo Montes in 1933, and entered the Jesuits at seventeen. After the usual early formation, including the second year of noviceship at Santa Tecla in El Salvador and a stint teaching chemistry and biology at the Jesuit high school in Nicaragua, he went to St. Mary's, Kansas, for theology studies and was ordained there in 1964. He returned to El Salvador and to the posts of prefect of studies and multifaceted teacher at the seminary until he was named master of novices in 1970. He developed a reputation as spiritual director and preacher, the latter somewhat of a surprise because he was so shy and retiring. He resonated a peacefulness and thus was called upon to serve as rector of the Jesuit high school during a turbulent period of attacks against the school that will be described later in the book.

Juan Ramón Moréno worked several years as spiritual director at Rome's Pio Latino seminary before going to Panama, where he founded the Centro Ignaciano de Espiritualidad and the journal *Diakonía,* an early source of liberation theology articles. In 1980, he moved this operation to Managua when he was made superior of the Jesuit community at Nicaragua's UCA. His leadership was recognized by election to head the conferences of major religious superiors in Panama and Nicaragua. In 1985, he came to the UCA in El Salvador to organize the Romero Pastoral Center library and to be secretary to the Central American Jesuit provincial superior.

Amando López was born in Burgos and entered the Jesuits at the age of sixteen in 1952. Like his martyred companions, he came to El Salvador for the second year of noviceship. After studies in Ecuador, he taught at Colegio Centro América in Managua. Ireland was the site of his theology studies and ordination in 1965, and the prelude to graduate studies at the Gregorian University in Rome and a doctorate in religious studies from Strasbourg. Shortly after his return to El Salvador and a teaching position at the major seminary, San José de la Montaña, he was named rector, but disputes between the bishops and the Jesuits led to the dismissal of the order from the seminary, and López went to the UCA as professor of philosophy.

In 1975, he left for Nicaragua and the rectorship of the Jesuit high school. In these final years of the Somoza dictatorship, López gained the confidence of many people who were pursued by the oppressors and to whom he gave shelter. His jolly, rotund figure, smiling face, and ever-present pipe exuded peace and gave hope to those who came for assistance. After the Nicaraguan revolution in 1979, he became rector of the UCA in Managua, and played a major role as advisor in the area of education and as a member of the human rights commission.

Back in El Salvador after his Nicaragua rectorship, López served as spiritual director and professor of philosophy and theology at the UCA and spent the weekends at his poor parish in Tierra Virgen.

Like Segundo Montes, Ignacio Martín-Baró, the youngest member of the group, hailed from Valladolid and entered the Jesuits just before his seventeenth birthday in 1959. After his second year as a novice in Santa Tecla, he studied in Ecuador and finished philosophy at the Universidad Javeriana in Bogotá. He taught for several years at the San Salvador Jesuit high school and then headed for theology studies in Frankfurt, Louvain, and back in San Salvador. He finished a psychology degree at the UCA and was dean of students and a member of the *ECA* editorial board before going to the University of Chicago, where he earned a doctorate in social psychology. He returned to the UCA to teach in 1979, and then from 1981 until his death he headed the psychology department.

In the turbulent early 1980s, the board named Martín-Baró acting vice rector for academic affairs, a position to which he succeeded after receiving the prerequisite of Salvadoran citizenship. He wrote eleven books and numerous articles and gave conferences throughout the United States, Europe, and Latin America, suggesting to his colleagues a "psychology of liberation."[6] In 1986, he became the first director of the university's opinion polling center (IUDOP) and directed twenty-five surveys on questions that ranged from presidential election preferences to economic conditions affecting the poor majority.

Martín-Baró strode off to his demanding classes with his umbrella and legendary attache case. His serious, intense expression belied a warm person who made himself available to his students. He never failed to bring bags of candy for the children in his weekend parish, Jayaque, and he regaled audiences with his guitar. "El Padre Nacho" integrated his scholarly and pastoral work in a breakneck schedule that saw him in his office at the computer by 5:30 A.M., and getting back to the residence after his final class at 8:00 P.M., and then managing a full weekend up in the Jayaque parish. He was the last one to go to bed at night and the first one up in the morning. There were some who alleged that he never slept. All the other assassination victims were found in bedclothes; Nacho was fully dressed as he lay dead in the garden.

These biographical details show us men who were human, talented, and pleasantly idiosyncratic. They had gotten used to living with danger over several decades, and in a phone conversation with the author just nine hours before their deaths, they gave no indication that they felt that they were in particular danger that night. In fact, Martín-Baró was already working on an analysis of the insurrection which he was due to send to the United States by fax the next day.

What motivated the Salvadoran armed forces to perpetrate such a bloody crime? What was their objective?

On that early morning of November 16, 1989, they sought to kill not just a few priests; they tried to kill the university by wiping out Ignacio Ellacuría, its president, and leaving no witnesses. They massacred the UCA's central administration and its key figures, who met death because of the kind of institution they ran: a university with academic standards, a faith vision, and a commitment to bring about a just society in El Salvador; a university that served as a creative and critical conscience for the nation, and an agent for genuine democracy.

Methodology

In preparation of this historical study, the author combed the archives of the Central American Province of the Society of Jesus (Jesuits) in San Salvador, the archives of the UCA itself, and major university publications, especially *ECA*. Because these events are relatively recent history, the archives would normally not have been available to scholars, but the author's long association with the Jesuits of Central America made this access possible.

In addition, surviving members of the past and present staff were interviewed, and use was made of many conversations with the martyrs themselves from 1976 to 1989, including telephone calls from the United States to El Salvador the night their residence was searched, and again two days later, just nine hours before the assassination.

Four months after the killings, the author was asked by the surviving Jesuits and the superior general of the Society of Jesus, Pieter Hans Kolvenbach, to succeed Ignacio Martín-Baró, S.J., as vice rector of the UCA, and he accepted the position for three years, until a Salvadoran substitute was ready to assume it.

The author also reviewed major UCA publications to identify examples of how the university presented itself to the community it sought to serve. Most of the quotations are limited to *ECA*, however, because in one way or another every important issue appeared in its pages, and the journal is readily available in major research libraries.

The secondary literature on Central America and related questions has also been studied to fill in the background. It is always difficult to know how much detail is necessary. There has been an attempt to avoid either extreme: skimpy references or a lengthy "life and times" of El Salvador that could distract the reader from the main subject: the UCA university model.[7]

The same is true of the vast literature on issues related to the political role of a university—the sociology of education, "political correctness," John Dewey's ideas on school and society, and even critical theory.[8] The basic thrust of the UCA curriculum will be studied, but not in such detail as to attempt to suggest the relevance of specific programs or courses to the goal of social transformation. The focus of the story is the university model itself and its interaction with Salvadoran reality since 1965. As we shall see, after more than a decade of civil war, there is need for an overhaul of the curriculum and pedagogy of the university to sharpen its focus and improve its methodology. A reorientation of its general direction, however, is not needed.

Being a participant observer brings advantages and disadvantages: access to people and places, documents and anecdotes, on one hand, and yet the fear that one might be too close to the events and the people to achieve neutrality. As a result, some observers will probably feel that admiration clouds objectivity, and others will see the analysis as too critical. The risk is worth taking, however, while so much of the story is fresh and when the past is so accessible through documents and survivors.

Every day visitors speak in hushed tones as they walk through the UCA Jesuit residence garden and the house where the six Jesuits and the two women met their deaths. They stop for a prayer at the simple tomb of the martyrs in the Romero Chapel, and they chat with their lay and Jesuit colleagues who remain. Until January 1992, these pilgrimages were often punctuated by distant explosions of the raging civil war or helicopters swooping overhead, about to land at El Salvador's version of the Pentagon a half-mile from the university, the place from which the assassins embarked that fatal night.

In looking at the UCA model it is important to try to separate myth from reality, hopes from actual accomplishments, and to ask what can be learned from this innovation. Every country and every university is different, and the UCA model cannot and should not be uncritically transplanted. But elements from this intense experience might be of help to others; the model might suggest what could be adapted elsewhere; it might save others from making some of the UCA's mistakes. Hence, this book, which was already in preparation almost two years before the shots rang out early on November 16, 1989.

Notes

1. For a detailed, insightful account of the assassination and the subsequent Jesuit case see Martha Doggett, *A Death Foretold: The Jesuit Murders in El Salvador* (Washington: Georgetown University Press, 1993), and Teresa Whitfield, *Paying the Price: Ignacio Ellacuría and the Murdered Jesuits of El Salvador* (Philadelphia: Temple University Press, 1995). The Whitfield text complements this book in many ways, such as with a rich panoply of details from interviews about Ellacuría's meetings with public figures and his role in the peace process.

2. These biographical notes are taken from Rodolfo Cardenal, "Ser Jesuita Hoy

en El Salvador," *Estudios Centroamericanos* 44 (1989), 1013–39.

3. See also Whitfield, 15–32.

4. For an overall view of Zubiri see Ignacio Ellacuría, "Aproximación de la Obra Completa de Xavier Zubiri," *Estudios Centroamericanos* 38 (1983), 965–82. For more details on Zubiri see Antonio González, "El Hombre en el Horizonte de la Praxis," *Estudios Centroamericanos* 42 (1987), 57–87. The best summary of Zubiri's influence on Ellacuría is Antonio González, "Aproximación a la Obra Filosófica de Ignacio Ellacuría," *Estudios Centroamericanos* 45 (1990), 979–89.

5. Whitfield, 245 ff.

6. For his principal articles on this subject in English see Adrianne Aron and Shawn Corne, eds., *Writings for a Liberation Psychology* (Cambridge, MA: Harvard University Press, 1994).

7. For this reason the complementary Whitfield text is very helpful.

8. Some helpful books on these topics are Henry A. Giroux and Peter McLaren, *Critical Pedagogy: The State and Cultural Struggle* (Albany: State University of New York Press, 1989); Darryl J. Gless and Barbara Hernstein Smith, *The Politics of Liberal Education* (Durham, NC: Duke University Press, 1992); Maria-Regina Kecht, *Pedagogy Is Politics: Literary Theory and Critical Teaching* (Chicago: University of Illinois Press, 1992); Gerald Graff, *Beyond The Cultural Wars* (New York: Norton, 1992); and Reginald D. Archambault, ed., *John Dewey on Education: Selected Writings* (Chicago: University of Chicago Press, 1964), especially 289 ff.

The Salvadoran Context

Stanley and Barbara Stein, in their classic *The Colonial Heritage of Latin America,* conclude that

> In Latin America political systems have long been designed and main-
> tained to limit popular demands. In many nations, high levels of il-
> literacy (between 40 and 50 percent), weak peasant and industrial
> labor organizations, well-organized and highly influential landowning
> and business associations, the widespread use of political funds to
> influence voting, and finally the recourse to military force to destroy
> the results of elections—all have concentrated political control over
> national decision-making in the hands of a self-perpetuating elite or
> oligarchy whose decisions are governed by narrowly defined class
> interests rather than national considerations.[1]

Unfortunately, this general description fits El Salvador like a glove, and serves as a backdrop for our story.

A separate political division, or intendency, within the colonial kingdom of Guatemala since 1785, El Salvador gained independence in 1821 as part of a shaky Central American federation that managed to stay intact until the various republics went their separate ways in 1839. Political chaos reigned: "Between 1841 and 1890 El Salvador participated in five wars with Guatemala, four with Honduras, and one with Nicaragua, while thirteen successful coups d'état occurred." Many of these battles were fought by poor soldiers who had been forcibly recruited.[2]

Indigo dominated the Salvadoran export economy from the sixteenth century until coffee took its place late in the nineteenth century.[3]

Very little was done to enable the majority of the population to take advantage of the opportunities created by international trade. By contrast, those who managed to engage in indigo production were subsidized by everyone else. Import taxes ultimately paid by consumers financed a transportation system designed to help exporters to take their products to the ports. Most of the budget was used to finance an army that kept order for the benefit of exporters while the educational system remained under-funded. Land policies were designed to favor coffee production. The state was created by and for the emerging oligarchy.[4]

Since colonial times, many of the poor had lived and worked on communal lands and *ejidos,* areas set aside for the general population to grow subsistence crops and some products for markets outside the community.[5]

Communal lands and *ejidos* were not devoted exclusively to subsistence agriculture. Trade and cottage industry were very much part of the rural economy. In the bigger towns there were fairs where many goods were traded. San Juan Nonualco, a predominantly Indian town, bought its food from other towns and concentrated in the production of hides, mustard, indigo seed, earthenware, and brown sugar. According to the 1858 census, the value of the nonsubsistence products was 48 percent of the value of the town's production.[6]

By the 1880s, indigo prices had started to drop and coffee took hold despite considerable start-up costs: tight credit and a wait of four years for the first crops.[7] By that time, the government had sold most of its vacant lands at bargain rates to the well-to-do for growing coffee.

Lindes-Fuentes points out that "in 1881, a law abolished the communal land system, and the following year this [legislation] was extended to the *ejidos.* These lands had to be purchased by their occupants within a term which was extended several times, but in the event most *comuneros* lost their holdings, which were acquired by the coffee growers."[8] Lindo-Fuentes shows that notices for claiming land were published in the newspapers, but the majority of the poor occupants were illiterate, and "skilled lawyers hired by rich landowners with friends in high office had an edge over illiterate peasants."[9]

In 1888, only 1 in 32 Salvadorans attended primary school, 1 in 530 secondary school, and 1 in 3,820 made it to the university which had been founded in 1841. In 1888, "only 528 Salvadorans had university degrees, 262 of whom were lawyers."[10]

It is important to note that "in the case of the *ejidos* 73 percent of the land was given to 5.68 percent of the new owners whereas the 50 percent less fortunate scrambled for a share of 3.45 percent of the land."[11] Sad to say, "by 1950 the situation had not improved. According to that year's census only 1.17 percent of all the agricultural properties in the country were greater than 100 hectares, but they accounted for 50 percent of the arable land."[12]

Not only did the poor fail to profit from the nineteenth-century land reforms, they also lost much land for food production. "Although there are no direct data on food production for the 1880s, it is clear that despite its fluctuations indigo production fell very slowly during the second half of the century. This implies that most of the resources used for the expansion of coffee were diverted from food production. . . . The liberal reforms, which affected Indian communities and *ejidos* traditionally linked to the production of foodstuffs, insured that coffee would expand at the expense of food."[13]

It is small wonder that there were Indian uprisings after these "reforms."

Hector Lindo-Fuentes, in his book *Weak Foundations: The Economy of El Salvador in the Nineteenth Century. 1821–1898,* upon which this chapter draws heavily, links the political and economic issues in the following manner:

> The main political issue was to find the best way to protect the coffee planters. President Ezeta (1890–1894) was overthrown when he mismanaged a financial crisis and dared to double the export duty on coffee. His successor, Rafael Gutiérrez (1894–1898), repealed the tax. Gutiérrez was overthrown when the drop in coffee prices in 1898 led to a financial crisis that he could not handle. From 1898, when Tomás Regalado overthrew Rafael Gutiérrez, to 1931, there were no coups d'etat and all the presidents were coffee planters. . . . There was a sort of *pax coffeana* [because] the elite had a firm grip on power and required stability to maximize profits.[14]

A descendant of President Regalado with the same name was an original UCA benefactor.

James Dunkerley, in "El Salvador Since 1930," adds that "wages and conditions on Salvadoran estates were among the poorest in the region and contributed towards the relative efficiency of the export economy."[15] This is a pattern that continues today—growth without equity.

Dependence on coffee made El Salvador the victim of international seesaw price fluctuations. For example, from twenty-five cents per pound in 1925, coffee dropped to nine cents ten years later; worker wages dropped from seventy-five to fifteen *centavos* a day.[16] "At the end of the Second World War (average of 1940–44), the quoted price of a pound of coffee in New York was about 11.7 cents; in 1949 it had risen to 28.7 cents, and between 1955 and 1957 it was worth 57.4 cents."[17] "The most recent cyclical downswing (since 1978/79), for example, has wiped out nearly three decades of increase in real GDP per head in El Salvador."[18]

Dominance by the coffee elite continued as the Meléndez-Quiñónez family passed on the presidency of the republic from one member to another from 1913 to 1927.[19] Members of this family were also founding benefactors of the UCA.

Enrique Baloyra, in *El Salvador in Transition,* points out that the power of the well-to-do resulted from close-knit ties within the oligarchic families and their "control of production, export, finance, and land tenure."[20] This is another pattern endemic to Salvadoran society.[21]

The Araujo administration came to power through fair elections of 1929 but ran afoul of the worldwide economic depression. A December 1931 coup placed General Maximiliano Hernández Martínez in the presidential palace, where he ruled El Salvador until another coup replaced him with one of his allies in 1944. Economic desperation provoked an uprising early in 1932, but the plot was discovered beforehand, the leaders arrested, and massive retaliation, known in history as La Matanza (the massacre), left at least 15,000 peasants dead.[22]

The insurrection was seen as "a rebellion that had some links with the PSC [Salvadoran Communist Party] but was at root an independent movement in pursuit of both immediate economic amelioration and a more deeply seated defence of the region's embattled communal culture."[23] Italo López Vallecillo, in an article on social change in El Salvador, characterized the Hernández Martínez coup as "a preventive reaction by the dominant class in the face of new political forces which had arisen from within the dominated classes of a society in crisis at many levels and dimensions."[24] From this point on, the military would rule El Salvador until the 1992 peace agreements began to curtail their power.

Hernández Martínez kept power "in a style broadly comparable to that of his peers in the neighboring states, through a cycle of unopposed elections and with the retention of no more than a veneer of democratic procedures."[25] His interim successor was trying to prepare the country for free democratic elections with civilian candidates, but he was toppled in a coup by Colonel Osmín Aguirre, who had helped suppress the 1932 uprising. No civilians ran in the January 1945 elections in which General Salvador Castañeda Castro came to power. Castañeda "presided over a four-year holding operation during which time the Cold War set in and the international conditions for a return to democracy deteriorated under the weight of a pervasive anti-communism. The same period also witnessed a steady economic recovery as coffee prices were freed from wartime agreements, opening possibilities of agricultural diversification and encouraging some industrial development."[26]

When Castañeda tried to extend his term, another coup turned him out of office in 1948. The new leader was Colonel Oscar Osorio. With that shift, "a regime of complete political prohibition and economic conservatism moved toward one that promoted an increased level of state intervention in the economy, tolerated a number of closely watched-over urban unions and civic associations, accepted some political competition within the middle class as well as the oligarchy, and gave a degree of support to those elements of capital seeking to invest in new sectors of agriculture, particularly cotton, and the manufacturing industry."[27]

López Vallecillo adds that "immediately after the Second World War and the reinforcement of our economy with the production and exportation of cotton and sugar, the agrarian-industrial sector became the leader of the political-military movements of 1944 and 1948–50, with the collaboration in both cases of influential coffee growers, especially those more inclined toward agricultural modernization and restricted political expression by the people."[28]

Strong anticommunism, "absolute prohibition of popular organization in the countryside and tight control of the urban unions through both co-optation and direct coercion ensured that for the mass of citizens, the system was only marginally different from its predecessors. . . . The governments of Oscar Osorio (1950–56) and José María Lemus (1956–60) consolidated military power in a period of generally buoyant coffee prices."[29] In the spring of 1960, however, election successes of an opposition party convinced President Lemus to declare martial law and to invade the national university. "A junta with civilian technocrats and sympathizers of democratic reform" overthrew Lemus in October.[30] But in January 1961 a countercoup restored military dominance with Colonel Julio Rivera as president. Colonel Rivera presided over the inauguration of the UCA in 1965.

The PCN [Partido de Conciliación Nacional] was created in 1961 following the military coup that put an end to the reformist tendencies of a civil-military junta (1960) and the cautious modernization projects attempted by Colonels Osorio and Lemus (1956–60). This coup marked the installation of a new period of political monopoly by the army, which, in totally controlled elections, secured the election of Julio Rivera (1962–67), Fidel Sánchez (1967–72), [Arturo Molina (1972–77),] and Carlos Humberto Romero (1977–79).[31]

After his "election," Colonel Rivera allowed some modest populist reforms such as proportional representation for opposition parties in the national and municipal assemblies, and he legalized the Christian Democratic Party (PDC).[32] Dunkerley says that this party "was permitted to win fourteen congressional seats against the PCN's thirty-two in 1964, and in 1966 one of the party's young leaders, José Napoleón Duarte, was allowed to take the mayoralty of San Salvador which he soon converted into a platform for the PDC's policy of social rapprochement and measured reform."[33]

Thomas Anderson concludes in *The War of the Dispossessed*, however, that such modest reforms as an increase in the minimum wage provoked resentment from the oligarchy, who "immediately took measures to cancel its effect, forbidding the workers to farm the small plots they had previously used on the estates, dropping the traditional daily noon meal of one tortilla and a handful of beans, and laying off as many workers as possible."[34] Baloyra says that Colonel Rivera "made his peace with the oligarchy, . . . enjoyed favorable coffee prices and was able to follow a pragmatic and fairly progressive course, . . . and [continue] some reforms, which, however, always fell short of damaging the interests of the oligarchy."[35]

These governments gave financial support to wealthy landowners by tax breaks, special arrangements to import machinery, and convenient credit arrangements, along with infrastructure such as access roads, improvements of the port at Acajutla, hydroelectric plants, and the "golden bridge" over the Lempa River, later destroyed by the insurgents.[36] Some of the funding came from Alliance for Progress loans, which were accompanied by an increase in military aid and introduction of the doctrine of national security and concern for the "internal enemy."[37]

Governments had ignored social problems for years and forced hundreds of thousands of Salvadorans into exile, many to Honduras. Feeling the pressure on its own resources, Honduras closed its borders and summarily deported many Salvadorans. Tempers ran high at a soccer championship and the rioting there spilled over into an international incident inaccurately called the Soccer War. This brief war, in fact, had its roots in the more important issues of poverty. This war effectively ended the Central American Common Market, one of the initiatives of the United Nations' Economic Council for Latin America (ECLA). The UCA published its first serious piece of social analysis on this war and its implications.

In 1971, a militant group headed by Salvador Cayetano Carpio broke from the Communist Party and founded the Fuerzas Populares de Liberación (FPL). Another guerrilla group, with roots in the leftist youth of the Christian Democratic Party, formed the Ejército Revolucionario del Pueblo (ERP), which included the poet Roque Dalton until he was assassinated. His followers then regrouped as the Fuerzas Armadas de Resistencia Nacional (FARN). With two additional groups, they all formed the Frente Farabundo Martí para la Liberación Nacional (FMLN) in 1981, which waged war against the government until the peace agreements signed at Chapultepec on January 16, 1992. These groups gained force in the early 1970s after the farcical elections of 1972.

The Social Democrats under Guillermo Ungo founded the Movimiento Nacional Revolucionario (MNR), which banded together with José Napoleón Duarte and the Christian Democrats in 1972 to form a coalition ticket (Unión Nacional Opositora [UNO]). With Duarte and Ungo ahead in the tallies, the army suspended the count, and on the next day announced that Colonel Arturo Molina had been "elected" by a small margin. The military captured Duarte after he took part in an attempted coup of democratic military officers to preserve the true election results. The military high command then sent Duarte into exile in Venezuela; Ungo was hidden in the Jesuit residence at the seminary until he could go quietly into exile. Similar fraud marked the 1977 presidential elections when Colonel Carlos Romero was "elected."[38]

In 1976, the Molina regime allowed some discussion of one of El Salvador's central problems—land reform. But the Asociación Nacional de Empresas Privadas (ANEP) and the Frente de Agricultores de la Región Oriental (FARO) put an end to these suggestions of change, "thwarting the proposed legislation and signaling to the high command that the limits of concession had been exceeded. This negative stance against even mild reform was brutally supplemented by the growing activity of right-wing vigilante groups (death squads) such as the FALANGE and the Unión Guerrera Blanca (UGB), which undertook selective assassinations and established a pattern of repression that was henceforth to be a sadly persistent feature of Salvadoran life."[39]

The UCA's reaction to Molina's surrendering to the right wing on land reform will be treated extensively later in this book, along with the story of the UGB's threat to kill all Jesuits if they did not leave the country within thirty days.

A fraudulently elected president and a surprisingly progressive archbishop, both named Romero though unrelated, came into office early in 1977. Colonel Romero stepped up military repression that was supplemented by civilian guards in an infamous group named Organización Democrática Nacionalista (ORDEN). Archbishop Romero rallied the faithful around him, especially after the assassination of the Jesuit pastor of Aguilares, Rutilio Grande, who had been a friend and colleague of the archbishop on the seminary faculty. Archbishop Romero refused to allow the cathedral to be used for the traditional "Te Deum," the hymn of thanksgiving, when the new president assumed office. As a protest against the repression, Romero canceled all the masses in the Archdiocese of San Salvador to focus attention on the funeral of Father Grande.[40] The three years of Romero's archbishopric were marked by close collaboration between him and the UCA, as will be detailed later.

On October 15, 1979, the lay rector of the UCA, Román Mayorga, and the 1972 vice presidential candidate of the UNO, Guillermo Ungo, joined another civilian and two military officers in a takeover of the Salvadoran government.[41] But opposition from the left that felt that its plans had been preempted, and continued repression by the military and their civilian allies on the right doomed the revolutionary government, which resigned in early January 1980.

The popular organizations BPR (Bloque Popular Revolucionario), FAPU (Frente de Acción Popular Unificada), and LP-28 (Ligas Populares 28 de Febrero) issued a call for insurrection on January 11, 1980, and organized a January 22, 1980, march that the government suppressed violently. These organizations joined together to form the CRM (Coordinadora Revolucionaria de Masas) to channel their demands.

In February 1980, Archbishop Romero pleaded with the Carter administration to stop military assistance to El Salvador, and a month later, on March 24, ex-Major Roberto D'Aubuisson, who was to be a 1984 right-wing party presidential candidate, sent an assassin who fired one bullet through the archbishop's heart as he was saying mass.[42] On April 1, 1980, the civilian political opposition united to form the FDR (Frente Democrático Revolucionario).

A second government junta lasted a few weeks, and then in March 1980 José Napoleón Duarte, recently returned from exile, joined the military and some Christian Democratic Party colleagues in a third junta, of which he eventually was named president. The junta attempted to implement a three-stage land reform that was seen by the right as too much, and by the left as too little too late. The junta nationalized the banks to make credit more accessible to a wider range of clients, and they exerted more control over external trade, especially coffee. The United States government had pushed for these "reforms" as an antidote to the low intensity war of the FMLN. But the next right-wing administration watered down or repealed these reforms.

Critics accused Duarte of repudiating the role he had enjoyed as a progressive in the 1970s to provide a cloak of respectability over the repression of the 1980s. Duarte, in turn, called his former UNO colleagues dupes of the communists who were unwilling to join the democratic process.[43] New elections brought to power a new right-wing party, Alianza Republicana Nacionalista (ARENA), whose founder, Roberto D'Aubuisson, the notorious death-squad leader, became head of the assembly in 1983, and set about writing a new constitution for El Salvador.[44]

With considerable pressure from the United States embassy, D'Aubuisson was kept from the Salvadoran presidency.[45] The voters turned out the ARENA-dominated legislature and elected Duarte to a full presidential term in 1984. Repression continued, however, since the military exercised real power in the country, and they were strengthened in their position over the next decade by at least four billion dollars of United States military and economic aid. Tommie Sue Montgomery, in her book *Revolution in El Salvador,* criticized United States policy in these terms: "What U.S. officials failed to understand was that pushing a 'law and order' line on the one hand and supporting private enterprise on the other played directly into the hands of the most conservative sectors of Salvadorean society."[46] It is difficult to understate the devastating effects of United States–supported military solutions initiated during the final months of the Carter administration, intensified by the Reagan years, and eventually wound down by the Bush administration.[47]

Secretary of State Warren G. Christopher of the Clinton administration, after the United Nations Truth Commission exposé of many human rights violations, set up a task force to review events of the 1980s.[48] Its disappointing report glossed over much of the complex reality of that period. But late in 1993 and early in 1994, the Clinton administration did release thousands of documents that show that American officials knew a great more than they wanted to admit about what was going on in El Salvador, including the funding of death squads and the truth about infamous massacres such as "El Mozote."[49]

In the 1980s, more and more victims of the repression fled the country or joined the FMLN in the mountains. The FMLN expanded in size and broadened in ideology, including in its ranks communists and Christians, university graduates and peasants.

Duarte died of cancer shortly after leaving office in 1989, and the new ARENA administration under Alfredo Cristiani, encouraged by Reagan's successor, the less ideologically strident Bush administration in Washington, stepped up negotiations with the FMLN, a slow process that led to the peace accords in 1992.[50] Other contributing factors to the beginnings of peace were the electoral defeat of the Sandinistas in Nicaragua, allies of the FMLN; the strength of the November 1989 FMLN offensive; the toppling of the Berlin Wall; and the deterioration of the Soviet Union; and the UCA massacre, which showed the futility of United States efforts to humanize the Salvadoran military.

The UCA analyzed key events in depth and thus became a major social force in the country. Criticized by both sides for advocating negotiations since 1981, the UCA identified potential conditions for a just peace in article after article of *Estudios Centroamericanos (ECA)*. Many of its suggestions formed part of the eventual agreements realized under supervision of the United Nations. But by the time the ink dried on the treaties, about 75,000 people had been killed, mostly by government security forces, and prominent UCA scholars were also in their graves.

In addition to this political history, it is important to look at data that show the depth of poverty and the gravity of the overall situation that motivated the UCA to dedicate its resources to develop solutions.

The concentration of wealth and income, and general conditions of life in El Salvador, are shared with the rest of the countries in Central America.[51] In El Salvador, the impact of inequities is sharpened because of size, population density, a major earthquake in 1986, and over a decade of civil war. A brief look at these factors is in order.

El Salvador is the smallest country in Latin America (the size of the state of Massachusetts), and the most densely populated: 250 people per square kilometer. In 1987, when El Salvador had 238 people per square kilometer. Guatemala had 77.49; Honduras 40.27; and Nicaragua 26.48. When one goes beyond Central America, El Salvador's total of 238 in 1987 compares even more negatively with Argentina (11.33) and Chile (17.1).

As a consequence of unequal distribution of wealth, and deterioration in real income, at least one-third of all Salvadoran families do not have sufficient resources to cover basic food costs for the average family, a situation that results in undernourishment and exhaustion. Low income means that affordable housing does not cover basic needs for shelter, and that children go to work early in their lives if they can find some employment, especially in the informal sector. As a result, illiteracy is still high, especially among the poor. And finally, health statistics show high infant mortality rates due to diarrhea and respiratory infections.

The marked inflation during the last decade, accompanied by only modest increases in the minimum wage, led to continual deterioration in real wages. Between 1980 and 1989, real minimum salaries in the agricultural sector declined by 58.3 percent; in the industrial, commercial, and services areas the drop was 64.4 percent. Average overall salaries dropped 51.2 percent in the private sector and 57.6 percent in the public sector.[52]

The productive sector of the Salvadoran economy has been unable to create enough jobs. In 1990, the "official" urban unemployment rate was 10 percent, but underemployment hit 49 percent. For that same year, 52.4 percent of the economically active population was absorbed in the informal market, where working conditions are worse and income lower.

There are no up-to-date statistics on rural employment, but it is important to remember that any work available there is seasonal, and employers feel no year-round obligations toward workers. As a result, already high underemployment is far greater in the rural areas.

There are no accurate data for income distribution in rural areas or for homelessness, but the Salvadoran Government's Multi-Purpose Survey of Urban Homes of 1990 gives some idea of overall distribution: 50.29 percent of income went to 20 percent of the inhabitants and just 19.7 percent went to 50 percent. If this is the picture given by official government sources, one can imagine how much worse is the reality, especially the percentage of income in the hands of the wealthiest.

Official data for 1990 show that 30.7 percent of the urban population live in extreme poverty, and another 32.3 percent live in relative poverty.[53] Two-thirds of the population do not have the means to get adequate clothing.[54] In 1994, the government added to the national income the almost one billion dollars sent by Salvadorans in the United States so that the poverty statistics would suggest improvement in job opportunities.

Government services have not been able to make up the difference, as can be seen by a comparison of expenditures from 1980 to 1991. Health services dropped from 10.8 percent of the total budget to 8.1 percent, and education dropped from 22.6 percent to 15.2 percent, while defense rose from 14.4 percent to 22.8 percent.

Data for 1985 showed that 59 percent of all housing, and 76.6 percent of rural housing, was constructed with fragile materials such as adobe, bamboo, and metal sheets.[55] In addition, much of this poorly constructed housing is perched on hillsides, next to high-risk areas such as contaminated rivers and barely accessible land. Official data indicate that 38 percent of these homes are packed closely together.[56] Forty-one percent of these poorer places in San Salvador house more than five persons per room. These figures rise to 44.2 percent for other urban areas and to 63.2 percent in rural zones. The total housing shortage for 1990 was 600,000 dwellings.[57] Again, it is important to keep in mind that these are official government figures.

Lack of schooling brings high levels of illiteracy, low educational achievement, and large numbers of school dropouts, with inevitable effects on income and health. Government figures that understate the case show urban illiteracy at 17 percent; in rural areas it rises to 42.3 percent. As many as 31.7 percent have not finished even one year of schooling; only 28.8 percent reach high school and 2.6 percent higher education.[58] The government's Social Development Plan indicated that for 1988, the average number of years of schooling completed by the urban population was 4.5, but only 3.1 in rural zones. These data reflect the tendency of rural children to abandon school so they can help their families survive economically.

A 1988 study by the Salvadoran Health Ministry concluded that as a result of low income and the lack of government services, 50 percent of families showed an energy deficit, and 50 percent of families and 34 percent of children were unable to obtain daily iron requirements. Vitamin A deficiencies showed up in 74 percent of families and in 63 percent of children. Protein deficits affected 61 percent of the children. Of all children from eight to fifty-nine months, 38 percent were undernourished and another 22 percent had a inadequate diet, with the result that 60 percent had energy level deficits.[59] El Salvador is one of the countries included in the so-called world hunger belt; approximately two million out of five and a half million Salvadorans are not able to eat regularly. It was not surprising to find in a survey completed in 1989 that 43 percent of pregnant women showed nutritional anemia.[60] One can just imagine the long-term effects on the general well-being of the population and its potential productivity.

Health Ministry data indicate a general mortality rate of 8.4 per 1000, while infant mortality totals 55 children for every 1000 live births (47.8 in San Salvador, 63.4 in other urban areas, and 80.9 in rural areas). Populations displaced by the war reported figures three times greater; 60% of infant mortality is caused by infectious diseases.[61]

Retarded physical growth has been common in 30 percent of children less than five years old. The prevalence of malnutrition in children less than five years old is at least 50 percent. Diarrhea affects 39.5 percent of the children less than five years of age, but highest prevalence is from twelve to seventeen months. At least one-third of children are without proper vaccinations. The most frequent causes of death in the country continue to be types of diarrhea and acute respiratory infections.[62]

The high level of respiratory illnesses suggests the existence of high levels of air pollution, but there are insufficient data to show this correlation. Watching the poison spew out of bus exhaust pipes on the roads and highways of El Salvador, however, gives one a good idea of what scientific studies would document in detail.

There is a high level of pollution in many of El Salvador's rivers because of the dumping of raw sewage, which spawns enteric illnesses. These waters are used by the rural population for all their needs. Only 39 percent of the total population has access to relatively safe drinking water. Sewerage is available for only 23 percent of the general population, and in rural areas the coverage is only 11 percent.[63]

This picture of centuries of repression and dependency, injustice and killing serves as the background for the development of the UCA and its mission—to have academic standards with a faith vision help form a just society in El Salvador and the region.

But what is the role of a university in the face of such conditions?

Let us turn in the next chapter to various models of universities, which we will examine not because of any direct influence on the UCA but rather to provide context for it.

NOTES

1. Stanley Stein and Barbara Stein, *The Colonial Heritage of Latin America* (New York: Oxford University Press, 1970), 197.

2. Hector Lindo-Fuentes, *Weak Foundations: The Economy of El Salvador in the Nineteenth Century, 1821–1898* (Berkeley: University of California Press, 1990), 55.

3. Miles L. Wortman, *Government and Society in Central America, 1680–1840* (New York: Columbia University Press, 1982), 277.

4. Lindo-Fuentes, 5.

5. Lindo-Fuentes, 129.

6. Lindo-Fuentes, 100.

7. Lindo-Fuentes, 116.

8. Ciro F.S. Cardoso, "The Liberal Era, c. 1870–1930," in Leslie Bethell, ed., *Central America Since Independence* (Cambridge, England: Cambridge University Press, 1991), 43.

9. Lindo-Fuentes, 147–8.

10. Lindo-Fuentes, 71.

11. Lindo-Fuentes, 150.

12. Lindo-Fuentes, 151.

13. Lindo-Fuentes, 139.

14. Lindo-Fuentes, 154.

15. James Dunkerley, "El Salvador Since 1930," in Bethell, 162.

16. Dunkerley, 163.

17. Edelberto Torres Rivas, "Crisis and Conflict, 1930 to the Present," in Bethell, 91.

18. Victor Bulmer-Thomas, *The Political Economy of Central America Since 1920* (Cambridge, England: Cambridge University Press, 1987), 269.

19. Cardoso, 61.

20. Enrique A. Baloyra, *El Salvador in Transition* (Chapel Hill: University of North Carolina Press, 1982), 28.

21. Jeffrey M. Paige, "Coffee and Power in El Salvador," *Latin American Research Review* 28 (1993), 7–40.

22. The best account of this revolt is Thomas P. Anderson, *La Matanza* (Lincoln: University of Nebraska Press, 1971).

23. Dunkerley, 164.

24. Italo López Vallecillo, "Fuerzas Sociales y Cambio Social en El Salvador," *Estudios Centroamericanos* 34 (July–August 1979), 559.

25. Dunkerley, 166.

26. Dunkerley, 169.

27. Dunkerley, 170.

28. López Vallecillo, 559.

29. Dunkerley, 170.

30. Dunkerley, 171.

31. Torres Rivas, 101.

32. López Vallecillo, 561.

33. Dunkerley, 171–2.

34. Thomas P. Anderson, *The War of the Dispossessed: Honduras and El Salvador, 1969* (Lincoln: University of Nebraska Press, 1981), 32.

35. Baloyra, 43.

36. López Vallecillo, 560.

37. Torres Rivas, 101. For a very helpful summary outline of major elements in the Salvadoran political system see Italo López Vallecillo, "Trayectoria y Crisis del Estado Salvadoreño (1918–1981)," *Estudios Centroamericanos* 36 (June 1981), 504–12.

38. Dunkerley, 176.

39. Dunkerley, 177.

40. James Brockman, *Romero: A Life*, rev. ed. (New York: Orbis, 1989).

41. For details on these rapidly unfolding events see both Enrique Baloyra's text already cited, and Tommie Sue Montgomery, *Revolution in El Salvador: Origins and Evolution*, rev. ed. (Boulder, CO: Westview, 1994).

42. "De la Locura a la Esperanza, la guerra de doce años en El Salvador: Informe de la Comisión de la Verdad," *Estudios Centroamericanos* 48 (March 1993), 269.

43. For Duarte's side of the story see José Napoleón Duarte, *My Story* (New York: Putnam, 1986).

44. On the death squads see *Los Escuadrones de la Muerte en El Salvador* (San Salvador: Jaraguá, 1994). This is a Spanish translation of a collection of major newspaper and magazine articles on death squads that appeared in the American press in the 1980s and 1990s. The Salvadoran editors of the text did not identify themselves because of the upsurge in death squad activity at the time of publication.

45. Cynthia J. Arnson, *Crossroads: Congress, the President, and Central America, 1976–1993*, 2nd ed. (University Park: Pennsylvania State University Press, 1993), 95 ff. This is the most comprehensive study of United States policy.

46. Montgomery, 20.

47. For details on the highly criticized role of the United States in El Salvador see Raymond Bonner, *Weakness and Deceit: U.S. Policy and El Salvador* (New York: Times Books, 1985).

48. George S. Vest, Richard W. Murphy, and I.M. Bestler, *Report of the Secretary of State's Panel on El Salvador* (Washington: United States Department of State, July 1993).

49. On "El Mozote" see Mark Danner, "The Truth of El Mozote," *The New Yorker*, December 6, 1993, 50–133.

50. On the peace accords see Terry Lynn Karl, "El Salvador's Negotiated Revolution," *Foreign Affairs* 71 (1992), 147–64.

51. The author is indebted for data in this section to Antonio Cañas and his staff at the UCA documentation center (CIDAI) and Dr. Ernesto Selva-Sutter and his staff at the UCA Department of Public Health.

52. DIES/CENITEC, "La Erradicación de la Pobreza en El Salvador: Elementos para un enfoque alternativo," *Política Económica* 4 (December 1990–January 1991), 5. UCA, *Proceso,* 457, 472. See also Carlos Briones, *La Pobreza Urbana en El Salvador: Características y Diferencias de los Hogares Pobres: 1988–1990* (San Salvador: Instituto de Investigaciones Económicos y Sociales [IIES], UCA, December 1991).

53. Government of El Salvador, GOES/MIPLAN, *Evolución Económico y Social,* 3rd Trimester Report, 1990.

54. Ministry of Public Health and Social Assistance, Republic of El Salvador, *Plan Nacional de Salud, 1991–1994,* 1992, 2. Hereafter cited as *Plan Nacional.*

55. Government of El Salvador, GOES/MIPLAN, *Encuestas de Hogares de Propósito Múltiple,* Chart A.07, 1985. Hereafter cited as MIPLAN.

56. Ministerio de Planificación y Coordinación del Desarrollo Económico, Republic of El Salvador, *Plan de Desarrollo Económico y Social, 1989–1994,* 1989.

57. Developed on the basis of MIPLAN, Charts A.02 and A.04.

58. MIPLAN, Chart E.02. For a comprehensive picture of the Salvadoran educational system see Fernando Reimers, ed., *La Educación en El Salvador de Cara al Sigle XXI: Desafios y Oportunidades* (San Salvador: UCA Editores, 1995).

59. Asociación Demográfica Salvadoreña, Ministry of Public Health and Social Assistance, Instituto de Nutrición de Centro America y Panama, *Evolución de la Situación Alimentaria Nutricional en El Salvador* (El Salvador, 1990).

60. Instituto de Derechos Humanos de la UCA (IDHUCA), "La Salud en tiempo de guerra," *Estudios Centroamericanos* 46 (1991), 653–73.

61. Ministry of Public Health and Social Assistance, Republic of El Salvador, *Memoria 1990–1991, 1992.* See also IDHUCA Health Study cited earlier.

62. Gobierno de El Salvador, *Salud Pública en Cifras* (San Salvador: Ministerio de Salud Pública y Assistencia Social, 1993).

63. Organización Panamericana de Salud/Organización Mundial de Salud, *Las Condiciones de Salud en Las Américas,* II, El Salvador, 1990.

3 WHAT IS A UNIVERSITY?

Although labels tend to blur nuances, it might be helpful to identify several emphases of universities, knowing full well that no university concentrates on only one function. Three useful categories are *teaching* (Newman); *research* (German universities of the late nineteenth century, and major United States institutions such as Yale, Harvard, Princeton, and the University of Chicago); and *social outreach* (as exemplified by the University of Central America [UCA]). These are emphases only and not rigid categories.[1]

We will review Cardinal Newman's *Idea of a University,* which celebrates knowledge as a value in itself and highlights the importance of teaching. Pope John Paul II's *"Ex Corde Ecclesiae"* offers the latest Vatican views on the Catholic university. Ernest Boyer, former United States commissioner of education, adds nuances to the meaning of research by calling it "scholarship"; he subdivides scholarship into discovery, integration, application, and teaching. His category of "application" sheds some light on an important part of the UCA social outreach model.

A. Bartlett Giamatti, the late former president of Yale, medieval scholar, and baseball commissioner, suggests a model closer to what we will see in the UCA as far as social outreach is concerned, but he gives greater emphasis than the UCA to Newman's notions on knowledge as a value in itself.

Though not studied here, some Latin American authors, such as Carlos Tunnermann, past rector of the University of Nicaragua, former minister of education, and Nicaragua's ambassador to the United States, have also given importance to the social role of the university because of the desperate conditions in their own countries.

UCA educators did not consciously adopt any existing model, but it is important to look at others in order to compare and contrast key elements.

The classic description of the university's role is John Henry Newman's *The Idea of a University*, in which he presents his new institution for mid-nineteenth-century Catholics of Ireland.

Ian Ker, a Newman scholar, suggests there are three areas in which Newman has made a permanent contribution to the "idea" of a university: (1) students learning to think clearly and exactly; (2) the university as an intellectual community; and (3) the autonomy of each field of learning and the value of knowledge as an end in itself.[2]

Let us look at Newman's own words; first, his stress on teaching and the training of the intellect: "When the intellect has once been properly trained and formed to have a connected view or grasp of things, it will display its powers with more or less effect according to its particular quality and capacity in the individual. In the case of most men it makes itself felt in the good sense, sobriety of thought, reasonableness, candor, self-command, and steadiness of view, which characterize it" (xliii). Newman emphasized the training of the mind: "this habit of method, of starting from fixed points, of making his ground good as he goes, of distinguishing what he knows from what he does not know . . ." (xlv).[3]

In Discourse VI, Newman says that the university's function is "intellectual culture; here it may leave its scholars, and it has done its work when it has done as much as this. It educates the intellect to reason well in all matters, to reach out towards truth, and to grasp it" (VI-1). Ker says that "intellectual culture" for Newman "did not mean reading 'great books,' but learning how to think."[4] We will see a different use of the word "culture" in Ignacio Ellacuría's description of UCA objectives.

Newman says that in the university "a habit of mind is formed which lasts through life, of which the attributes are, freedom, equitableness, calmness, moderation and wisdom" (V-1). He cautions, however, that a liberal education will not guarantee a life of virtue. "Knowledge is one thing, virtue is another; good sense is not conscience, refinement is not humility. . . . Liberal Education makes not the Christian, not the Catholic, but the gentleman" (V-9). He defines the "gentleman" as one who has "a cultivated intellect, a delicate taste, a candid, equitable, dispassionate mind, a noble and courteous bearing in the conduct of life. . . . Liberal Education, viewed in itself, is simply the cultivation of the intellect, as such, and its object is nothing more or less than intellectual excellence" (V-9).

Let us turn now to the second area that Ker cites as a Newman contribution—the university as a community to achieve "universal knowledge" (xxxvii). Newman insists on the totality of all knowing; the various disciplines make sense only as part of a whole, which does not take away from their individual value, their autonomy as disciplines with their own methodologies and their own unique contributions. As part of a totality, each discipline adds nuances both to the others and to the whole; none should dominate the others (V-1). When one understands the connections among the various branches of knowledge, one arrives at what Newman called "philosophy," not in the technical sense of the term, but rather as the act of grasping meanings.

Ian Ker points out that Newman did not intend a university to offer courses in all subjects. Instead, says Ker, Newman felt that "a university must be in principle hospitable and in practice not hostile to any kind of knowledge. What subjects a university explicitly teaches will depend on a number of educational and practical factors; but implicitly it is ready to teach any genuine branch of knowledge because by its very definition a university cannot exclude or refuse to recognize any part of human knowledge."[5] We will see, however, different criteria chosen by the UCA for its decisions on what to include in the curriculum.

And now, a brief look at the third contribution Ker attributes to Newman. He is perhaps best known for his insistence that knowledge is a good, in and of itself, before it can be transformed into a means for something else, something more "useful" in the many senses of that word.

What is the end of university education, according to Newman? "Knowledge is capable of being its own end. Such is the constitution of the human mind, that any kind of knowledge, if it be really such, is its own reward. . . . an object, in its own nature so really and undeniably good, as to be the compensation of a great deal of thought in the compassing, and a great deal of trouble in the attaining" (V-2).

He goes on to say that "knowledge is not merely a means to something beyond it[self], or the preliminary of certain arts into which it naturally resolves, but an end sufficient to rest in and to pursue for its own sake. . . . Further advantages accrue to us and redound to others by its possession, over and above what it is in itself, . . . but, independent of these, we are satisfying a direct need of our nature in its very acquisition. . . . Knowledge . . . is valuable for what its very presence in us does for us, . . . even though it be turned to no further account, nor subserve any direct end" (V-2).

In Discourse VII, Newman looks at the mutual relationship of the good and the useful. "Though the useful is not always good, the good is always useful. Good is not only good, but reproductive of good; this is one of its attributes; nothing is excellent, beautiful, perfect, desirable for its own sake, but it overflows, and spreads the likeness of itself all around it. . . . If then the intellect is so excellent a portion of us, and its cultivation so excellent, it is not only beautiful, perfect, admirable, and noble in itself, but in a true and high sense it must be useful to the possessor and to all around him . . ." (VII-5).

He also affirms that "a cultivated intellect, because it is a good in itself, brings with it a power and a grace to every work and occupation which it undertakes, and enables us to be more useful, and to a greater number" (VII-6).

In contrast to Newman, we will see less emphasis at the UCA on knowledge as an end in itself and more on its usefulness for changing the reality of El Salvador.

Cardinal Newman delivered his nine discourses as part of a campaign to justify the university that the Irish bishops wished to establish for Catholics to have the educational advantages until then available only to Protestants. In the preface, he remarks that it was a concern of the church "that their people should be taught a wisdom, safe from excesses and vagaries of individuals, embodied in institutions which have stood the trial and received the sanction of ages" (xlvii).

Newman spoke to his own times but he also points out to later generations the timeless values of the intellectual life and how such educational advantages should be available to Catholics, at least to Catholic gentlemen. He was an Englishman, but he spoke to an Irish audience, a nation that had been oppressed for centuries. Even though once called the isle of saints and scholars, Ireland had been subjected to cultural oppression that destroyed its language and gave its best lands to the conqueror. Newman saw the new university as a bulwark for the faith of these people and a means of earning a respectable if not equal place in that society.

But his vision left that society basically unchanged. Social change was only beginning to be a part of the vocabulary of his age, at least in Catholic circles. He crossed swords, instead, with those who would deprive Catholics of a university education. In the course of his arguments he clarified the value of knowing in itself, and thus responded to those utilitarians who scoffed at liberal education as useless, and at theology as unintellectual. His university attempted to deal with the "national reality" of Ireland as he saw it. It is a vision with depth and relevance today, despite some of its time-bound limitations.

John Paul II and the Catholic University

In his apostolic constitution, *"Ex Corde Ecclesiae,"* Pope John Paul II calls the Catholic university a "center of creativity and dissemination of knowledge for the good of humanity"(265).[6] It is "distinguished by its free search for the whole truth about nature, man and God" and it does "research on all aspects of truth in their essential connection with the supreme Truth, who is God" (267).

The pope asserts that the university's "Christian inspiration enables it to include the moral, spiritual and religious dimension in its research and to evaluate the attainments of science and technology in the perspective of the totality of the human person" (268). In a statement that some critics might have difficulty reconciling with his later insistence on fidelity to magisterial teaching, he says that "by its Catholic character a university is made more capable of conducting an impartial search for truth, a search that is neither subordinated to nor conditioned by particular interests of any kind" (268).

He wants what he calls the "Christian mind" to have "a public, persistent and universal presence in the whole enterprise of advancing higher culture and that the students of these institutions become people outstanding in learning, ready to shoulder society's heavier burdens and to witness the faith to the world" (268).

After these preliminary descriptions the pope defines the Catholic university as "an academic community which, in a rigorous and critical fashion, assists in the protection and advancement of human dignity and of a cultural heritage through research, teaching and various services offered to the local, national and international communities. It possesses that institutional autonomy necessary to perform its functions effectively and guarantees its members academic freedom, so long as the rights of the individual person and of the community are preserved within the confines of truth and the common good" (268). He does not indicate who determines the "confines of truth."

The Catholic university has four essential characteristics:

1.   A Christian inspiration not only of individuals but of the university community as such.

2.   A continuing reflection in the light of the Catholic faith upon the growing treasury of human knowledge, to which it seeks to contribute by its own research.

3.   Fidelity to the Christian message as it comes to us through the church.

4.   An institutional commitment to the service of the people of God and of the human family in their pilgrimage to the transcendent goal which gives meaning to life. (269)

He goes even further in saying that "Catholic ideals, attitudes and principles penetrate and inform university activities in accordance with the proper nature and autonomy of these activities . . . [it is] an academic institution in which Catholicism is vitally present and operative" (269).

Along with Newman, he affirms "the church's belief in the intrinsic value of knowledge and research. In a Catholic university, research necessarily includes: (a) the search for an integration of knowledge, (b) a dialogue between faith and reason, (c) an ethical concern and (d) a theological perspective." And as for theology, it is to be "taught in a manner faithful to Scripture, tradition and the church's magisterium . . ." (269–70).

Then he turns to the relation of the university to the church "that is essential to its institutional identity. . . . [and] institutional fidelity of the university to the Christian message [which] includes a recognition of and adherence to the teaching authority of the church in matters of faith and morals" (271).

The bishops have "a particular responsibility to promote Catholic universities and especially to promote and assist in the preservation and strengthening of their Catholic identity. . . ." The relationship between the bishop and the university should be "characterized by mutual trust, close and consistent cooperation and continuing dialogue." Then the pope comes back to the special role of the theologians: "Since theology seeks an understanding of revealed truth whose authentic interpretation is entrusted to the bishops of the church, it is intrinsic to the principles and methods of their research and teaching in their academic discipline that theologians respect the authority of the bishops and assent to Catholic doctrine according to the degree of authority with which it is taught" (271).

A crucial question, however, is who will determine the "degree of authority" at any given time and place. As we will see at the UCA, the theological writings of Ignacio Ellacuría and Jon Sobrino were under regular surveillance when these theologians tried to push back existing boundaries and plow new ground.

When it comes to the problems of society, however, the papal teaching strikes a chord more responsive to UCA priorities. "Included among its research activities, therefore, will be a study of serious contemporary problems in areas such as the dignity of human life, the promotion of justice for all, the quality of personal and family life, the protection of nature, the search for peace and political stability, a more just sharing in the world's resources, and a new economic and political order that will better serve the human community at a national and international level" (271).

This resonates with the UCA's concern for the "national reality" and the need to look for solutions to El Salvador's basic problems, especially injustice and oppressive socioeconomic structures.

The pope even goes so far as to say that "if need be, a Catholic university must have the courage to speak uncomfortable truths which do not please public opinion, but which are necessary to safeguard the authentic good of society" (271). And indeed, the truths spoken by the UCA made some people very uncomfortable.

There is extensive elaboration by the pope of the university pastoral ministry, which should encourage prayerful reflection and participation in the sacraments, especially the eucharist. The Catholic university is also the forum for intercultural dialogue and evangelization (272–3).

The Catholic university is

a living institutional witness to Christ and his message, so vitally important in cultures marked by secularism or where Christ and his message are still virtually unknown. Moreover, all the basic academic activities of a Catholic university are connected with and in harmony with the evangelizing mission of the church: research carried out in the light of the Christian message which puts new human discoveries at the service of individuals and society; education offered in a faith context that forms men and women capable of rational and critical judgment and conscious of the transcendent dignity of the human person; professional training that incorporates ethical values and a sense of service to individuals and to society; the dialogue with culture that makes faith better understood and the theological research that translates the faith into contemporary language. (273)

A crucial concern is how church authorities will exercise their supervisory function over all these activities, especially in the light of what some have called the "restoration" mentality current in Rome, perceived as an attempt to slow down or even roll back the effects of the Second Vatican Council that will be discussed in the next chapter.

The last part of the papal document spells out general norms and insists that a teacher of Catholic theology have a "mandate" or permission to teach theology in the Catholic university. National conferences of bishops are supposed to come up with specific regulations by which these general norms are to be implemented. The United States bishops sent a draft to the universities late in 1993; that text has garnered heavy criticism because of the lack of due process and clarity on the nature of the bishops' authority. In 1994, Roman officials and United States bishops came to realize that the drafted regulations were unworkable and that more dialogue was needed before the issue would be revisited.

In El Salvador, the UCA has a unique status. Technically speaking it is not a Catholic university, (and we will see the reasons why it sought independence from ecclesiastical officials), but it does pride itself on its "Christian inspiration" and agrees in principle with many of the values expounded in "*Ex Corde Ecclesiae.*"

The local bishops have some say in determining the orthodoxy of what is taught as Catholic theology. There has usually been a cooperative relationship between the archbishops of San Salvador and the UCA, especially in the time of Archbishops Romero and Rivera, but if another kind of bishop were to head the archdiocese in the future, this could change the atmosphere dramatically. As we will see, some other bishops take a rather dim view of what is taught at the UCA and would be inclined to intervene in ways that would cause much controversy.

Like Newman, Pope John Paul's apostolic constitution praises the notion of knowledge as a value in itself, and gives great importance to research, especially in those areas where there is to be dialogue between faith and reason. It even describes service to the communities as an important role of the Catholic university, but there is greater concern for theological orthodoxy than urgency on justice issues that others, like the UCA, see as more intimately linked with the lived faith experience of individuals and communities.

We will see that the UCA worries less about orthodoxy and pastoral attention to students and turns its attention much more to dramatic issues of poverty and oppression. It is a difference of emphasis rather than a direct contradiction, but the emphases are significantly different and make for what appear to be very different kinds of universities. Thus it will be easier to understand why the UCA guarded with such intensity its autonomy from ecclesiastical officials, especially in the light of the broad authority over the Catholic university given to the local bishops by Pope John Paul II.

ERNEST L. BOYER

Ernest L. Boyer, the former commissioner of Education for the United States and a noted author and teacher in the field of education, talks about another important aspect of the university—its obligation to do research. Although his context is the United States, his insights will help illustrate a dimension of the UCA mission.

He prefers the word "scholarship" to "research," and he distinguishes four aspects of scholarship: discovery, integration, application and teaching.[7]

Boyer laments that too many universities see their role in scholarship as limited to "discovery," with the other three dimensions relegated to subordinate positions. Rewards come mainly with the discovery of new knowledge.

Some scholars contribute by "integrating" this new knowledge into a larger picture by critical analysis and interpretation. These studies often use interdisciplinary techniques and stretch beyond the more narrowly defined field in which the original discovery was made. "By integration, we mean making connections across the disciplines, placing the specialties in larger contexts, illuminating data in a revealing way, often educating nonspecialists, too" (18).

Boyer continues, "Application [of knowledge] moves toward engagement as the scholar asks, How can knowledge be responsibly applied to consequential problems? How can it be helpful to individuals as well as institutions? And further, Can social problems *themselves* define an agenda for scholarly investigation?" (21).

Boyer does not posit a separation between discovering and applying. "New intellectual understandings can arise out of the very act of application—whether in medical diagnosis, serving clients in psychotherapy, shaping public policy, creating an architectural design, or working with the public schools. In activities such as these, theory and practice vitally interact, and one renews the other" (23).

Boyer sees teaching as a form of scholarship—a creative, dynamic activity. "Teaching at its best means not only transmitting knowledge, but *transforming* and *extending* it as well. Through reading, through classroom discussion, and surely through comments and questions posed by students, professors themselves will be pushed in creative new directions" (24).

This expansion of the notion of scholarship to include more than the discovery of new knowledge brings the university into the community. "This deeply rooted professional concern reflects, we believe, recognition that teaching is crucial, that integrative studies are increasingly consequential, and that, in addition to research, the work of the academy must relate to the world beyond the campus" (75). Boyer argues that "the human community is increasingly interdependent, and higher education must focus with special urgency on questions that affect profoundly the destiny of all: How can the quality of the environment be sustained? Should the use of nuclear energy be expanded or cut back? Can an adequate supply of food and water be assured? How can our limited natural resources be allocated to meet our vast social needs? What new structures of world order can be devised to cope with the challenges of the post–cold war era?" (77).

The application of scholarship plays a major role at the UCA. But some critics will point out that the discovery, integration, and teaching dimensions need much greater emphasis for the full UCA potential to be realized.

A. Bartlett Giamatti

A. Bartlett Giamatti, the Renaissance scholar who served as president of Yale University in the 1980s and ended his days as United States baseball commissioner, writes imaginatively about what should happen in a university. He describes the world beyond the campus as an important concern of the institution, and he sees this commitment exercised when students participate in "that serious and splendid conversation that is any great college or university."[8]

He sees higher education as serving a democracy "by maintaining faith with a national history that at its best aches for equality as well as quality, for accessibility as well as excellence" (27).

While routine matters have importance and are the responsibility of the administrator, the "leadership in such an institution must define institutional shape, that is, define its standards and purposes—define the coherent, sustainable, daring, shared effort of learning that will increase a given community's freedom, intellectual excellence, human dignity" (37).

Essential to achieving its purposes is "civil conversation—tough, open, principled—. . . that must be preserved. If it is, a community is patiently built. If it is not, the place degenerates into a center of crisis management and competing special interests." Crucial is the conversation: "the sound of voices straining out the truth" (45).

Giamatti urges, "If there is a vision we press for, let it be of our nation's schools and colleges as free and ordered spaces, for those who live there, for the country at large; let the institutions for education be strong in their vision of themselves as both a source and a symbol for the freely inquiring mind, supportive of the right of other minds freely to inquire" (46).

He criticizes those institutions that have isolated themselves in ivory towers, "for they have chosen to be sanctuaries from society and not tributaries to it." He feels that a university's "basic strength derives from our common sense of what we do, why we do it, and whom we mean to teach" (50).

These words resonate with how the UCA also sees itself—as an institution with an unambiguous commitment to service the nation.

In his university, Giamatti stresses that

freedom of thought is the necessary precondition to political freedom.

If freedom, with all its freely chosen constraints, does not first reside in the mind, it cannot finally reside anywhere. Such an education, with a sense of history at its core, does not magically confer freedom of mind and spirit. Rather, by pursuit of learning for its own sake, by the pursuit of truth wherever it may lie, by the pursuit of those limits that must be learned in order to be surpassed—by these pursuits the mind and spirit are exercised. The mind and spirit are toughened and made capacious in the habits and conditions of freedom, a freedom based on an order, giving of itself so that others may pursue the same compound of boundary and boundlessness, restraint and release, and order earned for freedom's sake. (92)

Giamatti picks up Newman's idea of knowledge as a value in itself and liberal education as its own end. He emphasizes integration of the intrinsic value of education and its usefulness, and insists that they can be realized at one and the same time—a notion that will help in our reflection on the UCA model.

And I believe that the good, for individuals and for communities, is the end to which education must tend. I affirm Newman's vision that a liberal education is one seeking no sequel or complement. I take him to be writing of the motive or tendency of the mind operating initially within the educational process. But I believe there is also a larger tendency or motive, which is animated by the pursuit of ideas for their own sake. I believe that the pleasure in the pursuit of knowledge joins and is finally at one with our general human desire for a life elevated by dignity, decency, and moral progress. That larger hope does not come later; it exists inextricably intertwined with a liberal education. The joy of intellectual pursuit and the pursuit of the good and decent life are no more separable than on a fair spring day the sweet breeze is separable from the sunlight. (123)

He concludes that "in the common pursuit of ideas for themselves and of the larger or common good, the freedom that the individual mind wishes for itself, it also seeks for others. How could it be otherwise? In the pursuit of knowledge leading to the good, you cannot wish for others less than you wish for yourself. Thus, in the pursuit of freedom, the individual finds it necessary to order or to limit the surge to freedom so that others in the community are not denied the very condition each of us seeks" (124).

Giamatti values education as an end in itself, "a self-fashioning," whose larger purpose is "to turn the self out, to reach into yourself so as to reach beyond yourself—out to others, in order to make a country, and the lives of your fellow citizens, better" (124). In this he integrates both the intrinsic and social values of learning and of the university itself.

Giamatti's insights will be of assistance later as we look at ways the UCA might develop more effectively its model in its own historical context.

SUMMARY

We have reviewed Newman's *Idea of a University* because of its seminal importance and the emphasis given to knowledge as a value in itself. Then we saw, from the pope, a more explicit "Catholic" vision of the university. Ernest Boyer breaks free of more restrictive concepts of research and poses a more expansive term, scholarship, as more appropriate for realization of a university's mission.

Each of these points out elements of value in the university, but perhaps Giamatti is most successful at suggesting the integration of the interior and exterior aspects of the "idea" of a university. In his book of Yale convocation talks he sketches out this vision, and highlights the notion of integrating key elements, a point we will question in relation to the UCA.

We now turn to the UCA and the new model it represents. In one sense, the early years of the UCA should be described first, because they occurred before the new vision began to take shape. But such a treatment would break up the historical narrative and suggest an abrupt break with the past, which would not accurately reflect reality. We therefore turn first of all to the external influences that fostered a new vision of the university.

NOTES

1. For a survey on Latin American universities see Orlando Albornoz, *Education and Society in Latin America* (Oxford: Malmoll Press, 1993), especially 9–51, and José Joaquín Brunner, *Educación Superior en América Latina: Cambios y Desafíos* (Santiago: Fondo de Cultura, 1990). On the relationships between public and private Latin American universities see Daniel C. Levy, *Higher Education and the State in Latin America: Private Challenges to Public Dominance* (Chicago: University of Chicago Press, 1986). For general treatment of the social role of the university see also Carlos Tunnermann Bernheim, *Ensayos Sobre la Teoría de la Universidad* (Managua: Editorial Vanguardia, 1990), which reprints reflections of this famous Nicaraguan educator written up to the mid–1970s. See also Francisco Javier Palencia, *La Universidad Latinoamericana Como Consciencia* (Mexico City: Universidad Nacional Autónoma de México, 1982). On the research emphasis see Karl Jaspers, *The Idea of the University*, ed. Karl W. Deutsch (Boston: Beacon Press, 1959). See also Philip H. Altbach, "Patterns in Higher Education Development: Towards the Year 2000," *PROSPECTS* 21 (1991), 189–203, for a general survey of pertinent issues.

2. Ian Ker, *The Achievement of John Henry Newman* (Notre Dame, IN: University of Notre Dame Press, 1990), 34. See also Ian Ker, *John Henry Newman: A Biography* (Oxford: Clarendon Press, 1988), especially chapter 9. For an additional

important commentary on Newman see Jaroslav Pelikan, *The Idea of the University: A Reexamination* (New Haven: Yale University Press, 1992), 88.

3. John Henry Newman, *The Idea of a University,* ed. Martin J. Svaglic (New York: Holt, Rinehart and Winston, 1960). Citations are from this edition; sections are noted in the text in upper-case Roman numerals, and the preface in lower-case Roman numerals.

4. Ker, *Archievement, 9.*

5. Ker, *Archievement, 23.*

6. Pope John Paul II, "The Apostolic Constitution on Catholic Universities," *Origins* 20 (1990), 265–76. Page numbers are cited in the text. An excellent commentary on this apostolic constitution is John P. Langan, S.J., ed. *Catholic Universities in Church and Society: A Dialogue on "Ex Corde Ecclesiae"* (Washington, DC: Georgetown University Press, 1993). It includes the major papers and commentaries of a Georgetown seminar in which the author participated.

7. Ernest L. Boyer, *Scholarship Reconsidered* (Princeton: Carnegie Foundation for the Advancement of Teaching, 1990), xii. Subsequent citations are in the text.

8. A. Bartlett Giamatti, *A Free and Ordered Space* (New York: Norton, 1988), 24. Subsequent references are in the text.

4 ROOTS OF A NEW VISION

INTRODUCTION

Before we study the historical development of the UCA model, it is necessary to examine briefly another part of the context—changes in the Catholic Church and in the Society of Jesus (Jesuits). These four events were a council of the church, called Vatican II or the Second Vatican Council, the first one to meet in 100 years; an important meeting of the Jesuit order in 1968 (the provincial superiors in Río); a historic meeting in 1968 of all Latin American bishops at Medellín, Colombia, to look at their church in the light of both Vatican Council II and the miserable conditions in which most of the faithful lived; and the Thirty-second General Congregation, the highest legislative body in the Jesuit order, which met in 1974 and 1975.

In addition, liberation theology, so controversial in some circles and so influential in others, including Central America, also enriches this context because two major proponents, Ignacio Ellacuría and Jon Sobrino, taught and wrote at the UCA. A brief look at these ideas is also essential to understand the internal changes that took place at the UCA in subsequent decades.

Then, finally, this chapter will examine the "New UCA," as seen in key documents of the university.

THE SECOND VATICAN COUNCIL

In 1870, Napoleon III withdrew his troops defending the last remains of the papal states, so that they could help fend off attacks against Paris in the final stages of the Franco-Prussian War. After the departure of the French troops, Italian nationalists entered Rome, completed unification of the country, and hastened the departure of the bishops gathered at the First Vatican Council. Anxious to shore up the spiritual authority of the pope, whose temporal realms had been disappearing over the previous decade, the bishops declared the pope infallible in matters of faith and morals, and they left in place a strongly hierarchical church structure that would go unchallenged for a century.[1]

Those who opposed this church model found themselves outcasts; for example, the so-called Modernists and Americanists condemned early in the twentieth century.[2] Studies of biblical texts in their original languages, which Protestants had long explored, received little encouragement in the Catholic church until the papal encyclical *"Divino Afflante Spiritu,"* but eventually these biblical studies forced a more critical reading of the original texts and replacement of theology manual "proof texts" common in Catholic seminaries until the 1950s.[3] Reform of the Catholic liturgy was an early product of this new approach, but the election of Pope John XXIII, thought to be an interim appointment because of his seventy-seven years, opened the Vatican to a process of *aggorniamiento* (a fresh look at things), and he called the Second Vatican Council into session.[4]

This council redefined the church as "people of God" and used terminology that stressed the common ties of believers rather than their differences. This new emphasis showed up most clearly in the "Constitution on the Church" *(Lumen Gentium),* and the "Constitution on the Church in the Modern World" *(Gaudium et Spes).*[5]

In four sessions from 1962 to 1965, the bishops reformulated Catholic teaching in many areas, such as the sacraments, education, and the missions, but especially on the very nature of the church, and they called attention to the terrible conditions under which many of the people of God were living.[6]

Reflecting on these changes, Avery Dulles, S.J. describes five models of church, five different emphases that would make the postconciliar period a confusing yet creative time.[7] A brief description of these models helps situate liberation theology, which was to be such an important part of the UCA university model.

The first model Dulles calls "church as institution," or, as T. Howland Sanks, S.J., describes it, "the juridical model."[8] Dulles says that this model "defines the Church primarily in terms of its visible structures, especially the rights and powers of its officers" (31). Sanks says, "The primary mission of this type of church is to preserve the deposit of faith and protect the members from falling away from the truth thus guarded. This model . . . is the one most familiar to Roman Catholics prior to Vatican II" (32).

Dulles's second model sees church as "mystical communion" (43), a model that stresses community over juridical structure.

The third model of Dulles combines elements of both previous ones— "church as sacrament" (58). "As a sacrament the Church has both an outer and an inner aspect. The institutional or structural aspect of the Church—its external reality—is essential, since without it the Church would be invisible. . . . [But] the offices and rituals of the Church must palpably appear as the actual expressions of the faith, hope and love of living men. Otherwise the Church would be a dead body rather than a living Christian community. . . . Sacrament has an event character; it is dynamic. The Church becomes Church insofar as the grace of Christ, operative within it, achieves historical tangibility through the actions of the Church as such" (64).

Sanks calls this model "a social or communal sign, not just an individualistic one. Such a model stresses the witnessing activity of Christians and hence requires active participation by the members. This model is found in a number of recent Roman Catholic theologians such as Karl Rahner, Edward Schillebeeckx, Yves Congar, and Latin American liberation theologians, as well as in the documents of Vatican II" (33).

The fourth Dulles model, "church as herald," finds more echo in Protestant churches. Dulles says, "It makes the 'word' primary and the 'sacrament' secondary, the Church as gathered and formed by the word of God. The mission of the Church is to proclaim that which it has heard, believed and has been commissioned to proclaim. . . . It emphasizes faith and proclamation over interpersonal relations and mystical communion" (71).

"Church as servant" is the fifth Dulles model, whose mission "is not primarily to gain new recruits for its own ranks, but rather to be of help to all men, wherever they are. The special competence of the Church is to keep alive the hope and aspiration of men for the Kingdom of God and its values. In the light of this hope the Church is able to discern the signs of the times and to offer guidance and prophetic criticism" (91).

Sanks says this servant model "embodies the command to feed the hungry, clothe the naked, shelter the homeless, and care for the least of the brethren in order to enter the kingdom of God" (34).

We will see many resonances between this model and the writings of the liberation theologians of the UCA.

POST–SECOND VATICAN COUNCIL EVENTS

Pedro Arrupe, the superior general of the Jesuits, met in Río de Janeiro in May 1968 with the Latin American provincial superiors. In their final communiqué, the provincials affirmed their commitment to transform their institutions to tackle the appalling conditions in which the poor majority lived. "We intend to orient our whole apostolate . . . to participate, as best we can, in the common quest of all peoples (whatever their ideology may be) for a freer, more just, and more peaceful society. We want the Society of

Jesus to be actively present in the temporal life of humankind today: having as its sole criterion the gospel message as interpreted by the church, exercising no power in civil society and seeking no political goals, seeking solely to shape the consciences of individuals and communities"(78).[9]

The implications for a Jesuit university in Latin America could be guessed from their "promise to work for bold reforms that will radically transform existing structures . . . to promote social peace. . . . The integration of societal life within the Christian way of life calls for theological and philosophical reflection that will take in the whole world and its pressing problems" (79).

To help with this reflection, the provincials proposed Centers of Research and Social Action (CIAS); the Central American version became CIASCA, and it was staffed by some of the best-trained young Jesuits, who later had roles in the UCA at important times in its history.

The Jesuits affirmed, "Education, for example, is a major factor for social change. We think it is most important that our schools and universities accept their role as active agents of national integration and social justice in Latin America. We will not have development for all until we have integral education for all. . . . First and foremost we must instill an attitude of service to society in all our students and a genuine concern for marginal groups. Our students must participate in the transformation of present-day society and in the work of bettering the human condition" (80–81).

They called for more work with adults, financial assistance for students, attention to the mass media, and close collaboration with the laity: "And we must not only work *for* the laity, we must also work *with* them. By virtue of their real priesthood, they are called to the apostolate; and we must help them to channel their immense energies into the work of transforming our continent" (81).

The provincials ended their document with provocative questions for the Jesuits of Latin America. "Are we capable of responding to the world's expectations? Are our faith and charity equal to the anxiety-ridden appeals of the world around us? Do we practice self-denial sufficiently, so that God is able to flood us with light and energy? Does personal prayer have its proper place in our life, so that we are united with God in this great human task that cannot succeed without God?" (82).

In sum, the provincials called upon the Jesuit order to examine all that it did to see if its efforts were benefiting the most needy and leading toward the transformation of society according to the ideals of the gospels. They challenged individuals and communities to reflect on the quality of their own spiritual lives so that their motivation would be genuine and effective.

A few months later in 1968, the Latin American bishops met in Medellín, Colombia. After an address by Pope Paul VI, they looked at their church in the light of the new perspectives of Vatican II, and wrote guidelines for its renewal.[10] In vivid terms they describe the abject poverty and misery that permeates the continent and the social structures that hold it in place and "cry to heaven."

They root their challenge in the Bible and in personal conversion of Christians who have to commit themselves to change these conditions, not just as an act of charity but as an obligation.

> Although we are encompassed with imperfections, we are persons of hope. We have faith that our love for Christ and for our brothers and sisters will not only be the great force liberating us from injustice and oppression, but also the inspiration for social justice, understood as the whole of life and as an impulse toward the integral growth of our countries. Our pastoral mission is essentially a service of encouraging and educating the consciences of believers, to help them perceive the responsibilities of their faith in their personal and social lives. (Hennelly, 99)

The bishops criticized all current models of political and economic development:

> The system of liberal capitalism and the temptation of the Marxist system . . . militate against the dignity of the human person. One takes for granted the primacy of capital, its power and its discriminatory utilization in the function of profit-making. The other, although it ideologically supports a kind of humanism, is more concerned with collective humanity, and in practice becomes a totalitarian concentration of state power. We must denounce the fact that Latin America sees itself caught between these two options and remains dependent on one or another of the centers of power which control its economy. (101)

The Medellín documents go into detail on all aspects of Latin American church life, and how it has to change in order to respond to the urgent challenges of vast majorities living in such a way that they are scarcely an "image of God." What comes across so forcefully is the sense of urgency and the need to create social structures that will make life truly human and a more accurate reflection of the value of the person as seen in the gospels.

Medellín calls upon the church to separate itself from the interests of the powerful from whom it has so often sought protection in the past, and to align itself with the struggle of the poor—not in the sense of fomenting class struggle, but in recognizing the diametrically opposed visions of life and actual situations of the "haves" and the "have nots."

It would bring us too far afield to go into more detail on the Medellín vision that was so influential on the thinking of the UCA Jesuits, but the same concerns will be seen in the documents from the university and the social vision it seeks to implement.

There is one final outside source that must be touched on briefly because of its authoritative nature: the Thirty-second General Congregation of the Jesuit order. In the ordinary course of history, the superior general is the chief authority in the order after the pope, but at the death of the superior general or at other special times, a general congregation is held. While in session, the general congregation is the superior's superior. In all, there have only been thirty-three of these meetings since the founding of the order in 1540. The Thirty-fourth General Congregation met in January and February 1995.

Pedro Arrupe and the 263 delegates gathered during 1974 and 1975 and produced documents similar to Vatican II and Medellín. Luis Achaerandio, former Central American vice provincial and later rector of the UCA and leader of what we will call the "gradualist" approach to social change, was the delegate from Central America.

In its decree on "Jesuits Today," the congregation asked the question, "What is it to be a companion of Jesus today? It is to engage, under the standard of the Cross, in the crucial struggle of our time: the struggle for faith and that struggle for justice which it includes."[11] These words are emblazoned on a bronze plaque over the tomb of the UCA Jesuits at the Romero Chapel on the campus.

This decree explains the motivation for renewed commitment of the order:

> Ignorance of the Gospel on the part of some, and rejection of it by others, are intimately related to the many grave injustices prevalent in the world today. Yet it is in the light of the Gospel that men will most clearly see that injustice springs from sin, personal and collective, and that it is made all the more oppressive by being built into economic, social, political and cultural institutions of world-wide scope and overwhelming power. Conversely, the prevalence of injustice in a world where the very survival of the human race depends

on men caring for and sharing with one another is one of the principal obstacles to belief: belief in a God who is justice because he is love. Thus the way to faith and the way to justice are inseparable ways. . . . They cannot therefore be divided in our purpose, our action, our life. (402–3)

The order had always supported a social apostolate, direct work with the poor, but this general congregation added a new note: "Moreover the service of the faith and the promotion of justice cannot be for us simply one ministry among others. It must be an integrating factor of all our ministries; and not only of our ministries but of our inner life as individuals, as communities, and as a world-wide brotherhood. That is what our Congregation means by a decisive choice. . . . that underlines and determines all the other choices embodied in its declarations and directives." (403)

The Thirty-second General Congregation is best known for its Decree Number Four and for its description of the order's mission as "the service of the faith, of which the promotion of justice is an absolute requirement."[12] The General Congregation called upon the order to fashion lasting solutions to the major problems of the world and to do so in the spirit of the Gospels. "Injustice must be attacked at its roots which are in the human heart by transforming those attitudes and habits which beget injustice and foster the structures of oppression" (423).

The congregation called for spiritual renewal through the "spiritual exercises" of St. Ignatius, the founder;[13] a serious prayer life; and thorough preparation of Jesuits to work for a just society through all apostolic endeavors: high schools, colleges, universities, parishes, writing, research and every form of apostolic ministry.

The decrees forced reexamination of all that the order was doing throughout the world. In Central America, however, this reexamination had already begun with the province "retreat" in 1969, which will be explained later. But it is important to realize that what was happening in Central America was a manifestation of a far more extensive phenomenon, an awakening to the implications of injustice in the world, and the need for religious orders and educational institutions to see this terrible reality as the context for their labors.

We will see that the election of Luis Achaerandio as congregation delegate was a reaction against some changes that had already begun in Central America. Passed over for selection as the delegate of the vice province was the vice provincial himself, Miguel Francisco Estrada, who was identified with the more "liberationist" groups of the Society of Jesus in

Central America. Estrada was to be named rector of the UCA after the 1989 assassination.

There were common strands in all these documents and meetings: the church and the Jesuit order had to examine themselves in preparation for renewal and for refocusing their apostolic priorities—especially because of dramatic needs of the faithful, the desperately poor vast majority, whom we saw earlier in the socioeconomic description of El Salvador.

Many new insights were embodied in liberation theology, a movement in which the UCA played a significant role once it changed its initial focus. In examining the development of liberation theology at the UCA, and by citing the writings of the UCA faculty, we anticipate our story of the future, but it is important to see this theological approach early in the book, and as part of the overall context of a university for social change.

Sifting through the UCA writings on liberation theology can be a bit tedious, but there have been so many misinterpretations and caricatures that it is important to review them thoroughly, and in the words of the UCA writers themselves. The UCA staff constantly went back to the theological or faith vision that motivated them to immerse themselves in the real world of poverty and oppression, not as politicians but as theologians and scholars. Bear with us as we try to summarize this vast field.

THE THEOLOGY OF LIBERATION

Liberation theology does not add doctrines to Catholic belief; it does demand, however, that the believer integrate religious faith and a commitment to solve the needs of the community, especially those in dire straits. Rather than start with dogmatic statements or divine revelation and then apply these values to one's personal life, liberation theology challenges one to situate oneself in the middle of the real world, to reflect on this experience in the light of faith, and then commit oneself to change this world to one more in the image of God. There is less concern for orthodoxy and more for commitment. When this real world is one of oppression, injustice, and constant violation of human rights, then committing oneself to making a difference takes on a special urgency. Such is the real world of El Salvador and Central America.[14]

The August–September 1975 issue of *Estudios Centroamericanos (ECA)*, the scholarly journal of the UCA, was dedicated to Latin American theological method. The introduction states that "the novelty of this Latin American theology is rooted in its fidelity to the profound historicity of the faith message and to the radical historicity of our concrete situation . . . which needs changing at its very roots." There is no doubt "about the strength of those who are in power, and that they see themselves attacked by those who cultivate this new theology . . . whose voices they wish to silence by caricaturing them as anarchists and subversives, when they are not formally calling them Marxists.

Latin American theology attempts a rereading of all dimensions of faith from the point of view of one's own situation, and at the same time, offers a reinterpretation of the current situation from the point of view of faith" (403–4).

In that issue of *ECA,* in his "Towards a Foundation for Latin American Theological Method" (409–25), Ignacio Ellacuría summarizes this goal as follows: to use the most critical approaches possible, applying this method to the facts and the words of the historical Jesus as deduced from the Gospel accounts, thus recapturing for christology the historical reality of the life of Jesus.

Ellacuría asserts that

> the problem of theology does not depend principally on either the wishes of the ecclesiastical hierarchy or the pretensions of theologians, but rather on the concrete reality of the people of God. The salvation of God and the salvific mission of the church and of faith achieve their universality here and now in the very precise forms in which the theologian should make inquiries, reflecting on those signs through which the salvific presence of God is manifested or hidden in a Jesus who throughout history continued to become flesh. (422)

The task, then, is to avoid the identification of theology with one form of language, whether it be Aristotelian or Marxist, "taking care that the language used does not disfigure the purity and fullness of the faith, so that theology does not become a sacralized version of some particular secular discourse." To identify the "mediación" through which one arrives at faith with the reality of faith itself is to absolutize a particular expression, and thus to distort reality.

He continues:

> It is impossible to do theology today leaving out Marxist theory, not only as an element for criticism but also for illumination. The campaign [against Marxism] both inside and outside ecclesiastical circles . . . is myopic and motivated by vested interests whether consciously or not. But the exaggeration of one side should not lead to exaggeration by the other. A critical reading of Christianity through

Marxist theoretical categories should be accompanied by reflection on Marxist actions from the point of view of authentic Christian faith. Faith and theological reflection cannot be exhausted by Marxism regardless of what Marxism might offer for the interpretation and transformation of the person and society. (424)

Ellacuría points out, however, that despite its usefulness, "one should not be naive as to the consequences for the faith if Marxism is used indiscriminately, and even more so, if its usefulness is absolutized. Precisely because it might be useful, and should be taken seriously, it must be constantly subjected to a criticism which shows its limitations" (425).

In the same 1975 issue of *ECA,* Jon Sobrino, in "Theological Understanding in European and Latin American Theology" (426–45), praises the accomplishments of European theology, especially its contribution to the preparation of the Second Vatican Council, but he sees it as an inadequate instrument for analysis of the Latin American scene because of its "ahistorical nature," its reflection "from the point of view of the geopolitical center," and because it does not take into account what is going on in "the periphery" (444). He sees European theology as liberating and pastoral but reduced in its clientele to elite groups. "What has moved them to do theology is threats to believers as believers. Whereas the fundamental theological problem for Latin America has been not so much a threatened faith but rather the need to recapture a threatened sense of reality, a reality that is miserable. To do theology in the sense of liberation has meant transformation of the reality of sin. The adversary of theology is not so much the 'atheist' as it is the 'in-human.' Clarification of both faith and practice go together. . . ." In sum, "To know the truth is to do the truth, to know Jesus is to follow Jesus, to know sin is to take on its burden, to know God is to go to God in justice" (445).

This edition of *ECA* also included two more articles on christology by Jon Sobrino, who says that this theme of "the historical Jesus" became a war cry of those opposed to the UCA, as if it were a heresy that boded worse things to come. And indeed, Sobrino confirms that on a television broadcast, President Molina listed liberation theology as a national enemy.[15]

ECA returned to the important topic of liberation theology and the nature of the Latin American Church in the November 1977 edition.[16]

In the lead article, Ellacuría defines liberation theology as "faith-based reflection on the reality and the historical actions of the People of God who continue the work of Jesus in their announcing and realizing of the Kingdom of God. Salvation is always 'historical' in the sense that someone is saved from something at some given time—overcoming sin and evil" (707).

He calls attention to St. Paul's imagery of the church as the body of Christ: "The historical bodily presence of the church implies that the reality and the action of Jesus Christ 'takes flesh' in the church inasmuch as she brings about an incorporation of Jesus Christ into the reality of history. . . . The mystical and historical Christ are unified; they are two dimensions of the same Christ, and not contradictions" (708–9).

Arguing against those who see the church as an end in itself, Ellacuría points out that "only in an emptying out of self as a gift for the most needy, even to the point of death, and death on a cross, can the church claim to be the historical sacrament of the salvation of Christ" (710).

For people in the developing world, "the realization of the history of salvation is presented as liberation because domination and oppression define their actual situation." When one lives "like the majority of the people, that is, like the poor for whom Jesus felt a special concern because they were subjected to inhuman conditions, it is not difficult for the believer to see that what is happening is a new death of God in people, a renewed crucifixion of Jesus Christ present in the oppressed" (714–5). Therefore, it follows that the believer has to do something about this—one cannot go on living a "spiritual life" that ignores this continuing presence of God in history, a God continuing to be crucified today.

He continues, "For one reading the Gospel from the reality of sin and structural violence, Christian love presents itself forcefully as a struggle for justice which frees and saves a crucified and oppressed people. . . . This is not just a question of a rich church concerning itself for the poor, but rather, a church becoming present among the poor, in the end, dedicating its life to them and dying for them. In this way the church can establish itself in a Christian way as the efficacious sign of salvation for all people" (715).

Ellacuría sees persecution as inevitable if the church lives its faith in authentic ways, taking the side of the poor. How prophetic in the light of what happened to him and his colleagues on November 16, 1989.

He cautions, however, that "the church's role could not be reduced to that of a pure sociopolitical force which accomplishes its task by fighting ideologically against unjust structures or which gives top priority to this ideological task. . . . [Some] do not realize the damage they do. . . . Some take advantage of these poor people in order to attempt a hopeless political project which does not even take into consideration the totality of existing material conditions" (719). Ellacuría concludes that "the little faith and confidence they have in the saving potential of the teaching of Jesus causes them to pass right by the historical following of Jesus and opt instead for purely political actions. . . . But they are not the same as the Christian faith and they cannot be its substitute" (721).

In another article in the November 1977 issue of *ECA*, Jon Sobrino comments on the theme of evangelization and the church in Latin America especially, as treated in Paul VI's encyclical, *"Evangelii Nuntiandi."*

"All church structures, its doctrines, sacraments, and organizations do not achieve their fullness except in the service of evangelization . . . whose ultimate horizon is the Kingdom of God." Its fundamental elements are

> (1) a proclamation of the word of God as a global expression of the meaning of history and its gratuitous nature; (2) the testimony in the lives of Christians inasmuch as they are the subjects of faith and can transmit it; (3) the transforming action of the world which brings into existence the content of the word of God, and the establishment of the kingdom of God; (4) since the world in which the church develops its mission is a world of sin, evangelization involves not only proclamation but also prophetic denunciation of all that impedes or formally denies the proclamation of the kingdom of God.[17]

The content of evangelization is made present in two intimately related ways: "The Good News as transcendent, that is the love of God for people as manifested in Christ, and the hope of ultimate fulfillment, and secondly, the Good News as historical reality, the realization of this love in determined historical eras. In our continent, without ignoring other necessary forms, love should take the form of justice as an indispensable vehicle for the creation of community of all persons and their relationships as children of God" (733).

Sobrino continues, "Evangelization should unify the moment of faith and the moment of praxis, without giving either aspect autonomy over the other. . . . Christian reality is the historical process of believing in the God of the kingdom while making the kingdom." The consequences of this vision will be "the conversion of the church itself, the unity of various church groups around this evangelizing mission, and subsequent separation of those who do not accept this mode of evangelization, the persecution of the church, not as institution but as missionary, but also credibility for the church in the world, especially with the oppressed, and the self awareness of the church as the Body of Christ in history" (736).

In a 1987 article in the *Revista Latinoamericana de Teología*, Ellacuría further elaborates the essentials of liberation theology, and gives additional insights into why this form of theology underpinned motives and mission of the UCA Jesuits.[18] The excerpts are lengthy, but it is better to see these views in the words of Ellacuría than in paraphrase.

> Liberation theology aims at a change not only in Latin American people and society, but also in its sociohistorical structures. . . . The liberation that can be stated in theological terms as a liberation by degrees from sin, from the law, and from death, can also be stated in historical terms as liberation from everything that oppresses people and prevents them from enjoying their call to be God's free children.
>
> This theology has its point of departure in the experience . . . that the greater part of the population of Latin America lives under conditions of dehumanizing poverty and social and political oppression [which] . . . result from historical structural injustice, and for which different social subjects (classes, nations, empires) and different economic and political dynamisms are responsible, whether by commission or omission. In light of this situation, liberation theology, first as a more or less reflexive movement of faith, and then as explicit rational reflection, asks itself what Christian faith has to say about causes and solutions. . . . and what actions should result from that faith in order to make sure that oppressed peoples succeed through liberation processes in becoming free peoples. . . .
>
> Liberation theology is not a sociology or a political science, but a specific mode of knowledge whose sources or principles are revelation, tradition, and the *magisterium*—at whose service certain mediations are placed. If among these mediations the social, economic, historical, and political sciences have a certain importance, that does not necessarily imply that theology is transformed into one of these sciences with theological language, any more than the [previous] classical preference for the mediation of philosophy necessarily made earlier theology a form of philosophy. In intention, in methodology, in the facts, liberation theology shows itself more and more to be a theology. (19–20)

Ellacuría sees liberation theology as a "total theology," not just of one region, not "a theology of the political, but a theology of the kingdom of God." There is a sense in which it is a political theology since it stresses the liberation of persons and peoples, "yet not in such fashion that all that matters is the theology's political significance" (20).

These distinctions became very important later on, when the university and the church were accused of mixing religion and politics as if the UCA authors were denying any differences.

Ellacuría continues, "the institutional church is and must be a force that moves directly and formally in the social arena and not in that of the state. And . . . the church must resort to social power and not political power to realize its mission." He adds that "efficacy in this case comes from social pressure, through word and gesture, and not from managing political power." Realist that he is, Ellacuría cautions that "conflict will doubtless come about when this social pressure is exerted wholly and entirely on behalf of the mass of the people and the people's movements, consequently provoking clashes with dominant classes and structures. But it will not be a conflict from acting against anyone; rather it will be a conflict from acting on behalf of the oppressed mass of the people" (31).

He further adds nuances to this view by stating that "only in exceptional cases does the occasion arise for the institutional commitment to go beyond favoring the structural changes demanded by the mass of the people to realize their own liberation. Archbishop Romero used to warn about the . . . danger of making absolutes of popular organizations, and of subordination to any popular organization as if it were an absolute" (32).

Ellacuría sees the role of liberation theology as to "try to strengthen the contribution of Christian faith to social change, because, even without being subordinated to any political enterprise, faith, those who live that faith, and the church of the faithful have their own power, which must independently be placed at the service of the historical realization of the kingdom. . . . Liberation theology will urge [political and social movements] to adjust their choice of means and their hierarchy of values to what Christian faith sets forth as the spirit of every possible liberation" (38).

Ellacuría then turns to the question of violence.[19]

> Oppression in all its forms and . . . every kind of structural injustice, is the worst form of violence, because it affects the majority of the population and does so in what is most sacred and profound: the preservation and improvement of life itself. . . . even though it presents itself in modes and manners that lack dramatic effect. Liberation theology sees as violence and as a source of violence everything that it calls social sin which, in the Latin American context, is in great part the result of the prevailing capitalism—both in the center-periphery, north-south relationships, as well as in the corresponding reflection within each country. The principal reflection of this violence, but not the only one, is the condition of poverty and destitution that fundamentally affects, not only the quality of life, but the very fact of living.

Liberation theology, then, accepts in principle the morality and even the Christian congruity of the violence that liberates from the other, more radical, forms of violence, provided that it takes place in the proper context and with the proper conditions. In this it follows classical morality, only in a more rigorous and restricted form, in that it permits certain forms of violence only in the face of structural, repressive, and oppressive violence. The violence of structural injustice, especially when it goes to the extreme of preventing the achievement of human life and closing off all less violent means of seeking redress, is a supreme evil that can and even must be combated with effective means, including armed struggle. . . . But, in spite of armed struggle's limited licitness, it is always an evil, and it can only be used in proportion to the greater evil that is to be overcome. . . . And when the good of the mass of the people is subordinated to the taking or the keeping of political power by a revolutionary movement, the right to armed struggle is invalidated.

On the other hand, not just any violent means can be employed. There are means that are so intrinsically and totally wrong that their use is forbidden. Hence revolutionary violence must never take the form of terrorism, . . . actions against helpless persons in a violent way, placing their lives or physical integrity in danger. (40–1)

Nor is hatred permitted. "The enemy do not cease to be human because one wants to liberate them from their role as oppressors or violent repressors" (41). This is a variation on just war theory, and a far cry from an indiscriminate stand in favor of violence.[20]

In an article published the year of his assassination, Ellacuría wrote of utopia and prophecy in Latin America—utopia not in the sense of some never-to-be-achieved idealistic world, but rather as an ideal to which one could and should strive. He saw prophecy—speaking out on a current situation—as a way of identifying the gap between the actual and the ideal, and suggesting ways by which Christians could live out their vocation by committing themselves to close that gap, using their own special talents and opportunities."[21]

Ellacuría specifies that it is "a Christian utopia that is under discussion and so it maintains very explicitly the transcendent dimension of the kingdom." And thus, "prophecy and utopia, history and transcendence, nourish each other. Both are historical and both are transcendent, but neither becomes what it is meant to become except in relation to the other" (50).

The so-called developed world, he says, "is not at all the desired utopia, even as a way to overcome poverty, much less to overcome injustice.

Instead, it is a sign of what should not be and of what should not be done" (51). The western world's life style "is not universalizable, not even materially, since there are not enough material resources on earth today to let all countries achieve the same level of production and consumption as that of the countries called wealthy, whose total population is less than 25 percent of humanity" (56).

He criticizes some in the church who refuse to accept the prophetic dimension and who dismiss it as the "parallel magisterium" that sets itself up as more genuine interpreters of the nature of the kingdom of God.

Ellacuría speaks also of the "poor with spirit" who, "when they become aware of their unjust condition and of their possibilities and even of the real obligation they have in the face of destitution and structural injustice, . . . are changed from passive to active subjects and . . . multiply and strengthen their salvific-historical values" (60).

He emphasizes the importance of the virtue of hope in liberation theology.

> It is a verifiable fact that hope, which animates the poor-with-spirit, inspires them in long and hard processes that to others seem useless and futureless. . . . hope against all hope—a very Christian characteristic—although once it appears, it is nourished by the results already achieved. It is not the secure reckoning that leads to making an investment with the calculated expectation of desirable fixed-term results; it is not an idealistic dream that removes one from reality. Rather, it is the accepting of God's promise of liberation, a fundamental promise that propels toward an exodus in which historical goals and objectives unite with transhistorical certainties. (61)

The UCA Jesuits sought to bring to life this theological vision by solid scholarship, teaching, and active involvement in the community, and thereby to assist a just society to emerge.

Having seen the historical and socioeconomic context, reflections on the nature of a university from various authors, and then the changes within the Catholic church and the Jesuit order and liberation theology, it is now time to see three important documents that express the vision of the new UCA before examining the history of the university itself. The first is from a 1970 speech at the Inter-American Development Bank, and the second from an article written by Ignacio Ellacuría on the UCA's tenth anniversary in 1975. The third consists of a short excerpt from the book by Román Mayorga, the third rector.

The vision of the new UCA saw the light of day as early as 1970 in the speech written by Ignacio Ellacuría and Román Mayorga and delivered by Father José María Gondra, S.J., at the 1970 signing of the first loan from the Inter-American Development Bank (IDB). This was an early example of lay-Jesuit cooperation in the elaboration and implementation of the UCA vision. It crystallized the new vision and signaled the beginning of a new era.[22]

The UCA saw itself as an institution dedicated to "development" defined as "human and social transformation" and "access to real enjoyment of fundamental human rights"—not just blind following of the same paths by which the so-called developed nations of the world achieved their economic status. The speech cites the Vatican document *"Populorum Progressio"* on the goals the university should foster—particularly "integral development" of each and every person. Such a challenge "requires profound renewal of the traditional structures of a university" (10).

In addition, "The mission of the university is to serve all people and not just privileged groups." In Central America, "the university cannot assuage its conscience . . . thinking that just through training professionals it is going to reach all the people. . . . because graduates sometimes take advantage of the privilege of a university degree to impede the just development and distribution of national resources" (11).

The unique way in which a university should "put itself at the immediate service of all is by directing its attention . . . to the study of those structures . . . which condition for good or evil the lives of all citizens. It should analyze these structures critically, and contribute in university fashion to the exposure and destruction of unjust ones." The university "should create new models which society and government can put into operation." Such a university will also be "beneficial to its professors and students because it will offer them the critical and creative task without which there is no truly university education" (11).

The university wants to "awaken in all a sharp awareness of human rights for Central Americans . . . who live in a region that is more and more exploited and oppressed" and therefore are tempted to resort to violence to right these wrongs. "The university has to raise consciousness, not with moralizing sermons but with studies that have an impact." Only in this way will it be possible to avoid "developmentalism" and to create the channels which will bring about "new resources and the political and social structures which will lead to equitable distribution of the fruits of development" (11).

In words that come up time and again because they are so crucial, the university defines its principal mission as "a critical and creative conscience of society." It requires "autonomy for its thinking and freedom to express it" (12). It sees this freedom as liberation—"that process which causes the disappearance of all kinds of oppression: biological, social, economic, political, and cultural" (12).

In sum, the university seeks

> the creation of a new person for whom freedom is not just a political attribute but of the very essence of one's existence. . . . There is no freedom without justice and truth, and truth is not complete until it shows its . . . capacity to effect justice. . . . To know what kind of development to promote and for whom, and to know how to subordinate development to liberation and freedom, requires a new vision and unusual courage in undertaking a university task. . . . The professionals whom the university forms should be at one and the same time agents of development and social change, and its research should foster the complete freedom of the Central American. (12–3)

On its tenth anniversary in 1975, Ignacio Ellacuría spelled out the meaning of the UCA in an important article in the scholarly journal of the university, *Estudios Centroamericanos (ECA)*.[23] (Later in this book there will be an in-depth review of university documents elaborated conjointly by the Jesuits and their lay colleagues, especially in 1979, but the Ellacuría article is more readily available and gives an overview that will help clarify the basic elements.)

Ellacuría says that "the criterion for measuring the ultimate significance of a university and what it is in its total reality is its impact on the historic reality within which it exists and which it serves." In this sense the university has a political dimension and a political mission because "it is a factor in the political situation." But this political mission must be exercised as a university, and he cautions against two false approaches:

> to help strengthen the prevailing system by responding positively to its demands or at least by not hindering it, by being devoted to knowledge and technical matters in an ostensibly neutral manner. The other way is to challenge the system head on, especially that part which is the state, in the manner of an opposition political party or popular organization, whose political activity is determined by their primary objective which is to take over state power. Because of its own critical character, and because of its fundamental need to be rational and

ethical, the university cannot be reduced to taking the side of any given political or social system indiscriminately. (178–9)

He divides his presentation into the following categories: (1) the horizon of the university; (2) its specific concerns; (3) the means it uses; (4) its manner or style; and (5) its objective.

The *horizon* of the UCA is the Salvadoran people, who live daily in a society which is structurally unjust, a society in which the vast majority scrapes out a living from one day to the next, while a privileged minority reaps the benefits—as was seen in the first chapter. The Salvadoran majority has lived under many centuries of oppression, going back to pre-Columbian times when they were held in subjugation by their local *caciques,* who were later replaced by Spaniards, and then by the sons of Spaniards and their descendants up to the present day.

Ellacuría points out another crucial element in the new university—that the UCA had to take sides; it had to place itself at the side of the vast, oppressed majority—"a majority so overwhelming that by its very magnitude it can be regarded as the authentic representative of the interests of the whole—but also an unjustly dehumanized majority" (181). He did not advocate class warfare; he simply acknowledged that the interests of the poor and the rich were diametrically opposed to each other, and that one could not be neutral in the face of this conflict. The university would take sides, however, using university methods and not those of other social forces in the country which might be justifiable in themselves but would not be appropriate for a university. The horizon of the UCA, therefore, was to be the Salvadoran people.

The *specific concern* of the UCA is culture. Ellacuría uses "culture" in the sense of "to cultivate," to develop an understanding of the national reality so as to transform it. "Culture has an essentially praxic meaning, insofar as it derives from the need to act and should lead to activity that transforms both the subject and his or her natural and historic environment" (182).

The university is to serve as "the critical and creative consciousness of the national reality," processing national reality through its intellectual and technical resources (184). The UCA is to foster a cultural revolution by "thoroughly examining the current system of values that has been internalized, destroying it if necessary, and developing new values that really respond to the new possibilities of Salvadorans at this particular moment of history and in this specific geographical context" (183). In a play on words, Ellacuría splits up the word *conciencia*. The UCA is to create *con ciencia*—"with understanding" or "learning"—that can be used to transform an unjust society into one that fosters human dignity.

Ellacuría does not deny Cardinal Newman's thesis in *The Idea of a University* on the value of knowledge as an end in itself; essentially, he ignores it, because he is so intent on responding to the urgent, life-or-death reality of El Salvador, and the task the university could and should assume in transforming this terrible reality.

The *means* to bring about culture is what Ellacuría calls *la palabra eficáz*—"the efficacious word." This "word" would go far beyond the verbal; it would include "culture" in the sense of cultivating understanding, elaboration, and analysis of reality, a process that would lead toward the transformation of reality (185).

This "efficacious word" is powerful because it is based on scientific data and careful analysis, and it serves as the basis for what he calls a "collective consciousness": the Salvadoran community becoming aware of itself, its potential and its problems, its values and its promise. And this consciousness would lead to transforming action; the "word," in a sense, would take flesh in the liberating actions of the Salvadoran people. The university would be a forum and a catalyst for this transformation.

The UCA's *manner or style* is one of struggle; the word in Spanish is *beligerante*, but "belligerent" is not an accurate translation. Translator Philip Berryman's translation is "aggressive," but this too tends to go beyond what Ellacuría was suggesting (186). The notion of "struggle" seems the most appropriate. The UCA is to engage in a rational struggle against the irrationality of oppression. It is to be a university-type struggle, but a struggle nonetheless.

Román Mayorga points out that Ellacuría ceased using this phrase in later writings and preferred to stress dialogical language to describe the university's manner of acting.[24]

The university would dispassionately produce new knowledge and stress dialogue, but it would do more; it would unmask lies, and it would denounce the actions of those who propagated them. And so the word *denunciar* would take on special importance especially in the struggles of the 1970s and 1980s.

The UCA's *objective* is nothing less than the "structural transformation of society" (187). The university will educate professionals who will have competence and social vision, but even more importantly, the UCA will tackle structures. Simply to train professionals who might ameliorate the status quo would, in the long run, be a disservice to El Salvador. "The only justification for focusing the university on training professionals as the primary thrust of its activity would be with the understanding that only through well trained professionals can the structural transformation of the nation be brought about—but we would thereby be reasserting that structural transformation is primary" (188).

There is clarity in this vision: a clear horizon, the Salvadoran people and their concrete reality; a new sense of "culture," to cultivate a new reality for the Salvadoran people; use of "an efficacious word" to transform society; realization that this commitment involved struggle, but a struggle appropriate for a university; and a whole university contributing significantly to the social transformation of the national reality.

Ellacuría's vision recognizes the obstacles to be faced in this struggle. This new kind of university would be resisted by the privileged. Ellacuría foresees that the powerful will attack the UCA for taking sides in the Salvadoran people's struggle. The UCA will engage in the struggle through its minds and its data, with committed teachers and researchers. The powerful, unable to match these arguments, will reply with calumny and bullets.

He touches on other obstacles: economic dependence for the functioning of the university, students more interested in being professionals than agents of change, teachers caught up in their academic subjects but unmindful of the struggle for justice that challenges every day. Then there is the cumbersome task of the day-to-day running of a university: payrolls, records, supervision of teaching, coordination of research. Another very serious obstacle is the lack of enough highly prepared faculty who could share and implement this vision.

Toward the end of this article Ellacuría discusses the Christian dimension of the university, which he says could be measured more by its commitment to the liberation of the people of God than by specifically religious tasks such as dispensing the sacraments and giving classes of theology, which he also recognizes as important. He feels, however, that these tasks can be accomplished by parishes and other religious centers.

Román Mayorga, third rector of the UCA (1975–1979), sees the role of the university in his *La Universidad para el Cambio Social* as "contributing to the elaboration of a National Project," a vision of what a just society should look like, and a process in which all university departments and functions are dedicated to the creation of such a society, a process in which one "struggles for the good of other people, especially the majority of the Salvadoran population who are oppressed and exploited."[25] In 1994, Mayorga said that what he meant by a "national project" is the following: "Any university that wants to have a significant impact on the history of a society should forge rationally developed images of the future of that society and of the paths through which these projections might be realized. To this end all disciplines of knowledge should contribute much more than personal inspirations."[26]

Mayorga stresses the importance of the "political" role of the university in the sense of dedication to the study of society's most serious problems and the elaboration of solutions. He equates the term "apolitical university" *(universidad apolítica)* with "paralytic university" *(universidad paralítica)*.[27]

This vision requires "constant dialogue with all sectors and permanent contact with their needs and real anxieties."[28]

He takes the phrase "critical and creative conscience" and explains its double dimension: first, conscience—"a criterion of human value which tells us the difference between right and wrong;" and then consciousness, "understanding or reason [*conciencia*], a determination to apply intellectual capacity and knowledge toward shedding light on the ethical criterion . . ., two basic human faculties—reason and ethical responsibility . . . which complement each other."[29]

> [This] critical and creative conscience/consciousness, arrived at through research and communication among those who work in a university fashion, has to be communicated in order to become operative and effective, through the channels of teaching and social outreach *(proyección social)*. Social outreach makes no sense unless there is a university '*conciencia*' [both conscience and consciousness] to project, and university people to project it. Teaching would be just uncritical transmission of irrelevant data, if it were not nourished by research and transformed into social outreach. We are dealing with three activities profoundly linked with each other, and which must be carried on in a closely coordinated way.[30]

We have seen the theoretical framework developed by key architects of the UCA university vision. Now it is important to begin the narrative of the UCA history, the ups and downs of what worked and what did not, and what is still to be developed.

NOTES

1. See James J. Hennesey, S.J., *The First Council of the Vatican: The American Experience* (New York: Herder and Herder, 1963), and Charles J. Beirne, S.J., "Latin American Bishops of the First Vatican Council, 1869–1870," *The Americas* 25 (January 1969), 265–80.

2. See James J. Hennesey, S.J., *American Catholics* (Oxford: Oxford Univer-

sity Press, 1981), 184 ff.

3. See Gerald P. Fogarty, S.J., *American Catholic Biblical Scholarship* (San Francisco: Harper and Row, 1989).

4. See Peter Hebblethwaite, *The Runaway Church: Post-Conciliar Growth or Decline* (New York: Seabury, 1970).

5. Walter Abbott, ed. S.J., *The Documents of Vatican II* (New York: Association Press and America Press, 1966).

6. These council documents were complemented by papal encyclicals from Pope John XXIII and his successor, Pope Paul VI: *"Pacem in Terris," "Populorum Progresio," "Evangelii Nuntiandi,"* and "Justice in the World," the final document of the 1971 synod of bishops. There is a comprehensive study of the Council and these other church documents in T. Howland Sanks, S.J., *Salt, Leaven and Light: The Community Called Church* (New York: Crossroad, 1992).

7. Avery Dulles, S.J., *Models of the Church* (Garden City, NY: Doubleday, 1974). Subsequent citations are in the text.

8. Sanks, 32. Subsequent citations are in the text. For sociological paradigms useful for analysis of the role of the Church see Carlos Alberto Torres, *The Church, Society and Hegemony: A Critical Sociology of Religion in Latin America*, trans. Richard A. Young (Westport, CT: Praeger, 1992).

9. Provincials of the Society of Jesus, "The Jesuits in Latin America," in Alfred T. Hennelly, S.J., *Liberation Theology: A Documentary History* (New York: Orbis, 1990), 77–83. All citations are from this source and are in the text.

10. Second General Conference of Latin American Bishops, "The Church in the Present-Day Transformation of Latin America in the Light of the Council" (August 26–September 6, 1968), in Hennelly, 89–119.

11. Society of Jesus, "Jesuits Today," *Documents of the 31st and 32nd General Congregations of the Society of Jesus*, ed. John W. Padberg, S.J. (St. Louis: The Institute of Jesuit Sources, 1977), 401–9. Page numbers are included in the text. This compendium will hereafter be cited as *Documents*.

12. Society of Jesus, "Our Mission Today: The Service of Faith and the Promotion of Justice," in *Documents*, 411. See also Jean-Yves Calvez, S.J., *Faith and Justice: The Social Dimension of Evangelization* (St. Louis: Institute of Jesuit Sources, 1991).

13. David L. Fleming, S.J., trans., *The Spiritual Exercises of St. Ignatius* (St. Louis: Institute of Jesuit Sources, 1975). Ignatius of Loyola wrote a spiritual journal which suggests a process of personal renewal that begins with the "first principle and foundation," a declaration that God is to be the center of one's existence, and all else subordinate to this primary goal. Then the exercitant meditates on personal sin and seeks to purify himself or herself from all obstacles to following Jesus. The second "week" (which actually runs closer to two weeks) takes the retreatant through the life of Jesus Christ so that he might be the model for one's own life. The third "week" brings the person through the passion and death of Jesus, to confirm the resolutions made in the second "week," and then the last "week" focuses on the resurrection of Jesus and a final contemplation on finding God in all things. In its full form the spiritual exercises take one month. Jesuits make an eight-day version of it each year.

For a witty, scholarly account of the development of the spiritual exercises and their influence on the early days of the Jesuit order and its work in education see John W. O'Malley, S.J., *The First Jesuits* (Cambridge, MA: Harvard University Press, 1993).

14. The seminal work on liberation theology is Gustavo Gutiérrez, *A Theology of Liberation: History, Politics, and Salvation*, rev. ed. (New York: Orbis, 1988). The most comprehensive review of liberation theologians and their critics will be found in Alfred T. Hennelly, S.J., *Liberation Theology: A Documentary History* (New York: Orbis, 1990). A text that gives more emphasis to opponents is Michael Novak, ed., *Liberation Theology and the Liberal Society* (Washington: American Enterprise In-

stitute, 1987). For a discussion of the relationship between Marxism and liberation theology and a critique of the Novak approach see Peter Burns, S.J., "The Problem of Socialism in Liberation Theology," *Theological Studies* 53 (1992), 493–516. See also Stephen J. Pope, "Proper and Improper Partiality and the Preferential Option for the Poor," *Theological Studies* 54 (1993), 242–71. For an animated attack against the UCA see Ricardo de la Cierva, *Jesuitas, Iglesia y Marxismo, 1965–1985: La Teología de la Liberación Desenmascarada*, (Barcelona: Plaza & Janes, 1986). A summary of this former Jesuit's attack was republished by the Salvadoran newspaper *El Diario De Hoy* on the first anniversary of the assassination! A useful bibliography for related topics is Edward T. Brett, "The Impact of Religion in Central America: A Bibliographical Essay," *The Americas* 49 (January 1993), 297–341.

15. Conversation with the author, April 24, 1992.

16. Interview of Jon Sobrino, June 1992. This issue of *ECA* produced a furious reaction from Bishop Aparicio, who saw it as an attack against the preparatory activities for the 1979 meeting of the Latin American bishops at Puebla, Mexico.

17. "Evangelización e iglesia en América Latina," *ECA* 32 (1977), 728–9.

18. Ignacio Ellacuría, S.J., "La Teología de la liberación frente al cambio socio-histórico de América Latina," *Revista Latinoamericana de Teología* 4 (1987), 241–63, translated in John Hassett and Hugh Lacey, eds., *Towards a Society That Serves Its People: The Intellectual Contribution of El Salvador's Murdered Jesuits* (Washington: Georgetown University Press, 1991) 19–43. An appendix of this book contains an extensive bibliography of the published work of the martyrs. Page citations are in the text.

19. For a treatment of the topic of violence from the psychological point of view see the comprehensive article by Ignacio Martín-Baró, "Violence in Central America: A Social Psychological Perspective," trans. Anne Wallace, in Hassett and Lacey, 333–46.

20. For additional details on just war theory, see National Conference of Catholic Bishops, "The Challenge of Peace: God's Promise and Our Response," in Hugh J. Nolan, ed., *Pastoral Letters of the United States Catholic Bishops* (Washington: United States Catholic Conference, 1984), 493–581.

21. "Utopía y profetismo desde América Latina: un ensayo concreto de soteriología histórica, *Revista Latinoamericana de Teología* 6 (1989), 141–84, in Hassett and Lacey, 44–88. Page references are in the text.

22. "Discurso de la Universidad Centroamericana José Simeón Cañas en la Firma del Contrato con el BID," in *Planteamiento Universitario, 1989* (San Salvador: UCA Editores, 1989), 9–14. Page numbers for citations appear in the text.

23. "Diez años después: es posible una universidad distinta?" *Estudios Centroamericanos*, 30 (November 1975), 605–28, in Hassett and Lacey, 177–207. Page citations are in the text.

24. Communication with the author, January 21, 1994.

25. Third ed. (San Salvador: UCA Editores, 1976), 6. Hereafter cited as Mayorga.

26. Personal communication with the author, March 24, 1994.

27. Mayorga, 11.

28. Mayorga, 13.

29. Mayorga, 15.

30. Mayorga, 17.

5 THE FOUNDING YEARS: 1965–1969

This chapter traces the early history of the UCA, starting with an idea for one University of Central America with several campuses, and then a bishops' plan for a "Catholic" university in San Salvador. But the university that actually began in 1965 was a *corporación de utilidad pública*—literally, "a corporation for the benefit of the public." It is an institution oriented toward the public good and the public's needs but neither owned by the state nor a private university in the traditional sense of the term.

After an elegant inauguration in the presence of the president of El Salvador, the UCA set up temporary quarters, was evicted because of some unofficial student activities, took refuge for a while in the Jesuit high school, and finally moved to its own campus.

Most important for the development of a truly new university model, however, was the December 1969 retreat and discernment process that set the Central American Jesuits on a new path with their lay colleagues to be a voice for those who had no voice. Along with a new vision there were new leaders, including some highly trained in the best universities in the world.

A New "Idea of a University"

In the late 1950s, when a university was still on the drawing boards, Jesuit officials in Rome urged that one university be established in Central America with campuses in Managua, Nicaragua, and Guatemala City.[1] Local Jesuits opposed this model because they felt that legal difficulties would arise in each country, and they foresaw that with no duplication of programs among campuses, only members of the socioeconomic elite would travel and support themselves for studies in another country.[2]

John B. Janssens, S.J., the superior general of the Jesuits, sent Paolo Dezza, S.J., for an on-site evaluation of the options.[3] After Dezza's 1958 visit, Rome endorsed the concept of one University of Central America (UCA) with branch campuses in several countries so that "cooperation and help from various nations would be made easier, and cultural and economic bonds encouraged."⁴ The superior general pointed out that in those countries where a branch could not be started by the Society of Jesus, one could be run "by the secular clergy or other religious orders." He insisted that all the usual conditions be met: civil recognition of degrees, prepared personnel, secure financial bases, classrooms, laboratories, and library. He approved several degree programs for Guatemala but said Nicaragua needed further study. He concluded that "the Catholic University should not be started hastily or lightly, but gradually and seriously." The following year, 1959, Janssens gave approval for a feasibility study of a branch in El Salvador.⁵

A 1961 letter by the vice provincial, Luis Achaerandio, gives a hint of why he felt universities were needed: "After a short trip throughout the vice province just after taking over this position I find myself really concerned about the advance of communism all over: in the social atmosphere, in the universities. This impression is widespread—even governments are beginning to perceive it."⁶

An alarmed Achaerandio wrote to Janssens on September 19, 1961, that the Central American bishops (CEDAC) had issued a declaration on a Catholic university without any mention that the Jesuits would run the institution. They considered it a "foundation of the Central American hierarchy."⁷ He worried "that the bishops would intervene directly in the administration of the University . . . which was founded, owned, and administered by the Society of Jesus with a Jesuit majority on the board." He points out to the superior general that "in the statutes approved for the University the hierarchy does not come into the picture for any reason." He refers to a 1957 request from the papal nuncio "that the Society [of Jesus] take charge of this work" and a February 2, 1958, letter from the Archbishop of Managua to the superior general asking that "the Society administer the university in Nicaragua."

Since the bishops felt the "Catholic University," whatever its legal form in each country, was theirs, they wanted to open a Panama branch run by non-Jesuits.

Achaerandio asked the superior general to get explicit word from the Vatican that the Jesuits had been asked to take on this university project, so that the order could fend off these incursions from the local hierarchy. John Swain, the vicar general, replied a month later that "the Holy See did not explicitly request that the Society of Jesus start a Central American University," but that it was clear that Rome was pleased by the Society's willingness to take on such a task, as indicated by many letters from bishops, nuncios, and laypeople. Swain told Achaerandio not to worry when the bishops said they might start branches on their own, even with other religious orders. "If we can obtain from the bishops the possibility of working in a university without undue interference, fine. If not, we would leave such an undertaking to others."

Achaerandio replied on December 21, 1961, that "we have the sensation that our backs are not sufficiently protected from actions by ecclesiastical authorities."[8]

The following month, Janssens replied that the "statutes submitted to the Vatican . . . make it clear that *full* [emphasis in original] liberty is given to the Society of Jesus in the administration of the University," and that "if some individual bishop wants to interfere, he should be told, in all humility, that the Jesuit provincial has jurisdiction and that he will take up matters with the episcopal conference and not with individual bishops."[9]

In March 1963 the autonomy issue cropped up again after the Managua and Guatemala City universities had already opened. Achaerandio informed Janssens that Bishop Ambrogio Marchioni, the papal nuncio for Guatemala and El Salvador, had written a set of statutes different from those approved by Cardinal Pizzardo in 1961.[10] The following February, Achaerandio was very concerned that Janssens intercede with the Holy See to get official approval of the university statutes so that the bishops would have no grounds for undue interference.[11]

Six months after Achaerandio's previous communication with the Jesuit curia on university autonomy, the six bishops of El Salvador sent a letter to the papal secretary of state, Cardinal Amleto Cicognani, asking for permission to begin a Catholic university in El Salvador.[12]

The bishops complained that "communist infiltration is clear in the National University," but they regretted that with "university autonomy no one can do anything to pull out the existing communist cells by the roots." They expressed particular concern about the university leadership, which showed a "marked and defined position and focus that was friendly to Marxism. . . . Within the government there is a strong desire for the opening of a Catholic university," as shown by "the promise of the president of the republic to provide scholarships (100 or 200) for its economic support. . . . In the light of such motivation and moved to create a propitious climate for the life of the church and the good of souls, we declare ourselves in favor of a Catholic University."

For leadership, they first thought of Miguel De Paolis of Uruguay, and they asked Cardinal Cicognani to intercede with the father general of the Salesians in Rome to get him as the first rector.

The bishops suggested that "for a start the University could open with the following faculties: law, economics, humanities and engineering, which are branches of learning in which we have to have great influence so as to counteract the communist penetration in the National University. In addition, these first three are ideological professions in which it is necessary to have a Christian vision of the world, so as to influence the life of the nation."

Three months later, on November 17, 1964, Luis Chávez y Gonzalez, the archbishop of San Salvador, Arturo Rivera Damas, auxiliary bishop and later archbishop of San Salvador, Pedro Aparicio, bishop of San Vicente, Giovanni Gravelli of the papal nunciature, Segundo de Bernardi, superior of the Salesians in Central America, Luis Achaerandio, vice provincial of the Jesuits, and Joaquín López y López, adviser to the Federation of Catholic School Parents, and later one of the six Jesuits assassinated at the UCA, met to continue discussion of the Catholic university in El Salvador.[13]

Aparicio guaranteed that the government would give scholarships— twenty-two at sixty-four dollars a month. Gravelli, the papal representative, insisted that the Sacred Congregation of Universities and Seminaries wanted the university property and assets under the control of the local hierarchy. Chávez y Gonzalez, Aparicio, and the Salesian superior were against this proposal.

The grand chancellor would be a bishop appointed by the Salvadoran hierarchy, and the board of trustees, the rector, and the faculty would be selected by the institution itself, which would have responsibility for academics and discipline. The hierarchy would have its representative on the board, and the rector would give the bishops an annual report of progress. "For all other matters the institution would have full freedom of action."

There was a "unanimous desire that the Society of Jesus take charge of the administration of this University, a request that came from the ecclesiastical hierarchy, the Catholic School Parents Federation, representatives of the business community, and explicitly from the president of the republic."

Archbishop Chávez y Gonzalez suggested that the university bear the name of José Simeón Cañas, a priest and political leader who was the first legislator to propose emancipation of the slaves early in the nineteenth century.

Immediately after this meeting, Luis Achaerandio went to Rome to ask for permission to open the new university, but not the university the bishops wanted. Permission was granted.

Although the Roman Jesuit curia would raise the issue from time to time, and consider each of the universities as "branches," the one University of Central America never came into existence. Separate institutions developed in El Salvador, Nicaragua, and Guatemala, even though both the Salvadoran and Nicaraguan institutions retained the name University of Central America or UCA for short. The university in Guatemala was named for Rafael Landívar, a Guatemalan Jesuit who lived before the 1773 suppression of the order. This book limits its coverage to the UCA in El Salvador.

The Central American Jesuit vice province commissioned a feasibility study for the university proposed for El Salvador, which recommended that the Jesuits "collaborate in the education of future professionals in patriotic and religious principles" (5).[14] It lamented that "at least 70 percent of the population does not enter the economic market of the country. The two most important socioeconomic consequences of this situation are the lack of the sufficiently ample markets needed for economic development, and the potential socioeconomic instability which such a structure presents. . . . wealth is very unequally distributed geographically" (11).

The general recommendations after a two-month study were that the university be founded.

> 1.   Given the socio-economic situation of El Salvador and its foreseeable evolution, it is urgent to give priority to studies that favor industrialization of the country, and even more generally, its social and economic restructuring.
> 2.   Studies concerned with agrarian activity should be oriented in such a way as to favor the processing and marketing of products, and in due time, an agricultural system geared toward domestic food consumption.
> 3.   All academic faculties should be set up with a sense of absolute priority for university graduates with a development mentality not only in the economic arena but also in the social realm. This priority is presented not only because of the evident danger from communism but also in the light of social justice. (38)

The study recommended that chemical, mechanical, and electrical engineering, economics, business administration, and accounting begin in 1966, medicine in 1967 on a separate campus in Santa Ana, and law in 1969. Humanities could be added when it seemed convenient. A plan of studies, modeled on the University of Deusto in Spain, was appended.

"To obtain income for the suggested budget the board of directors would have to stimulate interest on the part of the government, the banks, business, national and international foundations, and individuals, etc. because of the urgent need to bring the new university into existence" (74). The report suggested tuition and fees of 500 *colones* ($200) a year and "naturally it is expected that there will be sufficient scholarships for those who cannot pay for their studies" (76).

The study did not touch on the country's desperate socioeconomic conditions, and it cited per capita income without analyzing its distribution, the structural causes of inequitable possession of wealth, far more serious indicators than the geographical factors mentioned in the report. The almost exclusive stress on economic development overshadowed considerations such as a Christian vision and the social doctrine of the church, which might motivate genuine social change. The study recognized the need for professionals to develop the country, but did not treat important questions such as who might be the ultimate beneficiaries of such development. The feasibility study was basically a market study.

The Jesuit order accepted the recommendation and initiated steps to found the university. Luis Achaerandio, the vice provincial, visited Colonel Julio Rivera, the president of El Salvador, who, according to the minutes of the first meeting of the university board of directors, "gave approval to the project and indicated his desire to collaborate in the promulgation of the Private School Law as long as the project was supported by the general public and desired by the Salvadoran people. The president also indicated his wish that the Society of Jesus take charge of the new university."[15] These minutes record that the Federation of Catholic School Parents had visited Catholic high schools in San Salvador, Santa Tecla, Santa Ana, and San Miguel to announce the new university project, and they had gotten 7,000 parents to sign a petition in favor of its establishment.

After much discussion, the Salvadoran legislature approved the Private School Law on March 24, 1965. The University of El Salvador, according to Román Mayorga, saw the UCA as "a threat to its hegemony in the realm of higher education, and political sectors on the left chimed in with this strong opposition.[16] Many legislators, alumni of the University of El Salvador, did not want the national university's monopoly challenged.

The university would be a legally separate entity, a special kind of not-for-profit corporation *(corporación de utilidad pública)* before Salvadoran law. As mentioned earlier, this title made the UCA a public corporation in the sense of one concerned with the interests of the public or society at large. It was "public," but not publicly controlled, as was the University of El Salvador, the national university.

Neither the church nor the Society of Jesus would be its owner. The university was owned by its board of directors, who were to administer it according to its "public" or "societal" purposes. This arrangement would protect the university from intervention by the Salvadoran and Vatican hierarchy. This status essentially changed it from the type of university envisioned at the meetings with the hierarchy the previous year when a "Catholic" university was being planned.[17] This issue of autonomy would crop up time and time again, especially in the Ellacuría rectorate (1979–1989).

One might wonder why the bishops accepted this significant change in the nature of the university, but it is important to remember the close relationships and similar thinking between most bishops and Jesuit superiors at that time. Few realized that this autonomy would become an issue later on.[18]

On August 15, 1965, the all-Jesuit board of directors took office: Florentino Idoate (president), Segundo Azcue (vice president), Joaquín López y López (secretary), José Ignacio Scheifler (pro-secretary), and Jesús de Esnaola (member).

INAUGURATION

On Independence Day, September 15, 1965, President Julio Adalberto Rivera and Archbishop Luis Chávez y Gonzalez joined the Jesuit vice provincial, Luis Achaerandio, S.J., and several hundred other guests in the Cine Dario to inaugurate the new university. The rector, Florentino Idoate, S.J., greeted the distinguished assembly, especially "the parents from all social classes who with a great many signatures on petitions have committed to us this task."[19] He said the Jesuits had accepted responsibility for the university because of a call not only from these parents but also from the church hierarchy and "the illustrious government and the president of the republic [with] their noble and ambitious desire to elevate all cultural levels of the nation, and to improve the preparation of citizens for the intense process of development that surrounds us. . . . It is our hope that tomorrow the history of El Salvador will confirm that you have not been mistaken."

He called for a scholarship program so that the lack of financial resources would not keep anyone away "from the sources of higher culture."

"We do not come into existence in order to be against anyone or anything—unless it be the lack of professional and technical personnel. We come on behalf of the country—100 percent positive." We have "commissioned a technical statistical study so that we can see in the precise language of data and concrete numbers an accurate reflection of El Salvador's reality." This study, he said, had detected "a shortage of professionals and an overwhelming need in the country for technical expertise to bring about desired socio-economic development and the proverbial push and spirit of initiative."

To the University of El Salvador, he announced, "we have come to collaborate with you and to share responsibility. . . . we have the same goal and the same task."

A university "should not only prepare people to bring about the development of the country but it should also prepare well-rounded people who can think for themselves and give direction to themselves and to others." These persons, who are "privileged because they have received more education, should serve as natural guides for the rest of the people; they should know where they are going and where they want to lead others. They should know what elevates people and what . . . takes away their dignity and leaves them in misery." He summarized the "mission" of the university as "to collaborate in human progress and advancement, in all the gigantic tasks to bring about the transformation of the world according to the plan of God, to make it more and more balanced, more comfortable, more human and more just."

In language typical of the age, Father Idoate's university concerned itself largely with the preparation of professionals who could take in hand the next stage of El Salvador's "development." His successors, however, would speak more of "liberation."

As would be expected, in the presence of the military government head, Idoate did not address the university's potential role in denunciation of human rights violations by the security forces under the president's command; in the presence of the oligarchy he did not address the issues of inequitable resource distribution and the abject poverty of the vast majority of Salvadorans. He said that the Jesuits had agreed to take on the university after their study of "the precise language of data and concrete numbers [which are] an accurate reflection of the reality of El Salvador." Ignacio Ellacuría would later use a different definition of the national reality—an unjust society in which the many were subservient to the few, a society that craved transformation. The early UCA wanted to "collaborate in human progress and advancement," but later, others would ask questions about who should be the ultimate beneficiaries of the university.

Almost anyone starting as UCA rector in 1965 would have spoken in similar terms as Idoate because of the religious and educational formation of Jesuits up to that time. It would be unfair, therefore, to use today's criteria to judge an era that was preoccupied with the cold war and communism, and a church that was just beginning to understand what had happened at the Second Vatican Council.

The first few months saw the appointment of deans in engineering and economics, and negotiations with the Salesian order for use of their Don Rua property as the university's temporary site. A young Jesuit seminarian received a full-time contract to organize the engineering faculty: Jon Sobrino, later the noted liberation theologian.[20] The board approved a scholarship plan on November 9, 1965, but six days later the rector, Father Idoate, took a 50 percent cut in pay to help make ends meet. The rector and the secretary of the board went to see President Rivera to hurry along the promised scholarships. He responded with thirty scholarships, each worth $52 a month.[21]

The first school term began in 1966 with 309 students (136 in engineering and 173 in economics); for the year as a whole there were 367 students instructed by fourteen professors.[22] A school of business administration received approval later that year.[23] Román Mayorga characterizes the climate of these first few months as "improvisation and basic struggle for the very existence of the institution." The school got off the ground, he says, because of three factors: the international prestige of the Jesuits as educators, negative impressions of the national university's quality and atmosphere, and the demand for the initial academic programs of engineering and business during this era of "developmentalistic optimism."[24]

Father Francisco Javier Ibisate described these early years as focusing on *el nacer*—bringing the university into existence: obtaining donations, buying the property, getting basic books, and recruiting students.[25] Fathers Idoate, Gondra, and López y López personally went to their friends and other potential benefactors to beg for early resources. People saw the nascent university as a serious project because a person like Father Idoate was rector. He was a noted preacher and had been rector of several schools of the province.

Even as the doors of the new university in El Salvador were opening early in 1966, however, a letter from Pedro Arrupe, the new Jesuit superior general, to the vice provincial indicated that the issue of one versus three universities was not settled in the mind of Rome. Arrupe wrote on January 28, 1966, that

> it is necessary to recall something . . . that gets lost from sight with some frequency even though it is essential. The three university sections of Guatemala, Managua and San Salvador—even though in the civil order and in the public eye they seem to be three *different* universities, since each confers its own degrees, and has a separate gov-

ernance structure and budget—in Jesuit and church terms they constitute *just one* university. Faculties should not be duplicated or triplicated. Each school should choose those fields most appropriate for Central America. There are not enough personnel to have multiple faculties in each country.

The independent spirit of the Managua university was already making the superior general nervous. He reminds the Central American educators about the authority of the provincial and that "there is need for clearer vision and greater control, as was seen in the case of the government loan to the Managua campus that involved such a large amount of money and consequently the very stability and future of the work."[26] In another letter that same day to Achaerandio, Arrupe raised questions about the University of Central America spreading itself too thinly. For example, that same year Arrupe insisted that all three campuses discuss another proposal from León Pallais, the flamboyant Jesuit rector of the Managua UCA and a cousin of Anastasio Somoza, the dictator and an early benefactor of that university, to take over a veterinary program abandoned by the Dominican order. The superior general refused permission. "In order that our universities in Central America achieve the goals to which they are called, the moment has arrived to *consolidate* what already exists."[27]

Just before the beginning of the Salvadoran UCA's second academic year, Ignacio Ellacuría and Francisco Javier Ibisate replaced José Ignacio Scheifler and Segundo Azcue on the board of directors; Azcue had been named Central American Jesuit vice provincial.[28]

The UCA 1967 budget was 211,000 *colones* ($84,400), and 541 students were taught by twenty-six teachers, mostly part-time. The board of directors, on May 12, 1967, got a bank loan of 600,000 *colones* ($240,000) to purchase land for the new campus. They obtained the thirty-four-and-one-half-acre property through a combination of purchases and gifts from the early benefactors.[29] The building blocks were moving into place.

Shortly after the school year began, the board expressed its dismay "at the alarming absentee rate of teachers in the evening division of the economics faculty," and they recommended that "the dean urge the teachers to fulfill their contractual obligations with the university and the students." The board "also judged that it would be convenient if the dean himself spent some time in the university each day"—a modest expectation.[30]

From the very beginning, the university lacked adequate personnel. The vice provincial replied to the rector's request for more Jesuits by saying that he could not meet all UCA faculty needs because the other universities, the parishes, and all other efforts in the province works were asking for personnel. He suggested that the UCA look for help from other religious orders.[31]

Just into the second academic year, Idoate sounded a pessimistic but realistic note to the vice provincial: "if keeping the seminary is going to be considered seriously, I do not see the university as viable. In this case, I would be in favor not of closing it but rather of passing it on to some others." He pointed out that even though twenty benefactors had formally promised to help purchase land, "the project is moving desperately slowly, and some have put on the brakes because of their nervousness at the publication of certain church social documents, and especially after the Catholic radio station's 'political activities' in the last election"; these same benefactors had originally funded the radio station. He suggested that land at the Jesuit high school, the Externado de San José, be sold and the proceeds given to the UCA to buy the land it needed for the university.[32]

As if financial problems were not enough to occupy the founders in those early days, with two months' notice at the end of the second year, students' partying got the UCA evicted from its original site. On July 28, 1967, Father (later Bishop) José C. Di Pietro, the Salesian superior, wrote to the Jesuit vice provincial, Segundo Azcue: "I have nothing to say about the music, dancing and happiness of the students at their parties, but what surprises me is that on these occasions they are given total freedom in our house to get drunk with barrels of beer at their disposal. . . . After my complaints to Father Esnaola they suspended the distribution of beer for a time, but the students continued with their supply of rum, and then threw the empty bottles from the second floor to the street." He added, "I am sure that such orgies are not the usual custom in your high schools and universities. . . ."[33] The UCA then moved its 719 students and forty-two teachers to temporary quarters at the Jesuit high school, where they stayed for a year until they moved to the new campus in February 1969.

When the UCA had to vacate the Salesian property, the vice provincial wrote to Pedro Arrupe: "Perhaps you will say it is time to leave or to close this university in the face of so many obstacles and unfulfilled promises." But he noted that everyone would be disappointed particularly since credits would not be accepted at the University of El Salvador, which "opposed the UCA's founding and since that time has expressed its opposition on many occasions."[34]

Arrupe responded within a month. Set up a committee to study the feasibility of three universities, he said, because "the current situation cannot go on. If we have to let go one or two universities, the sooner we do it, the fewer problems we will have."[35]

There is evidence of continued concern on Rome's part, as, for example, when the vice provincial asked Arrupe's permission to take out a loan for the UCA in El Salvador. The superior general urged him to await the results of a general sociological study in which the entire order was engaged to determine ministry planning for the next decades.[36] This sociological survey in Central America was to play a major role in redefining priorities, and it will be studied in more detail later.

By the beginning of the 1968 academic year, the UCA had a budget of 336,440 *colones* ($135,000), a second dean in engineering, and a third dean in economics.[37] Four UCA faculty members received Fulbright-LASPAU [Academic and Professional Programs for the Americas] scholarships for graduate studies in the United States, the beginnings of an important faculty development resource for the university throughout its history, with fifty-two recipients in total. Of these fifty-two, twenty-nine are no longer teaching at the UCA, twelve are still on the staff, two have died, and nine are still in studies.

During the 1968 academic year, the UCA proposed the establishment of a new faculty, or division—Philosophy, Letters, and Human Sciences, with a department of education. This would bring the number of faculties or divisions to three, since business/economics and engineering had begun with the university itself. The new entity would have "as its objective not only the preparation of people who do not want to pursue a professional career, but also secondary school teachers." The faculty would not be called "humanities" because "this title has lost its prestige and is understood in an overly restricted way."[38]

When the vice provincial wrote the superior general in Rome about the new faculty, he added that Jesuit seminarians in undergraduate and philosophy studies would also take classes at the UCA, and that the minister of education had requested a program for public school teachers and administrators.[39]

Responding on behalf of Pedro Arrupe that same month, Paolo Dezza, who had visited the Central American region and had insisted from the beginning on one university with three campuses, brought up this same objection to starting a new faculty in San Salvador.[40] But Arrupe finally agreed to the proposal in October.

By the end of 1968, the board of directors authorized the move to the new campus, where two multipurpose/laboratory buildings awaited them. Most administrative and teaching functions were held in those two buildings and in some provisional structures. The following data show the overall growth of the UCA in its first years:

Year	Budget ($)	Faculty	Students
1966	32,760	14	367
1967	84,400	26	541
1968	135,000	42	719
1969	190,000	57	1039

On August 19, 1969, Luis Achaerandio, the former vice provincial, was named rector.

CIAS: A COMPLEMENTARY INNOVATION

As mentioned in the last chapter, parallel to Jesuit universities in Latin America was CIAS (Centro de Investigación y Acción Social), a set of think tanks established by the Jesuit order throughout Latin America to reflect on and to propose solutions to the continent's major social problems. In 1962, John B. Janssens, the superior general, urged all provinces or regions to set up CIAS teams. He saw them primarily as centers for studies and publishing about the causes of poverty rather than for direct work with the poor.[41]

The Central American Jesuit vice province selected various promising young men for this task, and encouraged the development of a team spirit by, for example, approving a December 1965 meeting in Paris of those who were studying theology in preparation for ordination and graduate studies.[42] These young Jesuits were to play a major role in the vice province "retreat" of 1969.

Among those sent to graduate school were César Jerez (political science) and Juan Hernández Pico (sociology) to the University of Chicago, Luis de Sebastián (economics) to the University of London, Ricardo Falla (anthropology) to the University of Texas, and Xabier Gorostiaga (economics) to Cambridge University. When some returned to the region in the early 1970s, they felt that working within the province's universities would bog them down in nonessential matters and stymie their research and policy reflections. Pedro Arrupe had strongly praised the thorough preparation of these men and reaffirmed the importance of CIAS. He wanted to see them cooperate with the universities without getting caught up in day-to-day details.[43]

CIAS team members worked in Guatemala from 1970 to 1980, but university, church, and political leaders saw them as a threat. Their role at the Salvadoran UCA at the time of the fraudulent presidential election of 1972 was crucial. During the Nicaraguan revolution they served as an *apoyo crítico,* giving support but also questioning. By the 1990s, however, their members tended to work more closely with the universities in El Salvador and Nicaragua, though they have retained their group identity.

DECEMBER 1969: THE RETREAT-DISCERNMENT PROCESS

Late in 1969, just months after Achaerandio's appointment as rector, and in the context of the Medellín and Río meetings described in chapter 4, an important event changed the Central American Jesuit vice province and set the stage for more changes to come. The Jesuits decided to meet in December 1969 for prayer and reflection on their apostolic efforts: universities, high schools, parishes, retreat houses, and other ministries.[44]

The original idea for this meeting came from Ignacio Ellacuría at a Madrid meeting of Jesuit seminarians studying in Europe.[45] The Central American vice provincial, Segundo Azcue, convened the vice province meeting and turned the planning over to Ignacio Ellacuría, who suggested that Miguel Elizondo be codirector of the retreat-reflection experience. Elizondo had been both master of novices and vice provincial, and was then a spiritual director famous all throughout Latin America. Florentino Idoate, the first UCA rector, and Ricardo Falla, a young anthropologist, also suggested subject matter for the gathering.

Ellacuría and Elizondo designed the retreat to stretch beyond the usual borders of individual spiritual reflection to encompass *institutional* discernment, an approach strongly resisted by more traditional members of the order.[46] The codirectors suggested reflection topics from key meditations of Jesuit founder Ignatius Loyola's "spiritual exercises." They also led discernment sessions to evaluate the efficacy of province institutions in the light of the dramatic needs of Central America's desperately poor majority. The participants devoted the last day to proposals for the vice provincial and approval of a vice province statement of purpose.

The retreat revealed deep polarization in the vice province. Ellacuría and Elizondo were supported by the younger generation of "liberationists" such as Miguel Francisco Estrada (soon to be vice provincial), César Jerez (Estrada's successor as vice provincial), Juan Hernández Pico, then a graduate student at the University of Chicago and later director of formation for the province, Ricardo Falla, Luis de Sebastián, and many others. In general opposition to their proposals and approach were the "gradualists" such as Luis Achaerandio (former vice provincial, named rector of the San Salvador UCA just four months earlier), and Santos Pérez, general secretary of the Rafael Landívar University in Guatemala.

After the retreat, Segundo Azcue, following the liberationist wing's recommendation, appointed Ellacuría as director of the formation program for all the younger Jesuits, from entrance into the society up to final vows. Both this appointment and the retreat itself sparked many letters of complaint to Rome. Arrupe wrote to Azcue, the vice provincial, that he should have asked permission much earlier for the December retreat-reflection so that clearer norms could have been set. He also expressed some concern about Elizondo's interventions on personal prayer. (This topic had provoked a public dispute between Elizondo and Achaerandio during the retreat.) But Arrupe still described the overall experience as "*positivo*."[47]

Azcue criticized those Jesuits who did not attend the retreat at all, and those who went but kept quiet there. Now they were all writing to Rome, even though they had had their chance to make their opinions known locally.[48]

As for Ellacuría's new position, Arrupe said that because the appointment was going to be controversial, Azcue should have consulted Rome before naming him delegate for formation. Speaking of Ellacuría, Arrupe said, "He made a good impression on me. But he has some ideas which are explosive and radicalized. He is a valuable 'modern' man whom we should help to realize all that everyone expects of him." As to his particular position as delegate for formation, Arrupe's judgment was that Ellacuría "was not the best choice, at least at this time."[49]

Responding to Arrupe's comments, Azcue wrote that some local Jesuits felt the same way about Ellacuría, but that there had been so much support expressed in the retreat for Ellacuría's appointment that failure to name him would have been seen "as a rejection of the wishes of the young and even some not so young members of the vice province."[50]

In April, Arrupe wrote to the vice provincial that after receiving more letters from the vice province, he was still concerned about the absence of personal prayer at the retreat. Arrupe asked about reports that the group assembled in the retreat could make decisions about the vice province, prescinding from the superior. Despite these criticisms, Arrupe remained positive about the overall effect.[51]

Azcue, in reply, admitted some dispute as to whether it was really a retreat, but he pointed out to Arrupe that most Jesuits that year had also made a traditional retreat.[52] The following month, Arrupe's assistant, Father Andrew Varga, S.J., wrote to Azcue that he should "proceed with firmness and clarity in positions taken against injustice and intrinsically unjust structures, without forgetting prudence." He added: "Father Ellacuría, especially, should exercise much tact in his university work and he should act slowly."[53]

During the retreat, Segundo Azcue had sounded out suggestions on his successor as vice provincial. He commented in a letter to Pedro Arrupe that the names of "current superiors practically disappeared from the lists." Azcue felt that this had occurred "not so much because of hope of spiritual renewal but rather for a more modern, up-to-date vision of the Society's role today with better organization and re-structuring of our ministries." The most popular suggestions for vice provincial were Miguel Francisco Estrada and Ignacio Ellacuría, with Estrada getting slightly more support from all age sectors.[54] At the age of thirty-six, Miguel Francisco Estrada became vice provincial in 1970.

In September 1970, vice province representatives met in Santa Tecla to finalize sociological survey results. Juan Hernández Pico presented the liberationist position and Antonio Pérez spoke for the gradualists. Guidelines for priorities in the selection of ministries were issued.

That same month there was still discussion of the retreat and the sociological survey in correspondence with Rome. Estrada insisted that all topics had been open to discussion. Opposition to the survey had come mainly from Luis Achaerandio, Antonio Pérez, José Ignacio Scheifler, Santiago Anitua, and Jesús Rodríguez Jalón. They pictured Ellacuría as controlling a younger group that did his bidding. This opposition group was influential when Achaerandio was vice provincial, Estrada said, and had continued to be influential in the Azcue period. Estrada answered their attacks against Ellacuría.[55]

In his reply, Arrupe praised the work of the sociological survey team and told Estrada not to be surprised by opposition. Arrupe urged the new vice provincial to try to keep differences of opinion from becoming a source of division.[56] Support from Pedro Arrupe on the main thrust of the retreat strongly encouraged the liberationists in their struggle with the gradualists. "The conclusions, presuppositions and results are worthy of approval and are within the spirit of the Vatican Council, the 31st General Congregation and the documents of Medellín." Arrupe suggested that the theme of apostolic unity should prevail over any undue stress on "national" concerns.[57]

In this letter, Arrupe raised once again the question of the three universities: "How can they be sustained? Is there any way that real cooperation among them can be achieved? I don't see how they can be sustained in the future if things stay as they are now with each one going its own way."

As to the liberation theology approach in the sociological survey documents, Arrupe said that "the statements . . . under the title 'sociological level' and 'theological level' are correct and they conform to recent developments of the social apostolate since Medellín. . . . and are consistent with the orientation of the Society of Jesus in Latin America." He urged caution because statements such as "liberation," true in themselves, can be taken out of context. He pointed out that the plans of the vice province would require a change in mentality and such changes would not come easily. He urged tact and patience so as to avoid divisions.

This short period—1965 to 1969—saw many changes. A university founded to protect its clients from a hostile outside world had begun to evolve into an agent for social change. A new generation took over responsibility for the Society of Jesus in Central America with approval from the Jesuit curia in Rome. The gradualists feared that their hard-fought efforts to start a university would be destroyed by alienation of affluent benefactors. The liberationists worried less about these practical questions and demanded a new vision. The Jesuit vice province stretched at the seams and threatened to come apart.

In a sense there was truth on both sides: A solid physical and academic structure was essential to make any real contribution to society in El Salvador, but a dynamic vision was also needed, or else the university could be counterproductive in achieving the goals of the church and the Jesuit order. In setting up the university as he did, Achaerandio, as vice provincial, guaranteed its independence and made it a flexible instrument for social change in the next decades. The UCA needed both the hard working pioneers and the critical thinkers, and it had the advantage of both in those early years.

Summary

We have seen the shaky but courageous UCA beginnings but also the seeds for a new university model. Crucial decisions got the university off to a good start despite its financially precarious position: insisting on the independence of the new institution by Achaerandio and his colleagues, working toward an appropriate campus and basic facilities, gradually gathering lay colleagues who could share and expand the vision, and soul-searching by an entire Jesuit province to develop a process by which a new vision would be implemented in all the order's apostolic activities in Central America. It was a risky but auspicious beginning.

Notes

1. ASJCA–G58/17 (Archives of the Society of Jeus, Central America). John B. Janssens to Miguel Elizondo, April 21, 1958. Originals of the correspondence between the superior general in Rome and the local superiors of Central America are kept in the archives of the Jesuit province in San Salvador, as are copies of the letters from local superiors to the headquarters (curia) in Rome. Hereafter they will be referred to

as ASJCA–G if the letter is from the general superior and ASJCA–P if it is from the provincial superior in San Salvador. The references will include the letter number and the date. Until 1976, the area was considered a vice province by Rome; then it became an independent province that included El Salvador, Nicaragua, Guatemala, Costa Rica Panama, and Honduras after 1982.

2. Interview with Miguel Francisco Estrada, July 22, 1992, former vice provincial superior (1970–1976) and rector of the UCA.

3. In a controversial move, Pope John Paul II appointed Dezza as his personal delegate to govern the Jesuit order in 1981 because of his dissatisfaction with the trends he saw under the direction of Pedro Arrupe. Dezza was influential as a frequent consultant to the Congregation for Seminaries and Universities (later the Congregation for Catholic Education), and he was also named a cardinal in 1991 shortly after Arrupe's death.

4. ASJCA–G58/35, Janssens to Elizondo, October 11, 1958.

5. ASJCA–G59/12, Janssens to Elizondo, June 3, 1959.

6. ASJCA–P61/13, Luis Achaerandio to John Swain, vicar general, March 27, 1961.

7. ASJCA–P61/45, Achaerandio to Janssens.

8. ASJCA–P61/65, Achaerandio to Janssens.

9. ASJCA–G62/4, Janssens to Achaerandio, January 20, 1962.

10. ASJCA–P63/12, Achaerandio to Janssens, March 8, 1963.

11. ASJCA–P64/12, Achaerandio to Janssens, February 7, 1964.

12. ASJCA, August 24, 1964. Copy in the UCA El Salvador file.

13. Copy of the minutes of the meeting in ASJCA, "Naturaleza Jurídica de la UCA."

14. "Estudio Preliminar para la Creación de una Universidad Privada en El Salvador." 1964. Recommendations in ASJCA. Page references in the text.

15. AUCA (Archives of the University of Central America), August 15, 1965. All references to the minutes of the board of directors of the UCA will be designated AUCA with the date of the meeting. These minutes are in the archives of the university.

16. Román Mayorga, *La Universidad para el Cambio Social* (San Salvador: UCA Editores, 1979), 25.

17. Interview with Luis Achaerandio, December 27, 1991.

18. Interview with Rodolfo Cardenal, November 15, 1993.

19. The full text is in *Planteamiento Universitario, 1989* (San Salvador: UCA Editores, 1989), 135–38.

20. AUCA, November 15, 1965.

21. AUCA, May 25, 1966.

22. *Plan Quinquenal, 1977–1981* (San Salvador: UCA Editores, 1976), 6.

23. AUCA, September 28, 1966.

24. Mayorga, 27, 28.

25. Interview with Francisco Javier Ibisate (November 1992), who became UCA rector in November 1995.

26. ASJCA–G66/4. Pedro Arrupe to Luis Achaerandio, January 28, 1966.

27. ASJCA–P66/10, Arrupe to Achaerandio, November 9, 1966.

28. AUCA, February 1, 1967.

29. Interview with Axel Soderberg, September 10, 1992.

30. AUCA, March 16, 1967.

31. ASJCA, Segundo Azcue to Florentino Idoate, March 20, 1967.

32. ASJCA, Idoate to Azcue, April 21, 1967.

33. ASJCA, Idoate correspondence folder.

34. ASJCA–P67/61, Azcue to Arrupe, December 12, 1967.

35. ASJCA–G68/2, Arrupe to Azcue, January 11, 1968.

36. ASJCA–G67/50, Arrupe to Azcue, September 2, 1967.

37. AUCA, February 22 and 29, 1968.

38. ASJCA, Idoate to Azcue, April 18, 1968.

39. ASJCA–P68/45, Azcue to Arrupe, August 2, 1968.

40. ASJCA–G68/47, Paolo Dezza to Azcue, August 26, 1968.

41. ASJCA–G62/57, Janssens to all Jesuit Superiors in Latin America, December 29, 1962.

42. ASJCA–G65/37, Arrupe to Achaerandio, November 21, 1965.

43. ASJCA–G69/26, Arrupe to Azcue, April 12, 1969.

44. The principal talks, discussions, and conclusions have been published in a mimeographed text that is in the archives of the Central American Province, San Salvador: "Reunión-Ejercicios de la Vice provincia Jesuítica de Centroamérica."

45. Correspondence between Juan Hernández Pico and the author, July 1993.

46. Interview with Miguel Francisco Estrada, July 22, 1992.

47. ASJCA–G70/8, Arrupe to Azcue, February 8, 1970.

48. ASJCA–P70/34, Azcue to Arrupe, April 29, 1970.

49. ASJCA–G70/21, Arrupe to Azcue, March 23, 1970.

50. ASJCA–P70/26, Azcue to Arrupe, April 20, 1970.

51. ASJCA–G70/26, Arrupe to Azcue, April 20, 1970.

52. ASJCA–P70/34, Azcue to Arrupe, April 29, 1970.

53. ASJCA–G70/33, Andrew Varga to Azcue, May 5, 1970.

54. ASJCA–P70/9, Azcue to Arrupe, February 12, 1970.

55. ASJCA–P70/50, Miguel Francisco Estrada to Arrupe, September 3, 1970.

56. ASJCA–G70/54, Arrupe to Estrada, September 29, 1970.

57. ASJCA–G71/15, Arrupe to Estrada, February 25, 1971.

6 DEVELOPMENT OF THE MODEL: 1969–1975

INTRODUCTION

This chapter will look at the six-year period in which Luis Achaerandio served as rector after his term as vice provincial of the Central American Jesuits. During his administration, the UCA began to move away from the goals of protection and narrowly conceived professionalism which had motivated its founding, and to take for itself, at first hesitatingly, a new role as agent for social change.

Its board of directors took the plunge with a loan of two million dollars from the Inter-American Development Bank (IDB); it assumed responsibility for the Jesuit publication, *Estudios Centroamericanos;* its faculty (mostly part-time) doubled from 80 to 164; and the student body jumped from 1,343 to 2,855.

With IDB funds and donations, the UCA sent potential faculty members to study abroad; it built nine buildings and reorganized the academic programs into a unique matrix configuration that sought to avoid the rigid structures that often characterize "faculties" in Latin American universities. Although spending most of their time on teaching, the professors began to venture into research and social outreach in areas vital to the country, such as rural electrification and low-cost housing.

Anxious for financial security but determined to admit students who could not afford to pay even low tuition, the UCA adopted a differentiated tuition structure *(cuotas diferenciadas)* in which students pay according to their means, and a unique salary scale that closes the income gaps among personnel of various ranks.

While building up the infrastructure, the UCA faced ideological problems from inside (some opposition, much indifference) and from outside (benefactors wary of a church that talks of social justice, and a government and oligarchy eager to keep their privileges). It struggled to define itself as a university of "Christian inspiration" with a commitment to social change, while trying all the while to deal with these issues in ways appropriate for a university.

Living out this mission provoked conflict among the Jesuits themselves, and the Jesuits with Rome. In the pages of *Estudios Centroamericanos (ECA)*, the UCA faculty analyzed such controversial issues as the war between El Salvador and Honduras, a teachers' strike, fraudulent elections in 1972, appropriate technology in the Cerrón Grande power project, land reform, liberation theology, population, the University of El Salvador and the Jesuit high school (Externado de San José). All these issues helped the UCA to define its mission ever more clearly, and will be examined in some detail.

This was an era of close cooperation between Jesuits and lay colleagues, which continued through the following rectorate of Román Mayorga.

Let us look at the Achaerandio years, an important period of development for the UCA model.

IDEOLOGICAL CONFLICT

Luis Achaerandio, age forty-seven, was elected UCA rector by the board of directors on August 19, 1969, just a year after the Río meeting of the Latin American Jesuit provincials and the landmark Medellín gathering of the Latin American bishops, and just four months before the turbulent retreat-reflection sessions of the Central American Jesuit vice province, where he was perceived as chief spokesman for more traditional or gradualist views.

Labels do not do justice to complex persons like Achaerandio, who was later considered "radical" in the more conservative atmosphere of the Jesuit-run university in Guatemala, the Rafael Landívar. He did not oppose change, nor was he insensitive to the need to reevaluate church and educational structures that might respond more appropriately to the enormous misery experienced by most people in the region. Still, he feared what he saw as an overreliance on vague concepts, Marxist analytical categories, and a desire to move too quickly to change traditional structures.

As we have seen, those in favor of a more liberationist approach gravitated to Ignacio Ellacuría, age thirty-nine, philosopher and theologian, director of the formation programs for Jesuit seminarians, and a member of the board of directors that elected Achaerandio. The majority on the board, however, tended to favor Achaerandio's gradualist approach, although they respected Ellacuría and engaged in dialogue with him. For about eight years (1967–1975), Ellacuría used to sum up his position on the board of directors as "being in a constant struggle and in the minority on votes."[1]

During this development decade of the UCA model, the gradualist and liberationist factions worked together, at times sparring, at times uniting their forces, especially when bombs began to explode after 1976 and after the assassination of Father Rutilio Grande, pastor of the rural parish of Aguilares, on March 13, 1977.[2] By this time the board had tilted toward Ellacuría's positions, thanks to a three-to-two liberationist majority (Ellacuría, Mayorga and de Sebastián).

The Jesuits lived in two physically separate communities: UCA I for the gradualists (Achaerandio, Gondra, Ibisate, Sáinz, López y López and Esnaola, and UCA II for the liberationists (Ellacuría, de Sebastián, Montes, Cortina, Sobrino, Martín Baró, Arroyo, Mariscal, and later, Rodolfo Cardenal). Both groups reached general agreement on goals statements such as Gondra's 1970 speech at the IDB loan signing, the operational manual of the UCA, and even Ellacuría's 1975 article in *ECA* that explained the basic characteristics of the university. On issue after issue, however, they disagreed as to timing, topics, and emphases. And yet, an integrated university model came out of the dynamic tension between the two communities.

Román Mayorga, Achaerandio's successor as rector, writes that "the liberation thesis could not but cause controversy and tension. It is important to note, however, that this occurred within a small group of people, and rarely reached the students." Mayorga also notes "a divergence between the spirit that animated the UCA leadership and the reality actually experienced in the university."[3]

The UCA organized a seminar in 1971 to talk about the role of the university, which Mayorga calls "the first public examination of conscience open to all sectors," and he sees it as "profoundly critical that the UCA with relative self-confidence would dare to have such an event, without worrying about the possible effect on the institution itself."[4]

Francisco Javier Ibisate confirmed this description of discussions on ideological differences. Ignacio Ellacuría urged becoming a university for social change. Gondra, and then Achaerandio, urged caution. Gondra feared the economic consequences of alienating benefactors who were already nervous with Pope John XXIII's *"Mater et Magister,"* Pope Paul VI's *"Populorum Progressio,"* and other social pronouncements of church officials.[5] But there was also concern that the younger generation was more wrapped up in *ilusión* (dreams) than *realidad* (reality).[6]

The UCA had launched a loosely drawn "faculty" system with major divisions in science/engineering and business/economics. Later, a division in human sciences was added. Early in Achaerandio's term, he and Román Mayorga traveled to South America, including Santa Catalina University in Marianopolis, Brazil, the Universidad Javeriana in Bogotá, Colombia, and the Catholic University in Lima, where they consulted with Felipe MacGregor, S.J., the rector. They returned to the UCA and began extensive discussion with colleagues on an organizational system that would give authority to departments rather than separate faculties or schools. They wanted to avoid duplication of positions and the creation of fiefdoms, and to give more importance to learning *(el saber)* than to student career preparation. In the next chapter there will be more details on how this system worked.

In this period, the university continued to be governed by a board of directors made up of five Jesuits, until Román Mayorga, rector from 1975 to 1979, joined the board in 1970 as its first non-Jesuit member. The rector was one of the five members ex officio. The university administration included an academic vice rector, a dean of students, a secretary general who handled all the financial and administrative details, and in the later years, a secretary of communications. But all major issues and many minor ones were handled directly by the board—an arrangement still functioning in the mid-1990s.

Approximately one-third of the faculty was full-time. By 1975, the UCA had eight departments: business administration, political science/sociology, economics, philosophy (including theology), engineering and natural sciences, mathematics, psychology, and literature.

Three "faculties" (like the "divisions" at the University of Chicago, but unlike the "faculties" more common in Latin America) administered student academic programs and the teaching function of the university: sciences of humanity and nature *(Ciencias del Hombre y de la Naturaleza)*, economics, and engineering. Each "faculty" was headed by a dean. All department heads, however, reported directly to the academic vice rector, not to the deans.

The organizational chart also called for "centers" and "institutes." By 1975, the only institute was the *Instituto de Investigaciones,* which coordinated research, and the only center was the *Centro de Servicio Social,* which supervised the obligatory community service programs of the students.

This unique organizational arrangement came about because the UCA administration wanted to coordinate the tasks of teaching, research, and social outreach. Since faculties traditionally concentrated on teaching, the other two functions might be neglected. UCA administrators also feared that the basic university mission would be more difficult to implement if there were too much autonomy in individual departments within a faculty. The board also saw "the problems of inflexibility, compartmentalization, and exaggerated professionalism" as endemic to a traditional faculty arrangement.[7]

Even from the beginning, UCA architects avoided designing buildings for exclusive use of faculties so as to discourage the formation of feudal duchies then prevalent at the University of El Salvador, the national university.[8] Even before the organizational manual spelled out the departmental system, the university architect, Juan José Rodriguez, was designing buildings in modular form that could be adjusted to various educational formats.

According to this administrative structure, no basic unit of the university was subordinated to any other; they were all to be coordinated among themselves under the supervision of the academic vice rector. Teaching questions would be determined by the dean of each faculty and department heads. Research and social outreach questions would be organized among directors of institutes and centers and department heads. Disputes between jurisdictions would be settled by the academic vice rector, who would also supervise the university library.[9]

The Higher Education Council of the University *(Consejo Superior Universitario)* was a representative, collegial body made up of the rector, the vice rector, the secretary general, the secretary of communications, deans, heads of departments, institutes, and centers, and a student and a faculty representative from each of the three faculties. This council defined the content of studies programs, admissions and graduation requirements, academic policy, and disciplinary matters. It also served as a consultative body for the board of directors.[10]

Mayorga maintains that during these years all emphasis was on teaching. There was little research, and personnel ranks increased more rapidly than the programs to integrate them into the UCA. Before the reorganization described above, "the lack of clearly defined functions caused diffusion of responsibility. There was a general feeling of not knowing exactly to whom one should direct oneself when there was a need beyond the most elementary ones."[11]

INTERNAL MATTERS

A quick look at enrollment, retention, and financial matters will fill out the picture at this point.

Fathers Florentino Idoate, José M. Gondra, Joaquín López y López (later martyred), and Luis Achaerandio did most fund raising in the early years, but additional resources were needed for the UCA to grow. Local funding sources for development could not offer low interest rates and long payback terms, so the UCA Jesuits established contact with the local head of the Inter-American Development Bank (IDB) and began to explore a loan. Father Gondra thought in terms of a few hundred thousand dollars, but

Román Mayorga recommended a goal of two million dollars. When Father Gondra recovered from his shock, the loan process began. Such negotiations had been made easier because the IDB had already begun to help the University of El Salvador.

On the initiative of UCA officials such as academic vice president Luis de Sebastián, and Román Mayorga of the Consejo Nacional de Planificación y Coordinación Económica de El Salvador (CONAPLAN), the UCA prepared this first IDB loan proposal that would provide for nine buildings, the basics of a library, laboratory equipment, more full-time personnel, graduate studies for faculty, and technical assistance. CONAPLAN declared the project "a high national priority" and the Central Reserve Bank of El Salvador indicated its willingness to give the necessary guarantees.[12]

In his book, Román Mayorga characterizes the proposal as "inspired by a certain 'developmentalism' *(desarrollismo)* without any explicit reference to the problems of class divisions and domination" that plagued the country.[13] But explicit reference to these realities might have frightened the IDB. The loan was approved and it provided the UCA with an excellent opportunity to state its goals publicly in Father Gondra's speech at the signing in 1970, as described in the last chapter.

As a result of these IDB resources, the UCA began to grow. The following data give an idea of its overall size in the Achaerandio years:

Year	Budget ($)	Faculty	Students
1970	370,000	80	1,343
1971	412,164	104	1,809
1972	545,700	135	2,034
1973	840,000	149	2,581
1974	940,000	155	2,480
1975	960,000	164	2,855

The drop in 1974 was due to a change in the number of secondary school graduates after implementation of the 1968 educational reform.[14] In the 1971–1975 period, 28 percent of the students were women: 57 percent in the sciences of humanity and nature; 25 percent in economics; and 12 percent in engineering.[15]

The first substantial number of graduates emerged in 1971—twenty-four in industrial engineering and forty-two in economics and business administration. A serious problem, however, was the student dropout rate. By 1975, 31 percent dropped out after first year; 18 percent dropped out after the second year; and 13 percent dropped out after the third year. Only about 25 percent ever finished a degree at the UCA.[16]

Up to 1974, there was no consistent salary scale.[17] The UCA made an effort to match salaries to actual needs so that the highest salary would be no more than three and one-half times the lowest.[18] In the early UCA years, personnel received whatever salary seemed best to the administrators. With the new salary scale, some maintenance staff and gardeners got a 100 percent increase, while some at the higher end took a cut. For those in engineering and computer sciences, this change meant sacrifice, but at that time the gap between salaries at the university and those in the private sector was not as great as in later years. There was general agreement that the plan was just and there was little opposition to its implementation.[19]

Until this point government annual scholarship subsidies had been worth on the average 50,000 *colones* ($20,000) in addition to direct payments of 100,000 *colones* ($40,000) in 1969 and 605,000 *colones* ($242,000) at the beginning of 1971.[20]

The tuition scale changed in 1974 to take into account student ability to pay. It had been a standard 65 *colones* a month ($260/year) for the day school and 50 *colones* a month ($200/year) for the evening program. The new monthly tuition ranged on a sliding scale from 20 to 120 *colones*— or from $80/year to $480/year.[21]

Even in these early days, the UCA board discussed the possibility of receiving economic assistance from the United States Agency for International Development (US-AID); Robert Henle, S.J., then vice president of St. Louis University and later president of Georgetown University, had proposed a regional plan for such assistance, but there are no indications that any funds ever came to the UCA.[22] In 1968, the UCA had received four scholarships from Fulbright-LASPAU for future faculty members. Ironically, LASPAU was negotiating to finance one scholarship with the United Fruit Company, one of the multinationals most criticized for unsavory practices in Central America.[23] In 1973, the board of directors approved the contract of Leonel Menéndez "even if US-AID does not cover the costs."[24] In 1974 the UCA accepted the offer of the United States embassy to finance a sociology professor.[25] But generally, there was little contact with the United States government, and even less in the following decades until the end of the civil war.

BEGINNINGS OF RESEARCH AND SOCIAL OUTREACH

The UCA made tentative beginnings of research in a few departments such as engineering, and cooperated on others with the Centro de Investigación y Acción Social (CIAS) think-tank team. In 1973, Guillermo Ungo was named director of the research institute. UCA faculty members began to accept invitations to international gatherings of scholars: Luis de Sebastián (economics) to Budapest, Ignacio Ellacuría (theology) to Buenos Aires, and Héctor Oquelí (population) to Bucharest.

The rural electrification study, funded by the World Bank, lasted from the second semester of 1972 to early 1974, and its director, Luis de Sebastián, produced a four-volume report that helped the UCA understand "the methodological problems involved in the application of social cost/benefit technique analysis."[26]

The great need for decent housing motivated the UCA to get involved early with *vivienda mínima,* low-cost housing units for the needy.[27] By 1975, Jon Cortina, S.J., had UCA engineering students participating in the project.

At the board of directors meeting on August 28, 1974, the UCA considered for the first time the establishment of a radio station, a topic that would come up almost a dozen times until the university finally went on the air in November 1991. In 1975, Italo López Vallecillo was named first director of the university press, which was to publish more than 200 books over the next two decades and serve as one of the main voices of the university's social outreach.[28]

The board of directors decided not to begin a department of education in 1975 because the university lacked trained personnel. This was another topic, like that of the radio station, which was to reappear on the board agenda only to be postponed again and again until 1991 for lack of human and financial resources. But the computer center did open in mid-1975, and became one of the best in the country.

Also in 1975, the board approved the start of the Centro de Documentación Política y Social, the forerunner of Centro de Documentación y Apoyo a la Investigación (CIDAI), which was to undergird so much of the social outreach research and analysis of the 1980s and 1990s.

Another important aspect of social outreach was theology for the laity. Even before the establishment of the Center for Theological Reflection (CRT) in 1974, the UCA offered theology courses that had considerable impact on the San Salvador archdiocese—as many as 300 persons attended these weekly sessions.

The Importance of *Estudios Centroamericanos (ECA)*

Five months before Achaerandio assumed the rectorship in 1969, the UCA took over *Estudios Centroamericanos (ECA)* under an agreement with the Central American vice province to which the journal belonged. It was in *ECA* that most research and social analysis conducted by UCA were to appear. Therefore, a brief review of some major articles serves as a comprehensive survey of UCA involvement in the national reality. Such use of *ECA* does not imply that this journal was the only source of UCA social outreach, but sooner or later most issues found their way into its pages. These articles indirectly help define the nature of the UCA model, and give hints as to how the model developed and was consolidated over the next two decades.

The War with Honduras

As indicated earlier, many Salvadorans had moved into Honduras looking for land and employment. When Honduras closed its borders to these immigrants and forced many to return to El Salvador, war broke out between the two countries.

The first issue of *ECA* under UCA direction, in November–December 1969, was dedicated to an analysis of the war. "The university would be failing in one of its most grave responsibilities, that of being an intellectual conscience for the nation, if it did not confront this crisis, and offer an intellectual diagnosis . . ."[29] This theme, and the phrase "national reality" *(realidad nacional),* occur over and over again in UCA documents that explain the context within which and for which the university exists.

In this issue, Sebastián Mantilla recounted the basic details of the war; Ignacio Ellacuría, human rights; Francisco Javier Ibisate, S.J., planning for the future; Luis de Sebastián, the economic situation; Abraham Rodríguez (one of the founders of the Christian Democratic Party and candidate for the presidency of El Salvador two years earlier), Organization of American States (OAS) involvement; Roberto Lara Velado, legal issues; and Jose Ignacio Scheifler, Central American comparative statistics. The project involved collaboration of Jesuits and their lay colleagues, with each author taking personal responsibility for individual articles, but the volume as a whole representing a team effort of the UCA.

In his treatment of human rights, Ellacuría touches on themes he would develop over the next twenty years: Central America's fundamentally unjust socioeconomic structures, the importance of respect for human rights, and the concept of "limit-situation."[30]

Ellacuría writes that "the situation of injustice is not only what the Honduran authorities have encouraged or permitted against Salvadorans living in Honduras; it is more complex, and it forces us to question the socioeconomic and political structures of both countries" (92). In the war, "ultimately what was at stake was the dignity of the person, but the protest would not have gone beyond remote sympathy if the offense had not been tinged with nationalism" (94). He lays the groundwork for saying later that the

Salvadoran government could not cite human rights as a justification for going to war with Honduras in 1969, and then ignore the same principles when it came to other violations of human rights, especially those perpetrated by the agents of the government.

He describes basic conditions in both Honduras and El Salvador as "limit-situations," a term "given currency by [Karl] Jaspers who used it to refer to those situations in which one cannot live without struggle and suffering . . . , situations which place our whole existence into question and flood it with light, so much so that it is in these situations and only in them that we grasp our true being" (96). Ellacuría transfers the "limit-situation" concept to the profound socioeconomic and political problems that overwhelm Honduras. "The thousands of Salvadorans in Honduras were a handy pretext for disguising the social situation. . . . and hence offered a ready explanation for unemployment and poor living conditions of Hondurans" (97).

On the other hand, "the fact that several hundred thousand Salvadorans were unable to find a decent livelihood in the country of their birth, is an irrefutable denunciation of an unjust situation" (97). As a result, "resistance to totalitarian regimes, and revolution against unjust structures, revolutionary violence, . . . demand a thorough rethinking of what a limit-situation is." And so, "first: the presence of a limit-situation itself is a condemnation of an unjust structure that demands radical change; second, when a person or a people enter a limit-situation, decisions are always ambiguous and therefore those who make and implement these decisions must refuse to be swept up by the passions aroused by the impact of that situation" (99).

A corollary of this assertion is that justice may come into conflict with law, and justice must prevail. Ellacuría does not dismiss the importance of law; he sees it as necessary for the coherence of a society, but he cites the letters of St. Paul, who urged early Christians not to be slaves of the law (99). Ellacuría says, "We would fall into anarchy if there were no laws and protection by the law; but we would fall into injustice if laws were absolutized and not subject to continual revision" (100).

He reminds the Salvadoran government of the current strategy's implications: "El Salvador has committed itself publicly to a great deal, and both inside and outside the country it is going to be held accountable for what it demanded at a difficult moment—the defense of the fundamental rights of the person is above other values, whatever the sacrifice might cost" (101).

In the 1980s, Ellacuría would also describe conditions in El Salvador as "limit-situations" and therefore urge negotiations to solve them.

The very next issue of *ECA* after the study of the war with Honduras (January–February 1970) picked up the perennial problem of land reform. The university sent representatives to the Land Reform Congress called by the Salvadoran Legislature.[31] The editorial points out that "not everyone who speaks about land reform means the same thing. For some it is just land distribution; for others it means merely an increase in productivity" (3). Talks at the congress had broken down, and the editorial warns that "we will not work our way out of this impasse unless a logical, objective, and scientific methodology is adopted . . . , [one] that is based on data drawn from the socioeconomic reality of the agrarian sector." It is important to know what is wrong, before attempting to fix it (3).

ECA called attention to problems and needs such as the land ownership system, low and static earnings of those who work the land, basic and vocational education, and community development. The UCA journal urged that production and work be adapted to both the large labor supply and new techniques—the maximum economic efficiency compatible with a high level of employment. Reforms should also include improvement of land productivity through fertilization, infrastructure, and appropriate crop cultivation, and farmer initiatives should not be frustrated by inadequate credit resources. It also touched on the need to improve national and international marketing techniques and quality control (3).

Román Mayorga said that the UCA interventions in the congress made quite an impression on the audience, which broke into applause at the words of Luis de Sebastián and Ignacio Ellacuría.[32] In his book, Mayorga observes that "for the first time, the UCA declared itself independent of the sector whose support had contributed toward giving life to the institution. It showed itself capable of going against the interests of this sector when honest perception of the truth required such a course of action. The UCA also demonstrated independence and a serious approach in the face of the repetitious, doctrinaire dogmatism of other representatives in the congress. This was the beginning of a gradual change of the university's external image."[33]

ECA picked up the land reform issue again in its July–August 1973 issue. All articles focus on the basic injustice of the socio-economic-political system, especially the distribution of benefits, and they imply that without political change, financially powerful people will resist any economic change. They will use "productivity" as an excuse for keeping control of the best land in their own hands. Although the UCA was not in a position to design a land reform program, it did want to keep basic issues before the public by reminding all that toying with one aspect of the problem would not get at the roots of the problem, namely; the unjust structures of land-holding.

But after Salvador Allende's socialist government came to power in Chile (1970–1973), interest in agrarian reform cooled, the minister of agriculture who had spearheaded the effort resigned, and another gesture came to naught.

The ANDES (Teachers') Strike

The legislature had passed a 1971 teacher salary scale law, but ANDES, the teachers' union, wanted a substitute plan to receive consideration. The government refused, and ANDES called the strike. By Decree 390, the legislature then declared the strike illegal.

An interdisciplinary study of the teachers' strike resulted in a UCA book, *Análisis de una Experiencia Nacional,* and an issue of *ECA.* According to Román Mayorga, "This little research project cost the UCA several hundred thousand colones; it caused the withdrawal of the 1972 national subsidy which the Executive branch had already presented to the Legislature. The subsidy disappeared by the wave of a magic wand, through instructions from the Executive branch just before the appropriation was to have been voted. High government officials claimed later that urgent public needs had come up at the last minute, and made necessary a pull back of the UCA subsidy." But too many coincidences, as well as the UCA's being singled out, made people in the university think that this decision "had much to do with the publication of the book."[34]

The July 1971 *ECA* editorial by Ignacio Ellacuría, although basically in sympathy with the strikers' demands, suggests that the teachers look beyond their own immediate interests.

The strike aimed to improve faculty salaries but, like the war with Honduras and the agrarian reform congress, it also raised the curtain on El Salvador's fundamental problems. *ECA*'s advice to the teachers served as a metonym for the UCA approach to other national problems.

In this strike, ANDES was seen as

> promoting social improvements. . . . but their involvement should . . . not stay closed inside their own interests. Nor should they confuse their mission with that of political parties. Their contribution to social change should follow its own path which means preparing teachers to be an independent group with real potential for stimulating consciousness for change, without entering into partisan politics. Only

a group of teachers with capability and dignity can promote social transformation and justice, and educate people who understand change and are prepared to bring it about. (398)

This statement is important because it shows that Ellacuría consistently wanted a strong civic society capable of being a social force against political forces such as the state and political parties. This goal led him in the 1980s to urge emergence of a "third (social) force" with an important role alongside the Salvadoran government and the FMLN insurgents.[35]

The August–September 1971 edition of *ECA* offered a whole issue on education problems, including an article on the methodology of the Brazilian educator, Paolo Freire, by César Jerez and Juan Hernández Pico, members of the CIAS think tank. The issue's introduction mentions an important characteristic that the UCA would try to follow across the board: "It is not enough to denounce, even when the denunciation is technical and not propagandistic. We have also sought to offer solutions, or more accurately, principles for solutions." (481).

ECA returned to the basic issue in April 1979—the right to strike. "We believe that a strong and responsible labor movement, operating within a legal framework that is not partial and vitiated in favor of capital, is a factor in the stability of a democratic and modern society. . . . On the other hand, we believe that labor power should not be transformed into arrogance, nor employ abuse against abuse, detrimental to the innocent majority who are caught in the middle of such opponents."[36]

The editorial points out that only 6 percent of Salvadoran workers were union members, and that "the labor code was too pro-capital in its definitions of strike legality. The judiciary has been partial in the application of the code. The result has been that almost no strike is ever legal . . . [and] the high principles and spirit of the constitution are left without effectiveness" (202).

Although sympathetic with the teachers' plight, the UCA book and the *ECA* summary attempt to offer objective evaluation and analysis, not polemical rhetoric on behalf of one side or the other.

The Invasion of the University of El Salvador

Despite the frosty relationship between the UCA and the national university which in 1965 had opposed its coming into existence, the July 1972 *ECA* editorial condemns the Molina government for sending in the military to take over the University of El Salvador.

"First of all, no one can deny the overall situation through which the

University of El Salvador was passing; it was frankly deplorable. Marxism or pseudodogmatism of a sectarian nature, rampant and superficial, dominated many academic units, and there were many doubts about honesty in the administration of budget funds. But these kinds of problems do not give a complete picture of the university. We are well aware of the honest and valiant work of many professionals and students" (436). Even though the *ECA* editorial recognizes genuine problems in the university, it condemns the action of the legislature and the military takeover, and the exiling of fifteen Salvadoran university personnel to Nicaragua (437).

A similar note was struck in 1977, when the government once again intervened violently in the University of El Salvador. The September editorial (633–8) admits that the national university is suffering from "the infantile effects of communism . . . a sectarian and dogmatic illness that puts ideology of one sector before the interest of the rest of the university community with serious deterioration of scientific and academic values as a result." But the government's intervention was "an incalculable evil which has generated a climate of violence and uncertainty in the university with devastating effects on studies. . . ."

Cerrón Grande

The August–September 1972 *ECA* took hydroelectric power as the topic for a special edition.

After a multidisciplinary technical analysis of the Cerrón Grande dam project, it concludes that although there is a need to reexamine ways to increase electrical power for 1976–1985, "there is insufficient proof that including Cerrón Grande as part of the solution is really economical. The study that supposedly proves that this project should be included contains errors and doubtful data which take away credibility. Even if these deficiencies could be corrected, it would still be necessary to come up with a detailed plan of activities . . . [and] to give just compensation to farm workers who will be affected by the flooding of the lands where they work" (615).

The project budget equaled the Salvadoran government's annual budget. The UCA study asks whether there are less expensive ways to achieve the same results, how many people will actually benefit, will it require a continuous flow of resources from outside the country when foreign exchange currency is scarce, and what are the effects on natural resources and the environment?

The UCA study uses this occasion to raise once again some land reform issues. "If on the basis of national opportunity costs the project should be deemed inappropriate, then the government should expropriate the lands that were going to be used in the project, and turn them over to a land reform program. Under no circumstances should large land owners be allowed to continue enjoying the use of these controversial lands, because that would identify national interests with those of a few private property owners" (619). The editorial adds that if the government expropriates the land it should give the owners an amount equal to the value listed on the tax rolls and not the market value. Needless to say, the UCA recommendations had no effect; Cerrón Grande was built.

The Elections of 1972

Ignacio Ellacuría proposed to CIAS members César Jerez and Juan Hernández Pico a research project on the 1972 election process. In an effort to minimize possible repercussions feared by some UCA board members, Román Mayorga proposed that the university publish the research in the form of a book that would have the UCA name on the cover and a prologue that would state the following: "(a) this is a scientific piece of historical investigation of ideas and falls within the mission of the university; (b) it is the sole responsibility of its authors and it does not commit the rest of university personnel for or against its content."[37]

The board also decided to send a commission to meet with President Molina to request a budget subsidy for 1973, "and, at the same time, let him know about the book, without giving the impression that he could put conditions on its publication." He gave the 1973 subsidy even though he knew the book was going to be published.[38]

There was controversy over any UCA officials meeting with President Molina. Some saw such meetings as "betraying the spirit proclaimed by the UCA and a sellout to the oligarchy." University officials later met with the students to clarify what actually happened in the presidential meetings— unambiguous dialogue with Molina on UCA's understanding of its role in the country.

At the end of Molina's first year in office, the September 1973 ECA editorial sees some slight rays of hope in three areas: establishment of a national financial council (Junta Monetaria), negotiations with Honduras to settle issues left over from the war, and an inkling of possible land reform. On the negative side of the chart are the takeover of the University of El Salvador, fear of the military's role, and the decision to go ahead with Cerrón Grande despite serious objections.

The July 1975 editorial, however, sounds a more sober note: Its hopes of 1973 had proved to be without foundation. "El Salvador has not moved. . . . This climate of violence gets worse." The editorial concludes:

"those who repress do not liberate" (325).

In the light of what happened over the next fifteen years, the words of the editorial are indeed ominous:

> Without a positive and well thought-out break with the current system and its way of running society with the interests of the dominating classes prevalent, it is impossible to respond to the objective need for transformation and to the ever more urgent needs of the people. . . . Instead of repressing those who protest their unjust situation, . . . the government should favor the protest. . . . To see in priests [several had been murdered by this point, including Father Rutilio Grande] subversion and communism is to look at reality through eyeglasses loaned by the dominant classes; it is political ineptitude, and even worse, it is culpable blindness. (326–8)

In the July 1977 editorial at the end of Molina's term of office, *ECA* concluded that he had left in place all the fundamental problems of the country (453–7).

Solidarity with the Jesuit High School

Another issue provided insights into the nature of the new UCA: controversy over the Jesuit high school. Government officials, Oscar Romero, then auxiliary bishop of San Salvador and later its martyred archbishop, and a number of parents attacked the Jesuit high school, Externado de San José, in mid-1973, as "communist" and "subversive"; they demanded the removal of some staff members and a revamping of the curriculum. The UCA Jesuits and their lay colleagues worked closely with the high school staff in its defense.[39] The UCA's official statement on June 29, 1973, said something very significant about itself as an institution—just eight years after its founding.

"Over these past few years, the UCA has grown in understanding of its own university mission at the service of the people of El Salvador. After its beginnings, when it tended to be considered as a bulwark of liberal capitalism, little by little, through the dynamism of its own university vocation, its Christian inspiration, and events that have demanded a response, the UCA has found its own line of independence and commitment" (523). The UCA had taken pains not to be used by any political party.

In summary, "the University, therefore, has no choice but to favor urgent and profound social change, an aim it hopes to help achieve through university means." The UCA saw the Externado as an ally in this process and joined its efforts to those of the high school. It decried the use of "anti-communism" as a cover for an attack against an institution committed to educate young people to be agents of social change (524).

Juan Hernández Pico feels that the Externado's public defense, prepared with the assistance of the UCA, and published as an advertisement in the nation's daily papers, deflected the judiciary from its attempt to bring the Externado authorities to trial.[40]

THE CHRISTIAN DIMENSION OF THE UNIVERSITY

The UCA defined its Christian dimension more by its commitment to the poor than by religious practices. One of the best treatments of this subject is Jon Sobrino's 1987 talk at the University of Deusto in Bilbao, Spain, which will be examined in the next-to-last chapter under events of that year.

In an early 1972 letter to the superior general, the vice provincial commented that "the elements of a Christian ambience or climate in a university can be sought in Christian practices such as masses and retreats, and in this sense the Christian climate of the university is close to zero." But he pointed to other signs that gave evidence of UCA efforts to live up to its goals, such as the Theological Institute, and "not putting itself at the side of the rich but on the side of justice . . . and at great sacrifice."[41] The vice provincial felt there were more signs of this Christian orientation in the faculty of human sciences, because of the presence of the Jesuit seminarians, than in business/economics and engineering, where students and faculty seemed more concerned about professional activities.

To show greater concern for social awareness issues than for the development of professionals, a number of Jesuits, including Ellacuría, did not want the excess from their salaries to go into a general UCA fund but rather for activities that the vice provincial described as *tipo crítico* (analytical). Father Gondra represented another point of view that stressed the precariousness of government subsidies and the growing reluctance of the original benefactors to support the university.

Later that same year, 1972, Vincent O'Keefe, S.J., assistant to the superior general, praised the UCA social justice orientation and the importance given to academic excellence, an achievement that had been reported by a recent Roman visitor to the region. He confirmed that this approach conformed to the guidelines of Pedro Arrupe, the superior general.[42]

The nature of the university—its autonomy and its "Catholic" or "Christian" nature—continued to be an issue in these early years. Cardinal Garrone, head of the Vatican's Congregation for Catholic Education, had complained about the independence of the Rafael Landívar University in Guatemala, and Father Estrada asked Father Arrupe for clarification. Arrupe replied that even though the universities of Central America have not been established canonically, they are Catholic universities, and they have a role to play. They should maintain good relations with the hierarchy . . . so as to find out what objections they have and to clear up any difficulties and misunderstandings. Then there would be no need to refer matters to Rome. The universities were established without canonical status to prevent the bishops from intervening in academic matters, but when it comes to important apostolic undertakings the bishops have full right to watch out for the university's general orientation in moral and religious questions."[43]

Estrada complained to Arrupe the following year that "I am seeing that this question of autonomy is bringing the Jesuits of all three universities to the point where they reject all external hierarchical or religious authority." He asked for a Roman visitor to help him clarify his role because he was running into opposition from people who said he did not have sufficient university experience.[44]

Estrada called a meeting of the rectors and religious superiors of the three universities later in 1973. He reported to Arrupe that "they discussed alternatives if the vice province could not staff the three universities, and the relationship between the Jesuits and the universities." The rectors suggested that the Society's influence would have to be indirect, through administrators, especially in Guatemala where a close connection with the Jesuit order would bring legal problems. They also discussed the Christian dimension of the universities and broached the possibility of bringing in some outside advisors on this topic. They asked for a year to think it all over and then to meet again.[45]

Concerned about the ideological polarization in the vice province, Arrupe urged the local authorities "to make every effort to arrive at the widest consensus possible on the style and timetable of change [in the communities and the institutions]." The colloquiums for apostolic renewal held in each community pleased the superior general, but he urged avoidance of what might be seen as "brain washing" to advance an exclusive way of thinking which some people think is what happens in Central America." He admitted that moving cautiously can "give the impression that one is going backwards, offering palliatives, when in reality what is intended is to avoid immediate difficulties that could prevent the realization of more fundamental goals in the long run." He added that "no one is trying to put the brakes on what is healthy but rather to avoid a polarizing political activism that at its roots is not Gospel-like."[46]

Estrada saw the UCA in El Salvador as "the most advanced in the sense of defining clear goals and objectives," but he felt that it still had a way to go in realizing some of its objectives, "especially those of Christian inspiration." He added that the two UCA Jesuit communities had to communicate more among themselves, but that "at the intellectual level the strength of the University comes from the group living at the liberationist UCA II."[47]

Arrupe agreed that the gradualist UCA I community should not be forced to change "because it was preferable that they live content according to hopes and customs which are fundamentally healthy and religious, even though they leave something to be desired as far as the current lines of renovation are concerned." Arrupe had difficulty understanding how two such different communities could conduct one university; differences, he felt, would inevitably surface. But he urged communication, and concluded by encouraging the general thrust of the university: "The plan and mission of the UCA are expressed with brevity and clarity and in agreement with the educational and social principles which the Society and I have underlined for many years."[48]

Later that year, however, he remarked: "I have the impression that the Jesuits from UCA II are very sure of themselves and that they look down a bit on the others."[49] He agreed that the time was not propitious to unite the two communities, but insisted that this arrangement not be considered permanent.[50]

A month later, Estrada reported to Arrupe on a recently completed meeting of vice province university personnel.[51] Achaerandio, the rector of the San Salvador UCA, gave a report about which he had not consulted the other Jesuits. The Managua UCA rector presented six pages that the team in Nicaragua had developed, and the rector from Guatemala also presented his own ideas without consulting his colleagues beforehand. Needless to say, it was a stormy meeting. Some felt that Ellacuría had come to the meeting with an already drafted vice province university plan that the other universities feared the vice provincial might impose on all of them.

After several hours of tense discussion and even personal attacks, several individuals made their own proposals, including Ellacuría. Antonio Gallo, the chief ideologue of the Rafael Landívar University in Guatemala, urged that the universities focus less on the critical function and more on what he called "the Christian mission." He thought the universities should reflect on the cultural reality, get to know the culture better, and not be so critical of it. He urged study of the indigenous peoples who were half the population, and the world of the Baroque.

César Jerez, then a member of the Central American CIAS team, the think tank on social issues, and later provincial of Central America and president of the UCA in Managua, disagreed. The proper role of the university was its critical function, and research on a country's immediate problems, even though such studies involved risks such as the loss of state subsidies or even expulsion from the country. Jerez claimed that oligarchic enclaves on the boards of directors were really running some of the universities, even though the Jesuits held administrative posts. His comments were aimed at both Nicaragua, which was linked to Somoza, and Guatemala, where a vice rector was a multinational corporation lawyer. Jerez also emphasized the importance of stimulating student social awareness. He agreed that the pastoral function was important but the critical function had first priority.

Some challenged the choice of programs such as business administration, and others asked how the popular movements might be served better.

The participants from El Salvador also stressed the critical function and the Christian mission; Achaerandio cited, as examples, the UCA organizational manual and the 1970 IDB loan-signing speech. Ellacuría warned against the transfer of First World models to the Third World.

The Nicaragua delegation insisted on what they called the Christian mission. The rector, Arturo Dibar, said the critical function was impossible as long as the Somoza government held power, but that they would bide their time until the climate might be more propitious.

Estrada concluded that "these three Christian conceptions of the university were not mutually exclusive but rather complementary. . . . El Salvador puts emphasis on its critical function but does not demean the priorities for which the others have opted; Nicaragua gives emphasis to pastoral activities; and Guatemala concentrates on preparing university graduates for a society with which they have to be as familiar as possible, without criticizing it so much." The vice provincial seemed overly optimistic in his attempt to resolve these points of view.

All three communities were asked to answer three questions when they returned to their respective places:

1. What is the Christian mission of a university in their country?
2. How is their university fulfilling this mission?
3. If it is not fulfilling this mission, what short-term plans does it have to change this situation?

Estrada told Arrupe that both El Salvador and Nicaragua showed a willingness to examine these questions, but "Guatemala kept quiet. When I insisted on a response they said they need more time, more than six months."

Many points did not get discussed, such as the relationship between the universities and the Society of Jesus, the practicality of maintaining three separate institutions, and distribution of human and economic resources.

José Luis Alemán, a major figure in the 1960s Jesuit sociological study and secretary general of the Latin American CIAS teams, was an observer at this meeting. He pointed out what he considered to be the excessive autonomy of the universities, and the possibility of losing their sense of "mission." He suggested an annual meeting of Jesuits from the boards of directors with the vice provincial to see whether these institutions should continue as they were.

Estrada said that the Jesuits from the Landívar University in Guatemala felt under continual attack by those from El Salvador, but he thought this impression arose because the younger Jesuits had many questions about the Landívar. Estrada felt that the exchange was helpful because differences came out in the open.

An important channel for realization of UCA goals in El Salvador was its theological reflection center (Centro de Reflección Teológica), known as the CRT. Arrupe saw its purpose as renewal for those already ordained, and he questioned whether Jesuit seminarians should do their theological studies there. But he gave his permission after he discussed the matter with Ellacuría.[52]

Then Ellacuría's book, *Teología Política*, caused considerable controversy with the Vatican.[53] When Arrupe asked for details, Estrada reported that theologians from Spain had reviewed individual articles from the book and had approved them before publication. Arturo Rivera Damas, auxiliary bishop of San Salvador, had also approved the text.[54] Archbishop Emanuele Gerada, the papal nuncio, produced a copy of a Roman document entitled "Nota Sobre la Publicación *Teología Política*" which Estrada saw as an implicit attack on Rivera Damas, who then took it upon himself to get the opinion of Latin American theologians so as to defend his original evaluation. Estrada requested that Arrupe have some theologians in Rome review the text so that no shadow would fall on the CRT.

Ellacuría sent a four-page letter expressing his surprise at the Vatican's criticism's lack of scientific rigor, and he suggested a closer reading of his text by the censor.[55]

Jon Sobrino's christology had also come under attack from Rome, and like Ellacuría, he was asked to respond. Estrada included with his letter of March 11, 1974, to Arrupe a twenty-six-page document in which Sobrino denies that his christology was unorthodox or based principally on Marx and European Protestant theologians. Sobrino stated that he does not deny the incarnation and the sacrifice of the mass or any of the other traditional teachings of the church. He defends his use of sacred Scripture as based on commonly available exegesis.

According to Estrada, Archbishop Luis Chávez y González responded to the nuncio, Archbishop Gerada, that he had met with the outgoing and incoming Jesuit provincials, Sobrino, and Ellacuría, and that he was quite satisfied with their responses to the criticisms. "With this meeting we feel we have fulfilled our responsibilities as zealous guardians of the purity of doctrine and as understanding friends of those who are in search of new paths. We consider these paths full of risks, but necessary" (see n. 54). Such support from the local bishop was crucial for the UCA.

Estrada evaluated the work of the CRT as "sufficiently positive for it to continue."[56] He praised a course on the theology and praxis of the "spiritual exercises" of St. Ignatius offered by Ellacuría and Sobrino, but he also indicated that a regular column published in *El Mundo*, entitled "Church and World," had to be suspended because it was seen by some critics as "polemical," and the advertisers were threatening to boycott the newspaper if it were continued.

Nonetheless, shadows did fall on the CRT, and Arrupe sent a letter to the vice provincial early in 1975 warning him to keep a close eye on the orthodoxy of the center. Arrupe criticized the reports from Central America sent to Rome for touching just on the academic and not on questions of "religious and community life, and the links of the young men with the Society." Arrupe added that he did not want Jesuit seminarians from other provinces to do their theological studies at the CRT.[57] These kinds of suspicions from Rome dogged the Central American Jesuits throughout these difficult decades.[58]

So many letters continued to make their way to Rome criticizing the new approaches in the province that Arrupe considered the possibility of appointing a new vice provincial to replace Estrada.

> Disunity in the vice province seems to suggest the appointment of someone who is not perceived as tied to one of the factions, even if this criticism has no basis. Such a person could work with freedom and try to solve the difficulties. In addition, there are concrete problems such as the formation program [of the young Jesuits] and the CRT, and it might not be easy for you to solve them even if you presented solutions which conformed to the orientation I have given when I have treated these matters.[59]

Estrada responded promptly and firmly to Arrupe's CRT criticism by pointing out that Ellacuría had written a serious evaluation of the center, and that he, the vice provincial, was annoyed by insinuations to the contrary. He questioned the objectivity of Arrupe's anonymous experts and asked that they be identified so that there might be face-to-face dialogue with them. He characterized their approach as idealistic and unrealistic.

> For me it is simply false that the CRT is obsessed with Latin American concerns and that it neglects the legitimate and appropriate study of universal theology. Equally false, and it is important to make this clear, is the charge that the gratuitousness of faith is forgotten along with the importance of Christ, and that merely sociological considerations are substituted. . . . We do not believe that there is a universal theology which merely has to be applied, but rather one that becomes concrete. This is a very different nuance, and it guides the work of the CRT.[60]

After citing many instances which he terms "unobjective" or "false," Estrada finds the experts' conclusions hard to accept: namely, that there is in the CRT *una decadencia teológica.*" Quite the opposite is true, he says; the students are enthusiastic and they see theology as something exciting, not just a step required for ordination. Estrada offers to have Jon Sobrino and Juan Hernández Pico go to Rome to talk with Pedro Arrupe or his "experts."

Arrupe did not respond in the same tone; he suggested instead conversations with his assistant, Eduardo Briceño, who would be coming to Central America.[61] Two months later, Arrupe invited Estrada to Rome and assured him that there would not be any change of vice provincial until the regular term was completed.[62]

In October, Arrupe wrote that he had enjoyed the visit of Estrada and Hernández Pico to Rome, and he praised the dynamism of all that was going on in the vice province.[63] (Hernández Pico had succeeded Ellacuría as delegate for formation.) Arrupe urged unity among the Jesuits, and he praised the men picked to train the seminarians, but he cautioned against "a tendency which concerns me, and that is excessive politicization." He clarified that his concern over the CRT had been whether the seminarians were so involved in their pastoral activities that they did not have sufficient time for study and reflection. He praised the quality of a number of professors, but wondered about the dependence on outsiders for staffing. A number of these concerns persisted in the mid-1990s.

Estrada also felt good about the visit to Rome because it had given him ample opportunity to explain the rationale behind so much of what was going on in the Central American vice province, and he was able to offset the effects of letter writers from back home.[64]

The following March, in the letter that announced César Jerez as the new vice provincial, Arrupe thanked Estrada effusively for "the important service you have given to the Society of Jesus in this position. It has been your task to guide the vice province in a moment of full evolution. There have been tensions which you have been able to handle with serenity, great spirit, and above all, with a keen sense of spiritual responsibility. In addition, you have been able to launch important projects and to encourage your colleagues to establish them solidly. Therefore, you should feel very content."[65]

Intra-Jesuit affairs have absorbed a considerable amount of space in these pages because of their crucial importance, but should not seem to explain the total picture of what was going on at the UCA at this time. While general guidelines for the university mission were strongly influenced by events inside the order, there was much ferment within the institution itself, including the development of a significant community spirit that involved both Jesuits and laity.

The development of drafts of the organization manual, salary scale, and differentiated tuition plans are examples of this collaboration, which took place not only in formal sessions on campus but also at social events in the homes of lay colleagues.[66] Jesuits and lay colleagues celebrated birthdays and anniversaries together, went to the beach for holidays, and became close friends. Luis Achaerandio, the rector, contributed significantly to encourage this community atmosphere. Although major decisions continued to be the sole responsibility of the board of directors, these decisions tended to represent a consensus from the university community rather than merely dictates from above. This spirit not only produced creative ways of being a university, it laid the groundwork for a solid community that would face adversity in the coming years, as the institution was perceived more and more as a threat to entrenched political and economic forces.

SUMMARY OF THE ACHAERANDIO YEARS

In looking back at this era, Román Mayorga observed that there had been no opposition or conflict with the right except for the agrarian reform congress, the *ECA* analyses were the main research projects, and the students were more interested in upward social mobility than in social change.[67] While Mayorga's analysis is basically correct, the stage had been set for changes in all these areas when he became rector in 1975.

One of Luis Achaerandio's greatest accomplishments was to help create an atmosphere of community—the feeling of a joint effort of Jesuits and lay colleagues to discuss alternatives and to bring about a new type of university. Achaerandio saw lay colleagues as an essential resource, and so he improved the salary scale to help retain them and radiated his own respect and confidence in them. Since he made these lay colleagues feel at home, they gained ownership of the university project and dedicated their efforts to its success despite their potential to earn a greater salary outside the university world.

Thus the UCA rectorate of Luis Achaerandio (1969–1975) and the vice provincialate of Miguel Francisco Estrada (1970–1976) ended. The UCA had the beginnings of a solid physical plant, academic programs in a wide variety of fields from engineering to theology, and a public presence mainly through the pages of *Estudios Centroamericanos*. This public presence, stretched across issues as different as agrarian reform and fraudulent elections, and took advantage of the talents of the Jesuit and lay team.

It was also a period of deep division within the Jesuit order, but also a time for clearer commitment of the whole vice province to change the thrust of its apostolic activities toward the needs of the poor. This local change had a deep effect on the UCA itself, and gave a preview of the types of changes that the Jesuit Thirty-second General Congregation would urge upon the whole order in the mid-1970s.

In the next stage, during the rectorate of Román Mayorga and the provincialate of César Jerez, the enemies of both the UCA and the Jesuit order would step up their attacks, testing the mettle of the university community and the vision that had been forged in its first decade.

NOTES

1. Correspondence of Juan Hernández Pico, S.J., with the author, July 1993.
2. Rodolfo Cardenal, *Historia de Una Esperanza: Vida de Rutilio Grande* (San Salvador: UCA Editores, 1986).
3. Mayorga, 46.
4. Mayorga, 40.
5. Interview with Francisco Javier Ibisate, November, 1992.
6. Interview with Román Mayorga, March 21, 1994.
7. *Plan Quinquenal, 1977–1981* (San Salvador, UCA Editores, 1976), 26. Hereafter this text is referred to as BID, the initials of the IDB in Spanish.
8. Mayorga, 43.
9. BID, 27.
10. BID, 71.
11. Mayorga, 45.
12. Mayorga, 31.
13. Mayorga, 31.

14. Most of this data is taken from *Plan Quinquenal 1977–1981,* which was prepared in December 1976, for the second Inter-American Development Bank loan of almost $10,000,000. There is a comprehensive picture of the finances on p. 75.

15. BID, 63.

16. BID, 64.

17. Mayorga, 60.

18. See "Consideraciones Justificativas y Aclaratorias Escalafón de la Universidad," in *Planteamiento Universitario, 1989* (San Salvador: UCA Editores, 1989), 15–36.

19. Interview with Román Mayorga, March 21, 1994.

20. Mayorga, 41.

21. Mayorga, 61–3.

22. AUCA, February 2, 1966. All reference to the minutes of the board of directors of the UCA will be designated AUCA with the date of the meeting.

23. AUCA, May 8, 1968.

24. AUCA, February 5, 1973. Ellacuría was not present for meetings of the board of directors that semester.

25. AUCA, May 9, 1974.

26. Guillermo Ungo et al., *Costos y beneficios de la electrificación rural en El Salvador,* 4 vols. (San Salvador: UCA Editores, 1974).

27. AUCA, October 29, 1973. See also Mayorga, 54.

28. AUCA, January 21, 1975.

29. *Estudios Centroamericanos* 24 (November–December 1969), 389. Hereafter referred to as *ECA* with dates and page numbers in the text. See also Thomas P. Anderson, *The War of the Dispossessed: Honduras and El Salvador, 1969* (Lincoln: University of Nebraska Press, 1981).

30. Ignacio Ellacuría, S.J., "Fundamental Human Rights and the Legal and Political Restrictions Placed on Them," in Hassett and Lacey, 91–104. Page references for citations of this article originally published in Spanish in *Estudios Centroamericanos* 24 (November–December 1969), 435–49, are included in the text. The translation is by Philip Berryman.

31. For details see Tommie Sue Montgomery, 82–3.

32. Interview with Román Mayorga, March 21, 1994.

33. Mayorga, 35.

34. Mayorga, 41.

35. Correspondence of Juan Hernández Pico, S.J., with the author, July, 1993.

36. "Los Sindicatos y el Derecho de Huelga," *ECA* 34 (April 1979), 199.

37. AUCA, November 9, 1972. The book on the elections was Juan Hernández Pico, César Jerez, Ignacio Ellacuría, Emilio Baltodano, and Román Mayorga, *El Salvador: Año Político, 1971–72,* (San Salvador: UCA Editores, 1973).

38. Mayorga, 52.

39. For a full account of the Externado controversy see Charles J. Beirne, S.J., "Jesuit Education for Justice," *Harvard Educational Review* 55 (February 1985), 1–19.

40. Correspondence with the author, July 1993.

41. ASJCA–P72/5, Miguel Francisco Estrada to Pedro Arrupe, January 30, 1972.

42. ASJCA G72/30, Vincent O'Keefe to Estrada, August 1, 1972.

43. ASJCA–G72/43, Arrupe to Estrada, September 15, 1972.

44. ASJCA–P73/21, Estrada to Arrupe, May 2, 1973.

45. ASJCA–P73/63, Estrada to Arrupe, November 9, 1973.

46. ASJCA–G73/89, Arrupe to Estrada, November 17, 1973.

47. ASJCA–P73/76, Estrada to Arrupe, December 21, 1973.

48. ASJCA–G74/7, Arrupe to Estrada, March 1, 1974.

49. ASJCA–G74/110, Arrupe to Estrada, December 20, 1974.

50. ASJCA–G74/76, O'Keefe to Estrada, August 12, 1974.

51. ASJCA–P74/69, Estrada to Arrupe, September 17, 1974.

52. ASJCA–G74/99, Arrupe to Estrada, December 21, 1973.

53. English ed., *Freedom Made Flesh* (New York: Orbis, 1976).

54. ASJCA–74/28, Estrada to Arrupe, March 11, 1974.

55. ASJCA–P76/23, Estrada to Arrupe, May 25, 1976. There is a copy of Ellacuría's response in the Estrada-Arrupe correspondence.

56. ASJCA–P75/1, Estrada to Arrupe, January 21, 1975.

57. ASJCA–G75/10, Arrupe to Estrada, March 5, 1975.

58. Hernández Pico, in correspondence of July, 1993, said that these "suspicions" from Rome were never seen by the progressive Jesuits of Central America as showing distrust of them by Arrupe, but more as useful criticisms and/or as a means for Arrupe to show that he paid attention to internal as well as external critics of the direction the vice province was taking.

59. ASJCA–G75/18, Arrupe to Estrada, March 17, 1975.

60. ASJCA–P75/29, Estrada to Arrupe, April 10, 1975.

61. ASJCA–G/32, Arrupe to Estrada, April 26, 1975.

62. ASJCA–G75/45, Arrupe to Estrada, June 14, 1975.

63. ASJCA–G75/61, Arrupe to Estrada, October 19, 1975.

64. Conversation with Father Estrada, July, 1992.

65. ASJCA–G76/16, Arrupe to Estrada, March 20, 1976.

66. Interview with Román Mayorga, March 21, 1994.

67. Mayorga, 38.

7 THE MAYORGA YEARS: 1975–1979

Román Mayorga joined the UCA board on June 18, 1970, and thirteen months later, he took over as the fifth economics dean in six years. He became rector on August 11, 1975, at the age of thirty-four. Vincent O'Keefe, Father General Pedro Arrupe's assistant, wrote to Miguel Francisco Estrada, the vice provincial, that Rome should have been consulted before the UCA made this decision because Vatican officials were now questioning it.[1]

But Mayorga was the choice of all factions for rector. Since his early days as a student in the Jesuit high school, he and his family had been close friends of the "gradualists" who played such an important role in the early days of the UCA. He also counted Ignacio Ellacuría and the other "liberationists" among his close friends. His education at the Massachusetts Institute of Technology (MIT) prepared him to deal competently with many of El Salvador's social and technological problems, and his gracious way of dealing with people won him many friends.

His time in office—just four years—was a crucial one for the university because of the quality long-term planning that took place inside the UCA, and the storm of persecution waged against the university and the Jesuits during the rest of the decade.

This chapter will describe the second loan from the Inter-American Development Bank (IDB) and the extensive development of the UCA campus and programs financed by this loan. We will trace the growth of the UCA full-time faculty, students, and budget. Governance issues will be important to study both in themselves and because of the light they will shed on the nature of the UCA model—some of its strengths and weaknesses. Government subsidies will disappear as the UCA takes a stand on land reform and raises its voice in protest against the increased repression of the late 1970s. The Jesuits will be given thirty days to leave the country, but they will stay.

The UCA makes a contribution at the Latin American bishops' meeting in Puebla, Mexico, as theologian Jon Sobrino accompanies Archbishop Romero to this conference. Within the UCA, a pastoral plan takes shape and a chapel and center are prepared.

Once again the pages of *ECA* will be one screen onto which much UCA social outreach will be projected—key issues such as land reform mentioned earlier, the 1968 educational reform revisited a decade later, and important social analyses of the tense political scene leading up to the overthrow of the government of General Carlos Romero by a combination of military and civilian leaders, including the UCA lay rector, Román Mayorga, and the director of the research institute, Guillermo Ungo.

Mayorga had a clear vision of what the UCA should be—and a realistic appraisal of how far it had to go to realize its aims. He had a deep appreciation for the work accomplished in the decade since its founding, and he was determined to build on this foundation. In his book *La Universidad para el Cambio Social* (The University for Social Change) he spelled out his research agenda—the central problems facing the nation.[2]

1. Agrarian reform
2. Demographic problems
3. Raw material needs for economic development
4. Appropriate technology
5. Tax reform
6. Educational reform
7. Public health and social assistance reform
8. Housing and urban renewal
9. Sociopolitical participation
10. External dependence
11. Central American integration
12. Overall situation of Central Americans

To make a difference in any of these issues, however, the UCA had to increase its resources—the number of well-prepared full-time faculty, laboratories, improvements in the library, and additional resources. This brings us to the IDB loan and the planning process.

PLANNING FOR 1976–1981

The UCA staff began a major planning effort that resulted in three volumes that detailed university and department goals and specific projects. The plan was divided into research, teaching, and social outreach.[3]

With *research* as a high priority, in the 1976–1981 period the university intended to double the number of full-time faculty while increasing the student body only 34 percent. The twelve doctorates and eleven master's degrees of 1976 would be increased to forty doctorates and fifty master's degrees (156). This increased capacity for serious research would require additional laboratories and equipment, expansion of the library collection and the computer center, and more infrastructure in the Instituto de Investigaciones (157). The plan even spells out the number of doctorates and masters degrees needed in each field (188ff.). Graduate studies would be financed through European sources, Fulbright-LASPAU, and IDB funds for loans that would be paid back by the faculty members through UCA service.

"The plan presupposes contracting sixty-seven persons full time with master's degrees and doctorates in the 1976–1981 period (twenty-eight with doctorates and thirty-nine with master's) in order to have a total of ninety in 1981. Of these ninety persons, twenty-three are already working in the university, twenty-four are studying abroad with a commitment to work in the UCA upon their return, thirty more will be sent for studies abroad and will return within this five-year period, and thirteen others will be given contracts, but they will not have to be sent outside to study" (290). There would also be in-service programs for other personnel, but sabbaticals were considered too expensive at that time. It was an ambitious plan.

The UCA reaffirmed its *teaching* goals as part of the plan: "to prepare professionals who want to and who can contribute to a process of social change which better satisfies the needs of the vast majority of the population and liberates them from the conditions of injustice and oppression in which they currently find themselves. This means in the long and the short run the production of goods and services, and profound structural changes in the distribution of wealth, income and social organization" (158). But the plan pointed out that "there is no prescribed sequence or timetable, nor a formal model of society which has been abstracted from other existing ones. . . . In the course of our university process we will be discovering and rediscovering the proper model of society to which we should aspire" (158).

The UCA hoped that the students would "acquire an ethical commitment and the necessary technical competence to contribute efficaciously to this process, even though it would imply personal sacrifice and inevitable contradictions with the dominant interests of the present" (158). The student body limit would be 4,500. Such a limitation was seen as necessary so that the UCA might achieve its goals for the country. By 1994, however, UCA enrollment had topped 7,300 students.

The curriculum was to be divided into four categories:

A: A nucleus of courses "to introduce the student to an understanding of the social realities of Central America, and the methodology and structure of thought in the various disciplines. This program would be common and obligatory for all undergraduate students." These courses would be spread throughout the program of studies but would usually be offered in the early stages (159).

B: Common courses for students within each of the three "faculties" or divisions of the university.

C: Courses that give students "the essential matter within an area of specialization that they would need to serve and to grow in a particular profession in Central America" (159).

D: Electives within the area of specialization or "C" courses (previous category) from some other profession, to complement the training in one's own field.

The plan proposed that this revision begin in 1977 (161).

In addition to revision of the current academic programs, the plan called for additional fields of specialization at the basic or licentiate level in agrarian sciences and mathematics, and perhaps biology and education at a later date (162). The revisions and the additions would serve as the basis for possible graduate programs in the 1980s.

There are two senses in which social outreach (*proyección social*) must be understood—the first is broader and involves the overall impact of the university on society, the cumulative effect of all university resources dedicated to social transformation. This theme has been treated already in the seminal documents.

The second sense is important but more narrow: publications, public statements, broadcasts, editorials, and social service activities, and so on—the products of the UCA's teaching and research. To improve this area, the plan focused on two aspects: written and audiovisual communications, and student social services (162). These means were chosen "to contribute to the formation of a 'collective consciousness,' as widespread and lucid as possible on the need for and the nature of the social changes that the country requires" (163). In this way, the university's teaching and research functions would have their full effect because they would be put in terms understood by and influential on decision makers and on the general public.

Student social service up to 1975 had resulted in 300,000 hours of unremunerated activities in the communities. The plan set a goal of 700,000 hours for the 1976–1981 period. This experience was supposed to deepen student awareness of community problems and to help them effect change by the use of their professional skills (164).

To assist all three major university functions, the Centro de Documentación Política y Social was approved on December 2, 1975, to provide a depository of basic research data. This center was the precursor of CIDAI, the documentary center so crucial in the 1980s and 1990s.

At that same meeting, approval was given to a research project by Nicolás Mariscal, S.J., on the political forces in El Salvador and their role up to the 1977 elections. In 1976, Luis Achaerandio, the former rector, attended a meeting of Jesuit research centers. A symposium-congress on seismology gained board approval in August 1977. In February and August of 1978, there was encouragement from the board for a study of the Nahuatl culture in cooperation with the University of Chicago. Several professors engaged in other individual projects, but much of the research in this period of UCA's history concentrated on preparation of articles that appeared in *ECA,* and the licentiate theses of the students.

A major part of the plan boldly called for the expenditure of $2,608,000 in new facilities: several classroom buildings, computer center and library expansion, faculty offices, laboratory equipment, a student common center that would serve as a cafeteria, an auditorium, communication facilities, and an agricultural experimental station.

Even bolder was the proposed student loan fund of $2,000,000, from which assistance would be available to students from the third year of studies up to graduation. The third-year limitation was placed on the fund because there was less chance of students' droping out from that point on. This decision raises questions, however, about the philosophy of admissions which tolerated high dropout rates at the earlier levels.

Plan financing was to come principally from an IDB loan of over $9,000,000 with forty years to pay back, ten years of grace, a 1 percent rate of interest for the grace period, and 2 percent afterward (243). Total project cost would be $12,400,000: 21.7 percent in construction, and the rest for improvement of research, teaching, and social outreach.[4] The IDB loan was signed on April 18, 1978.

Román Mayorga says there was to be additional revenue from a series of businesses sponsored by the UCA, such as computer services to outside consumers, production from the agricultural experimental station, consultation fees for UCA faculty expertise, book sales, and research project income.[5] The plan included financial projections on all potential income from 1976 to 1981 and then beyond. Inflation and civil war, however, were to wreak havoc on these projections over the next decade.

Crucial to the success of the plan was faculty and staff morale—their *"mística,"* which the plan defined as

> dedication to a cause or an ideal, along with determined efforts toward its implementation. Positive symptoms that persons have this quality are the following: to see in the university the best place to work even though remuneration is less than in other institutions; to feel a sense of personal accomplishment in university work; to persevere fully dedicated to university tasks even if this implies criticisms and risks for themselves [in 1976 five high explosive bombs went off at the UCA]. On the negative side, there is no "mística" if the exclusive motivation for working is economic or for security and tranquility. (291)[6]

What would motivate such people? It would be "the sad reality of extreme necessity and oppression in which the vast majority of Salvadorans are forced to live, and the consequent clash of the university with this reality. . . . To serve the people in a university fashion is the appropriate way to be a Christian." But the document hastened to add that "the university is not confessional; and it does not oblige or force anyone to follow any creed or religion" (291).

Even though financial remuneration was not to be the primary motive for working at the UCA, the plan was conscious of the "obligation to attend to the basic needs of the staff" through a salary scale linked to the cost of living; disability, health, and life insurance; emergency loans; and a friendly, physically suitable work place (292). The effect of inflation on the workers continued to be a concern of the university board.[7]

The plan established ambitious goals and a special office of planning and implementation (294). The third volume of the plan gave details on each individual unit's goals and activities.

As we shall see, events overcame ideals and prevented implementation of some of the plan: Inflation made repayment of the IDB loan far more difficult than anticipated, turmoil in the country forced talented people into exile, financial problems made it difficult to pay adequate salaries to staff with marketable skills and training, and then, most important, came a civil war with devastating effects on the teaching and research functions, and the concentration of the university's energies on the turmoil of the 1980s. This will be detailed in the next chapters.

The following budgetary, faculty, and student data show the dramatic growth of the UCA from 1975 to 1979.

Year	Budget ($, millions)	Faculty	Students
1975	.95	98	2,855
1976	1.10	109	3,229
1977	1.32	125	3,894
1978	1.83	137	4,519
1979	2.13	151	4,925

Despite shortages of trained personnel, the UCA was thinking about possible programs for the future. Some had to be postponed indefinitely, like clinical psychology and economics, but the M.A. in theology, the *profesorado* (associate's degree equivalent) for high school teachers of philosophy, and a program in religious and moral sciences became realities. In the next decade, starting an M.A. in sociology was even proposed as a solution for enrollment problems at the licentiate level.

In order to guarantee that the UCA vision would be implemented at each level, much decision making occurred in the almost weekly board meetings. They reviewed all matters, from major policy decisions to individual salaries.[8] Even resignations of secretaries had to be approved by the board if these persons had been on the permanent staff. All board members were internal to the university—the rector, the academic vice rector, and several professors. They were reluctant to delegate authority to other administrators.

In October 1978, for example, the board voted four to one to retain authority over which candidates proposed by the departments would be sent to studies with UCA or other scholarships, even though there was a separate review committee that included two vice rectors, the personnel director, the head of the psychology department, and the head of the candidate's department. Román Mayorga, the rector, strongly opposed this decision because he termed it an example of "a pattern of excessive concentration of power in the board of directors."[9] The argument in favor of board control was that ultimate responsibility for contracting these people when they returned to the UCA from studies was the board's; therefore, they felt they should have final say in selecting the candidates for studies. They responded to Mayorga's objections by pointing out that the board had made some poor decisions on contracts in the past because of uncritical acceptance of recommendations from below.

In an April 2, 1979, board meeting, there was further discussion of the IDB scholarship candidates: How to integrate forty persons trained outside El Salvador back into the faculty. Some members questioned the costbenefit analysis of studies: "to spend $23,000 in the formation of one person, is this the best investment for the UCA?"[10] They also expressed special concern because the funds for these studies were borrowed, and had to be paid back eventually. They gave some consideration to training people in El Salvador, and "reserving studies abroad for the more reliable." The minutes observe: "It is necessary to keep in mind the 'opportunity costs' of not having a team of teachers formed for tomorrow, to accomplish the task that the UCA hopes to realize."

It was a good discussion that touched on issues even more relevant in the 1990s: problems of inbreeding of ideas when most faculty are trained in El Salvador, and questions of what degrees are necessary for faculty qualified to teach and research in future programs of the UCA. Some administrators speculated that if they sent faculty for studies abroad, they would become more marketable upon return, and then leave the UCA after completing the required years of service. And indeed, experience shows that some did just that.

The UCA continues to be run, in the 1990s, in a highly centralized way, with all authority in the five-man board of directors. The strengths and weaknesses of this approach will be reviewed in the last chapter.

OTHER KEY UCA PLAYERS

Opponents usually aimed public attacks at the Jesuits, especially those later martyred, and against Luis de Sebastián and Jon Sobrino, but these priests were not the only significant players at the UCA. Lay colleagues, other Jesuits, and a diocesan priest, Jesús Delgado, also figured prominently.

The community spirit described at the end of the last chapter extended into the Mayorga rectorate. Jesuits and lay personnel continued to gather informally and enjoy mutual friendships.[11] At these gatherings, they shared reflections on the national crises and designed ways the UCA could respond, and they shared informal celebrations of the eucharist. Francisco Javier Ibisate, Jon Sobrino, and the martyred Amando López inspired special affection in the group.

Jesuits other than the martyrs figured prominently in those years at the UCA. They included those mentioned in the founding period, such as Fathers Achaerandio, Gondra, Idoate, Ibisate, and López y López. But behind-the-scenes contributions were also made by Fermín Saínz (psychology), Nicolás Mariscal (political science), Jon Cortina (engineering), Juan Ricardo Salazaar-Simpson (engineering), and Rogelio Pedráz (administration).

To mention names of some lay colleagues runs the risk of leaving out others, but a such list would include Italo López Vallecillo whose skill with publications and his wide contacts in Salvadoran civilian and military society provided many valuable insights into the national reality. Communications were coordinated by the very versatile Eduardo Stein, who wrote dramatic productions such as "El Prisionero," composed music, and served as a key person in the inner circle. Axel Soderberg developed much of the engineering phase of the UCA and has served for many years as financial and administrative vice rector, and, during several Ellacuría exile periods, he served as acting rector. Guillermo Ungo, prominent in the national and international political arenas, coordinated the early research efforts of the UCA and provided political analysis of current questions before the nation.[12]

STUDENTS

There was always some ambiguity as to the role of students at the UCA. The plan for 1976–1981 spoke of them as potential agents of social change, but with the shortage of university resources, most energy was invested in speaking out on the social issues of the time. Ignacio Martín Baró, one-time dean of students and later academic vice rector and UCA martyr, confirms the limited interest in students as compared to the university's role as a platform for social change.[13]

In his book, Román Mayorga gives more emphasis to the potential role for the students in the realization of the UCA's goals.[14] He feels that students should:

1. Be conscious of their privileged position in society; they form part of the 3 percent who receive any postsecondary education in El Salvador.
2. Commit themselves to service.
3. Possess technical excellence in their own disciplines.
4. Use technical excellence in a social context.
5. Be educated in an integral way.

He adds, "If you consider the hypothesis that at least 20 percent of the UCA graduates would have the desired characteristics at a sufficient level, the UCA will prepare annually some 100 to 200 professionals who could form the human foundation for leaders of social transformation."[15]

He also shows that "it would be unrealistic to pretend that one could launch a liberating process of social transformation, and construct in the present century a committed society, without people to lead it. If such leaders are not formed intentionally to serve for the liberation of all, it is highly probable that they will be educated to oppress, structurally and personally, the immense majority."[16] He sees 5,000 as the best number of UCA students.

Mayorga writes in favor of fostering student organizations: "In the current situation of the UCA, one of apathy and lack of participation on the part of considerable student sectors, a tendency derived from the inevitable class-divided composition of the student body (mainly bourgeois with some from the oligarchy, among whom we find paradoxically some socially aware students), we believe it is *necessary to develop* the vitality of student organizations and the capacity of these organizations for social awareness, without exaggerating their potential to achieve these goals."[17]

The dean of students position was established to help integrate social outreach activities inside the school. The social services office was meant to coordinate social outreach activities beyond the campus. Hector Oquelí Colindres, later assassinated in Guatemala, became full-time dean of students on October 29, 1973. Then Ignacio Martín-Baró held the position until he assumed responsibilities for *ECA*, and was replaced by Oquelí again. On November 18, 1975, the board accepted an Oquelí plan for operation of this office. In 1979, the students asked for more involvement in the university, and on April 2, 1979, Knut Walter was appointed dean. The board had high praise for a student affairs report by Walter, but he himself felt he had no power and that the UCA administration saw the post as a buffer between them and the students.[18]

Francisco Ibisate says that in the early years, student organizations played a positive role in the UCA.[19] But with the closing of the University of El Salvador, student activists wanted to play the same role at the UCA. UCA officials, however, opposed such activities in the 1970s and later in the 1980s because they felt that such groups would interfere with academic programs and would draw unnecessary fire from forces opposed to the UCA. Professors complained about loudspeaker announcements by students during class hours "at times with an insulting and abusive tone," but the board decided to play down the problem, hoping that the students would get tired and stop of their own accord, or that other students would protest against the disturbances.[20]

Rodolfo Cardenal also stressed the potential problems of encouraging student organizations of that era because they were not like the groups familiar to United States universities but rather student counterparts to the country's political forces. He reaffirmed the concern that giving space to such organizations could put in jeopardy any serious intellectual activity at the university as had been the case at the University of El Salvador.[21]

In his book, Mayorga addresses briefly the problem of student dropout rates mentioned in the earlier statistics. He feels that testing and recommendations are no substitute for the actual experience of the first two semesters to see who has the qualifications. But he sees a problem: "This has produced enormous numbers of course failures and dropout rates, which account for 50% of those who enroll." He seems to take these statistics as inevitable; he does not discuss the potential of programs like the Jesuit high school's *turno vespertino* (the evening program) that would give students with fewer economic resources a more solid academic base for university studies.[22] He sees the failure rate as due not only to inadequate testing but also to "insufficient academic attention for students at this level." He feels that the educational reform of 1968 would provide a wider pool of students by the mid-1970s. But there is, however, no study of correlations between the socioeconomic levels of the students and the dropout rate.

He points out that "the UCA's admission procedures *are not* a socioeconomic or class-divided selectivity process (in addition to what is inherent in the educational pyramid), but a selectivity based on the potential of aspirants to contribute more to the social transformation of Central America, which would benefit *all* people, and especially those most oppressed by current structures" (170–1). The criteria for this judgment, however, were not fully explained, and there were no longitudinal studies to test the thesis.

DENUNCIATION OF INJUSTICE: THE BOMBS BEGIN

As repression grew, so did the number of UCA protest statements; the crisis of 1975 illustrates this point. After government troops fired on demonstrators and killed several dozen, the University Higher Education Council published an official statement in *ECA*.[23] "In the first place, we condemn as unjust, the inhuman sinfulness against God which has roots in our society: the violence of tremendous inequality in the distribution of land and income and social and political power which favors a small portion of the population, and oppresses and pillages the majority of Salvadorans, and denies them the possibility of a life of dignity."

The statement condemns repression by police and security forces "and its culmination in the very violent repression of a student demonstration on July 30th in which an undetermined number of persons were killed, wounded or jailed." The university community "cannot accept the simplistic, unscientific and definitely false explanations that attribute all protest demonstrations, denunciations and popular struggle to a vast international communist plot. . . . [Instead, it is] a threat against the freedom to analyze, formulate and explain in the most appropriate terms the social reality of El Salvador."

Less than six months after Román Mayorga became UCA rector, the first bomb exploded on the campus where the journal *Estudios Centroamericanos* was published. The university board discussed the matter and approved an editorial written by Ignacio Martín-Baró.[24] "It has already become evident who might be disturbed by this voice and who wants to silence it—those who want to hide truth with myths, those who benefit from the injustice and structural oppression in which our society lives, those who cannot accept that the people will free themselves and will be transformed into the subject of their own history. This change would affect the interests of their exploiters." The editorial goes on to say, "In the face of this anonymous and senseless violence from those who try to support the rule of force and terror, *ECA* reaffirms its vocation with humility but without any vacillation. Neither bombs nor any other type of violence can silence the liberating word of *ECA*, which is committed . . . to the Salvadoran people, and only them."[25]

ECA did not let up. In the next issue, the editorial was entitled, "Neither Elections nor Elected." It questions the validity of elections in which only the official party, PCN, participated. The opposition forces (UNO) had decided not to run because electoral "reforms" had made their participation more difficult, and the harassing of popular organizations and labor unions made organizing impossible. The editorial is a variation on previous and subsequent themes—elections held under oppressive conditions simply legitimize the power of those who run the elections; they are the trappings but not the reality of democratic processes; Campaigns degenerate into mutual exchanges of invective—*de fascista y de comunista*—but they offer no serious analysis of issues. The editorial ends with a call for a government that wants to get at the root of the country's problems and benefit the vast majority instead of the oligarchy.[26]

In August, there were student reports that security forces were coming to the UCA campus and concern that these incursions might be a threat to university autonomy.[27] That same month a second bomb exploded in *ECA*.

LAND REFORM REVISITED

In September 1976, *ECA* published another whole issue on land reform: its ethical, legal, economic, historical and technical aspects. But the November issue was a watershed because it featured the famous editorial of Ignacio Ellacuría after the Molina government caved in to opposition against its modest land reform efforts. The editorial stirred up a hornets' nest and caused the cancellation of government subsidies to the UCA—a loss of 600,000 *colones* ($240,000).[28]

The editorial recalls that the UCA had supported the original land reform measure of President Molina and, therefore, felt obliged to criticize government backsliding under pressure from the wealthy. Ellacuría, the writer, calls the campaign against the measure "technically like a class struggle . . . brought about by one social class, the oligarchic class, which has gathered around itself the other forces of capitalism." Not all the bourgeois joined the attack, but "those who were not in agreement with this class struggle did not publicly manifest their disagreement. Class interest won the day" (638).

The government "could have decided to stop being the guardian of oligarchy interests by attempting real change in land holding. It was only a first step, but it could have been a step in the long process of creating a state for all Salvadorans" (639). But the government backed down.

The editorial reminds Molina of his bold words—"I only promise what I am sure of accomplishing" (540). The editorial goes on: "In the face of pressure from national capital . . . the Government has caved in; it has surrendered. After so much preliminary hoopla . . . the Government has ended up saying: Aye, Aye, Sir [*a sus órdenes, mi capital*] (641). Shortly after the editorial appeared, another bomb exploded at the UCA.

On January 6, 1977, Román Mayorga presented the board a plan for fund raising with embassies and other international entities to offset the effects of the subsidy cut. Pedro Arrupe, superior general of the Jesuits, sent moral and financial support at that time.[29]

In June 1977, three economics teachers left the country "for studies and for security."[30] At about that same time, Ignacio Ellacuría and Luis de Sebastián left the UCA for security reasons. Axel Soderberg became acting vice rector and Jon Sobrino substituted for Ellacuría as philosophy department head.[31] As late as March 31, 1978, the board still felt that "this was not an auspicious time to consider [Ellacuría and de Sebastián's] possible return. . . ."[32] Rubén Zamora, a political scientist and later a political leader and presidential candidate of the center left, asked the opinion of the board as to the prudence of his return from exile. They recommended that he not come back at that time either.[33] But by August, Ellacuría and de Sebastián had returned to El Salvador. A sign of the times, however, was the January 29, 1979, discussion of the board about the problem of early morning joggers coming to use the UCA track, accompanied by their armed guards!

EDUCATIONAL REFORM REVISITED

Undaunted by controversy and death threats swirling around the university, in August 1977, *ECA* reviewed the results of the 1968 educational reform of Minister of Education Walter Benecke.[34] Salvador Samayoa, later minister of education in the 1979 revolutionary government and one of the FMLN leaders, set the stage for the evaluation by examining the government philosophy of education and its strong ties with economic policy.[35]

Samayoa sees the governments of the 1960s and 1970s "appealing desperately to reform of the educational system as a mechanism that would make possible the developmentalistic/modernistic stance on which they had built all their policies . . . a state thinking in terms of 'national security.'"

Samayoa is not evaluating the reform itself; instead he points out the criteria that should be used for evaluation, and the premises on which the reform had been based. He offers nine theses on what to expect, and they all boil down to a chaotic struggle for dominance of both the educational system and the wider political process. Of particular concern, he says, is the "incompatibility of the economic system and the objectives of the educational reform, [for example] . . . the preparation of students for entrance into the job market . . . which will not be able to absorb them." He calls the secondary-school diversification plan a "dream," and he shows that the reform had left the pyramidal structure of the schooling system intact. While he compliments the ANDES teachers' union for its concern to improve teaching, he also criticizes "its more recent succumbing to political immediacy." As a result," he says, "the teacher organizations have contributed little or nothing to the political process and very little to the educational process."

Early in 1978, *ECA* returned to this issue in a very comprehensive editorial that cited much skepticism about anything government-inspired after the disappointments of the agrarian reform process.[36]

As for the Reform of 1968 itself, it was "a significant break with educational patterns which expressed and consolidated a hundred years of stagnation. . . . even though it was not exempt from defects worthy of evaluation." For example, there was not "sufficient analysis of the national educational situation, nor a needs assessment, nor were personnel sufficiently prepared before implementation."

The editorial becomes even more critical when it points out that "the crisis of our educational system is not where the dominant minority groups and their technicians and pseudointellectuals tend to put it. The ongoing failure to find solutions to our problems and social tensions shows that the social structure is nearing the point—or has already arrived at it—that the only possible solution is precisely the transformation of the social structure itself."

Two months later, on March 6, 1978, the UCA board accepted an invitation from the minister of education to send representatives and observers to the Seminar on Educational Reform. Participation in this seminar provided material in August of that same year for a whole issue of *ECA*. A closer review of its articles gives a good illustration of the UCA's careful, multidisciplinary approach to the country's most complicated and important issues.[37]

The editorial states that "education in El Salvador has lost its way. . . . For some time it has not found a way to . . . help the people on whose behalf education supposedly consumes one-fourth of the national budget. The people remain sunk in complete illiteracy or at levels and types of schooling which contribute little or nothing to liberate them from a naive fatalism about their own personal, social and historical destiny. They have not encountered a sense of direction nor paths to make the transition toward . . . a process of liberation" (563).

The editorial laments that "those who hold power not only do not want liberation of the people, they are disposed to stop it with blood and fire. . . . They will prevent a literate people from being prepared, because then the ignominious oppression of which [the powerful] are the beneficiaries would no longer be maintained" (564).

Guillermo Manuel Ungo, director of the Instituto de Investigaciones and Luis Fernando Valero Iglesias, from the faculty, write that "the educational reform has had unbalanced and ambivalent development because its sociopolitical presuppositions and aims were in large measure contradictory of the national reality."[38]

Ungo and Valero praise the development of educational television because it introduced some changes to the traditional system, creating more opportunities for students and involving them more actively in their own education (573). But they see nonschool issues as the primary obstacles to achieving the educational goals of the program: "malnutrition, hunger, unemployment, the need to contribute to family income"—these are "social and economic factors that impeded access to studies in the first place, and to the continuation of studies already begun." In 1957, 80 percent of the children left school after sixth grade; twenty years later, it was still 73 percent (573).

Segundo Montes, S.J., one of the 1989 martyrs, feels that there is too much money for the top of the educational pyramid and irrelevance in much of the education received at the more elementary levels. Montes also says that all this points to basic problems in the socioeconomic system and not just in the educational sector.[39]

Luis Achaerandio, S.J., the former rector, does not deny the problems, especially deficiencies in implementation, but he cites what he considers some positive aspects: taking student psychological levels into account, active and individualized learning, and program flexibility as compared to the previous traditional system. He concludes that "the worst results were due to *external factors* which were relatively independent of the study plans and the psycho-pedagogical methods suggested. The problem of Salvadoran education lies with the *teachers* and the negative *structural socioeconomic conditions* which fossilize the educational process for the students."[40]

Gorka Gárate calls for an educational system in which "critical analysis of the national reality would be a constitutive element in its development."[41] He sees curriculum as "a series of structured educational experiences within a school system which would have as their goal contact of the student with reality" (620).

Joaquín Samayoa explains positive elements that have to be included in any serious educational reform, especially teacher training.[42] He points out problems with the 1968 educational reform, such as teachers' seeing educational television as a threat and the government's insistence on quantity over quality, such as its campaign for "a school a day." Samayoa, author of the document "Exigencias de la planificación curricular," which the UCA presented at the National Seminar, points to difficulties in retraining current teachers: They are more set in their ways, and they have to hold many jobs to make ends meet—they will resist change.

Samayoa underlines the value of an interdisciplinary approach: It avoids repetition and aids the integration of knowledge for the student (634). He sees the need for teachers to experiment under supervision. He spells out steps that have to be included in any program: "observation, experimentation, communication, diagnosis, instructional design, evaluation, and analysis of reality."

This treatment of educational reform is an important example of UCA criticism of the status quo, combined with practical suggestions for improvement.[43] Such criteria were to guide similar UCA efforts on educational reform in the mid-1990s.

SUPPORT AND STORM CLOUDS FROM ROME

Pedro Arrupe wrote to the provincial on February 5, 1977, that he had heard about the attacks against the UCA and had concluded that "the cause of all this has been the valiant stand taken by the university, especially by the journal *ECA*, in the problem of land reform. I want to express my happiness and my congratulations to all of you for defending the cause of the poor and for suffering persecution for this reason."[44]

While supportive of the UCA's stand against injustice, some people at the Jesuit Roman curia were still critical of the Central American province's basic orientation. These criticisms, although directed more toward internal questions of religious life, nevertheless imply criticism of the UCA, whose principal staff members were actively involved in determining province policy.

On June 15, 1976, the new provincial, César Jerez, sent the superior general the working document of the Commission on Ministries. On December 1, 1976, Pedro Arrupe sent his strongly critical comments. He admitted that the work showed "all the time, intelligence and energy that has gone into describing the reality of the province and to orient it according to the norms of the thirty-second General Congregation. . . . but some of the theses presented in the document seem unacceptable, and others need nuancing and correction." He felt, however, that there was "rich and valuable material for the discernment process which under your direction should continue in the province."

Enclosed was the official response—eleven pages. It criticizes what it terms a fixation with the "new" and dismissal of the "old," and "exaggerated dualisms." Not enough importance is given to religious obedience, the eucharist, and spirituality. In the eleven pages, the reviewer does not cite any analyses of which he approves; texts are cited only to criticize them. The words of praise about the "rich and valuable material" seem more like an effort to keep the Central American Jesuits from total discouragement, rather than genuine praise.[45] Later in the month, Jerez expressed the disappointment of the province with the curia's analysis of the ministries document: "It was like a pitcher of cold water."[46]

A Surprising Ally: Archbishop Oscar Romero

Just as the forces of the right turned up the heat on the Jesuits, an important event occurred that was to have a great impact on the church of El Salvador and on the relationship between the San Salvador archdiocese and the Jesuits: the appointment of a new archbishop.

Church progressives in El Salvador apprehensively greeted the 1977 retirement of Archbishop Luis Chávez y Gonzalez because they feared the appointment of someone less sympathetic. Their hopes rested on Chávez's auxiliary bishop, Arturo Rivera Damas, but the traditional sectors favored Oscar Arnulfo Romero, who had attacked the Jesuit high school as "communist" just a few years earlier, and strongly criticized the christology of UCA theologian Jon Sobrino just months earlier in the cathedral during the principal feast day of the country, August 6, the Transfiguration.[47]

When Rome announced the Romero appointment, some Jesuits suggested to the provincial that he refuse to attend the new archbishop's installation. But Jerez went anyhow. He and Romero became close colleagues in the three years of Romero's archbishopric. But Jerez was not so positive at first about Romero's prospects. In his letter to Arrupe reporting the appointment, he reflected the sentiments of many church people in El Salvador. Romero is "weak in health and psychological makeup; I consider his categories to be behind the times. He has a strong spirituality but with an emphasis on piety. He is undoubtedly a good man. It seems to me, however, that his appointment does not represent a help for the Jesuits in the difficult times of persecution we are experiencing. He is very influenced by Opus Dei [a conservative religious group]. . . . For the young clergy who are living in the midst of the problems of the country's forgotten majority I fear that Archbishop Romero will not be the pastor they need." He saw Romero as an opponent of modern theology and of the Jesuit's Thirty-second General Congregation decree on faith and justice.[48]

History proved this judgment to be shortsighted, as César Jerez himself readily admitted later on.

On March 14, 1977, Rutilio Grande, S.J., pastor at Aguilares and a longtime friend of Romero's, was shot to death on his way to say mass. His death deeply affected the archbishop, deepened his own conversion to the needs of the poor, and contributed to bringing Romero and the Jesuits closer together.[49]

Stepped-up Persecution

Just two months after Rutilio Grande's death, Jerez wrote to Arrupe that "from a reliable source in the president's house . . . the archdiocesan chancery office has been advised that a team of six lawyers is working on a plan to expropriate the Jesuit high school, Externado de San José, and to deport the UCA Jesuits." Archbishop Romero and César Jerez were working together on this problem but experiencing difficulties from the papal nuncio, Archbishop Gerada, who had not even attended the funeral of the recently murdered Father Alfonso Navarro. There were reports that the terrorist group Union Guerrera Blanca was going to kidnap César Jerez and hold him in ransom for the foreign minister who was later killed by kidnappers.[50]

Meanwhile, persecution against the Jesuits grew more ominous. At a meeting attended by the incoming president, General Romero, members of his staff, the new archbishop, Oscar Romero, and Fathers Jerez and Estrada, President Molina maintained that he had nothing personal against the Jesuits.[51] Father Estrada insisted that they discuss specific cases and engage in dialogue, rather than have the president presenting the Society of Jesus with *faits accompli* such as the deportation of the priests from Aguilares after Rutilio Grande's death. Estrada also asked about rumors of closing the UCA, but Molina responded that he felt the UCA was beneficial for the country.

Molina asserted that he could not guarantee the safety of Ignacio Ellacuría and Luis de Sebastián, and that it would be better if they stayed out of the country. He mentioned he was hurt by the November 1976 ECA editorial "A sus ordenes mi capital," especially since no one had come to talk to him about it in private.

Less than three weeks later, Jerez sent Arrupe the first of six installments of the Jesuits' response to attacks against them.[52] Fearing distortion of their statements, the Jesuits took out advertising space in the local papers to publish "Los Jesuitas ante el Pueblo Salvadoreño" (The Jesuits before the Salvadoran People). Jerez also sent a copy of the Union Guerrera Blanca (UGB) announcement that the Jesuits should leave the country by July 20, 1977. This terrorist group claimed that "their struggle is not against the church but against the Jesuit guerrilla movement." They threatened that if the Jesuits did not leave, the UGB "would proceed with the immediate and systematic execution of all Jesuits who stay in the country, until we have finished them all off." They warned family members, students, and personnel, that they "consider Jesuit property and the places they visit to be military targets."

César Jerez warned Pedro Arrupe that the papal nuncio, Archbishop Emanuele Gerada, would probably be negative about Archbishop Romero and Bishop Rivera, who had been very supportive of the Society of Jesus in those times of conflict.[53] Two months later, Jerez described a meeting with President Romero, who had complained about Pedro Arrupe's declarations in support of the Jesuits.[54] Jerez invited Arrupe to come to El Salvador to see the situation for himself, but Arrupe felt it would not be prudent to come then.

At this time, Jerez described the UCA of El Salvador to Arrupe as "the university which has been the most successful in realizing Jesuit aims; it has been a critical conscience for the country, and it has had great impact in the face of what is going on in the country."[55] Arrupe responded two months later, in February 1978, that "it is evident what great influence a university apostolate can have when it is capable of offering well-founded thought in the service of the truth, and when it responds to the exigencies of real life."[56] In October, Jerez reiterated to Arrupe his high opinion of the university: the UCA of El Salvador is "a work of great influence in the country . . . in many ways a pioneering university. I mention just a few points: profound study of the country's problems, preparing researchers who are full-time and of high quality, the system for tuition adjusted to student ability to pay, a salary scale for the workers, etc."[57]

Pressure on the Jesuits continued, however, as indicated in a March 4, 1978, Jerez letter to Arrupe: "The President of the Republic [Romero,] alleging pressure from big business and the military, did not permit Ellacuría and de Sebastián to come into El Salvador even for the few days of the provincial congregation of the order. . . . and it was necessary to send one of the seminarians, Rodolfo Cardenal, out of the country."[58] (Cardenal was later a survivor of the UCA assassination, and became vice rector for social outreach and editor of *ECA*.) On July 11, 1978, Jerez reported that the Jesuit residence UCA II had been occupied and searched by Salvadoran security forces. The Central American Jesuits maintained close contact with Rome during these days. For example, Jerez sent Arrupe a background paper on the Salvadoran situation written by the UCA Jesuits at the request of Archbishop Romero.

Another sign of support in difficult times came from Georgetown University president Timothy S. Healy, S.J., who traveled to El Salvador and conferred an honorary doctorate on Archbishop Romero in the San Salvador cathedral despite pressure from the Vatican to stop it.

At this same time, the Latin American church was trying, although less dramatically, to continue in the steps traced at Medellín in 1968. A decade later, they met at Puebla, Mexico. Jon Sobrino reports on this meeting that because of the slant of preparatory texts, liberation theologians feared bishops would reverse the progressive direction set at Medellín.[59] The Pope had invited Pedro Arrupe, superior general of the Jesuits, to attend the conference, despite the objections of conservative leaders like then Archbishop and later Cardinal Alfonso López Trujillo, a leading opponent of liberation theology. At a Puebla press conference, Arrupe vigorously defended the Central American Jesuits against attacks by Bishop Aparicio of El Salvador.

The organizers of Puebla had invited "safe" theologians to join the bishops at the meetings, but a group of theologians and scholars, including Jon Sobrino, gathered outside the official meetings, producing position papers and serving as resources for the bishops who came out to consult them. Sobrino writes that "there was a sensation of disgust and even fear of ridicule for the poor quality of the texts produced by the bishops and the 'approved' theologians. Referring clearly to the theologians outside, one bishop said 'we are in front of a sick person whom we all wish to cure. But the doctor is outside.'" Still, his final note is more optimistic: "the letter and the spirit of Medellín are present in the final document. What is not present is the qualitative leap that Medellín signified" (133).

Meanwhile, back in El Salvador, on December 7, 1978, Ignacio Ellacuría and Luis de Sebastián, recently returned from exile, and Axel Soderberg went to see President Romero and the minister of education about three problems: (1) the need for a climate of dialogue in the country; (2) immigration problems of UCA personnel, one more form of harassment; and (3) a subsidy for the UCA, which had been cut off since the 1976 Ellacuría editorial on land reform. Romero agreed with the need for dialogue and asked for a confidential memo on the specific immigration cases in question. As for the subsidy, he answered ambiguously that the government would fulfill the commitments it had made.[60]

ECA continued to denounce the attacks against the church, thereby making itself a target of the opposition. Early in 1979, an editorial condemns the security forces attack against a retreat house, El Despertar, where a priest and several youths were slain and their dead bodies propped up to simulate attack positions. Police had kept reporters from the scene until all the props were ready, but their efforts were so amateurish that the farce was publicly exposed. The editorial joins with the statement of the Archdiocese of San Salvador and its priests—"basta ya" (we've had enough)—and it criticized the disorientation of the armed forces, which were told that priests and others who spoke out against oppression were communists.

"It should not be surprising that some security forces, not well-trained intellectually or morally, and subjected to systematic indoctrination of hatred against certain priests and people through the mass media, and through the messages of those who represent authority, should commit evils and abuses so cruel, so disgraceful, and so embarrassing for the government as the massacre at San Antonio Abad."[61]

The editorial implicitly criticizes some of the bishops. "Even though the bishops do not speak or act in agreement, that is not grounds for the conclusion that there are two churches: one that is faithful to the oligarchy and the government and consequently enjoys their favor, and another which denounces abuses and exposes the evils of structures that support abuses, and can therefore be persecuted in word and action. . . . The root of the problem is that the church demands changes in the socioeconomic structures of our countries as an indispensable stage in the establishment of the Kingdom of God."

Amidst all this controversy, Ignacio Ellacuría wrote to Rubén Zamora that "the general situation of the university has normalized . . . within the national context of crisis which seems more critical every day, a situation which has repercussions for the UCA. Let me tell you about the latest little problem: This year, [the government] has suddenly taken from us the subsidy of 500,000 *colones* which they had given us each year to pay part of the first IDB loan. Apparently they are going to distribute this amount among the 'new' universities, leaving us with practically nothing. . . . But everything is not just problems. For example, we have just finished a symposium on appropriate technology for underdeveloped countries, which had considerable international success."[62]

But the storm clouds thickened. On May 22, 1979, President Romero sent a telegram to the UCA inviting the university to participate in the National Forum on the problems of the country. Government security forces had recently killed fourteen persons outside the Venezuelan embassy. Román Mayorga met with Archbishop Romero and then sent the following telegram to the president's private secretary: "I am greatly disturbed by recent events. I ask that you give my regrets to the president for not attending the meeting called for tomorrow. We believe that the ambience has to improve, conditions must be clarified and procedures organized with more time, so as to increase the possibilities of success of the good idea for national dialogue which might lead to democratization."

The UCA board felt that "there should not be hurried participation in a meeting which was put together at the last minute because it could be interpreted as political support for the government under very controversial circumstances, and serve as propaganda for a formalistic type of national conciliation."[63] The board indicated that it wanted "(a) to work on serious and university-type analysis of national problems and solutions, as falls within the competence of a university; and (b) inside the university it was necessary to have wider consultation (with the Consejo Superior Universitario and some heads of departments) concerning the opportunities and the conditions for our participation in these national meetings, so that we might be able to provide a university contribution."

At this same meeting the board expressed concern about student organizations: "'student power' as it is understood at this time is prejudicial for the country"—as had been seen in the University of El Salvador and now in the UCA. "When students politicize themselves in partisan and radical fashion, they consider themselves owners of part of the university (indiscriminate use of loud speakers, occupying buildings, taking over classrooms and other spaces)." The board's fear was that "especially under present circumstances (an official state of siege) student activities could generate a false image of the UCA outside the campus, giving the impression that we university authorities are encouraging and protecting this type of partisan, radical, and noisy criticism which is far removed from the constructive criticism by the university."

That day three board members met privately at the president of El Salvador's office. Government representatives expressed their surprise at the UCA's reluctance to participate in the National Forum, but the UCA representatives said that the Mayorga telegram had explained their reasons. They expressed reluctance to participate because their fingers had been burned before when they supported the mild land reform of President Molina, who then backed down in the face of criticism from the right. The UCA refused to be used.

At the May 29, 1978, meeting, some board members expressed concern that the UCA's refusal to participate might be interpreted as "a boycott and opposition to the National Forum, which would give credence to the thought that the UCA is more on the side of those who prefer alternatives other than dialogue." The decision to call the Consejo Superior Universitario to make the final determination was approved three votes to two.

The Consejo gave approval to participation and asked Román Mayorga, the rector, to appoint a group to determine what might be needed for the UCA to respond as a university, and to be careful not to be caught up in temporary "solutions" that would distract from the deeply rooted problems of the country.

Groups opposed to the government set up the Foro Popular because they saw the National Forum as too dominated by government and oligarchy points of view. The UCA avoided identification with either group but sent observers to their meetings. To assist in the development of solutions for the country, UCA Jesuits and lay colleagues, forty in total, developed *Una Salida Democrática a la Crisis Salvadoreña* (a democratic approach to the Salvadoran crisis), known as "the yellow book" for the color of its mimeographed edition. Although never published, according to Román Mayorga, the book

contained a kind of government platform to rescue the country from the tremendous crisis in which it found itself." The book circulated, however, in a surreptitious way and some military officers who later overthrew the government, after hearing about or reading the document concluded that the UCA was the only institution in the country with sufficient vision and teams of competent people to govern under these circumstances. History showed, naturally, that they were wrong, for the country was already so polarized that our suggestions were not viable. But the incident shows what the UCA was capable of doing in 1979, in just a few weeks of work, and it also says something about the kind of people on whom the university could count."[64]

On May 30, 1979, Jerez reported to Arrupe the massacre of people on the steps of the cathedral, including two UCA students. The Jesuits celebrated a special memorial mass for them in a large classroom-auditorium. Jerez added that "this time Ignacio Ellacuría has been threatened with death."[65] Nevertheless, such threats did not stop the UCA later from protesting events such as the disappearance of one its students.[66]

Arrupe praised the university statement on the massacre as "one of high quality: serious and balanced. I believe that it will give clear orientation, and I hope it will do much good. I congratulate the authors."[67]

PRELUDE TO OCTOBER 15, 1979

Late in 1978, with attacks mounting against the UCA, the university found itself pulled in three directions. Some young Jesuits, most of whom subsequently left the order, and a number of lay colleagues and politically active student organizations wanted the university to take a clearer stand in favor of the revolutionary process. Some called them *bloquistas* because of their sympathy with popular groups such as the Bloque Popular Revolucionario (BPR) and what became the Farabundo Martí para la Liberación Nacional coalition (FMLN).

A second group included the UCA II Jesuit community and key laypeople such as Román Mayorga; they favored social change but stressed the importance of keeping the UCA independent of any particular group. Ellacuría and de Sebastián from this group were in exile during much of 1978.

The UCA I group argued for caution and a lower profile. They feared the consequences of even the UCA II approach, and were strongly opposed to the *bloquistas*.

With the nation more polarized and the UCA's role more important, some lay colleagues expressed concern that two important board members were not in the country. They felt that Ellacuría and de Sebastián should return and take their chances; others felt it was too risky. Although there seems not to have been any organized movement to replace these two Jesuits on the board with laypeople, it was a topic of conversation because of their extended absence.

The UCA seminal documents needed reexamination and updating, and this stimulated a process to produce a new document that would reaffirm the university's commitment to its basic goals. Discussions began in mid-1978 and Jon Sobrino was asked to bring the various suggestions together into a working document. This collegial process mirrored those that had preceded the development of important documents in the past—the manual of organization, the salary scale, the differentiated tuition plan, and the pronouncements of the University Higher Education Council on important issues before the country.

The final document, entitled "Las Funciones Fundamentales de la Universidad y su Operativización," gained board approval in May 1979. It summarized the role of the UCA as follows: "The UCA seeks to be a university, an institutional response to the historical reality of the country, considered from an ethical perspective as an unjust and irrational reality which should be transformed. It functions, therefore, with a finality: to contribute to the social change of the country. It does this in a university fashion and with Christian inspiration" (47).[68] Then the text elaborates on the meaning of each element in the summary, and explains in detail the university's three main functions: social outreach in the wider sense, research, and teaching.

Describing this important document in detail would repeat much of what has been said in chapter 3 and elsewhere. More important than the document itself was the process that led up to it, in which the basic principles enunciated earlier were reaffirmed by the university community of Jesuits and lay colleagues at a time of crisis in the country, and when various forces threatened to pull the university in different directions. The UCA tried to step back from the national polarization, and yet take a stand for social change.

In this spirit, the document warns that the

UCA should always be attentive to the real direction of the change process and the social forces that move it in the correct direction. It should, therefore, concretize its ideal aspirations in the light of real possibilities for the country at each historical moment. Without accepting those steps that would in the long term make impossible the ideal society project, it should give support to others, who while not the best, could help to advance the process. This implies a sane political realism that maintains the tension between what should be and what can be achieved at any given moment. This does not mean surrender or betrayal. Precisely because it is not in the world of political power, the university never has to identify itself with this power. It can maintain its ability to critique situations, which does not exclude certain cooperation to benefit the majority. (58–9)

The document calls for the UCA to support an "opening to democracy that allows place on the political stage to all social forces who do not have violence or terrorism for their banner, and who struggle to make the country a state of rights, one that respects the constitution and the fundamental rights of life and persons. It is of little use to promote willingly those concrete steps for which there are no objective or subjective conditions. Without neglecting the ideal nor shying away from necessary social criticism . . . the UCA should not fail to do anything that is good and necessary just because it is dreaming of the best" (59). The UCA's hope was that the poor majority "would recognize in the university's social outreach strong support to satisfy its most just needs"(59). These words seem to address directly the demands of those who wanted a more specific UCA commitment to their particular political platform.

While this process of document elaboration was already in progress, both Ellacuría and de Sebastián returned to the country and joined the discussion.

In a sense the UCA had a new charter—a fresh statement of the goals elaborated almost a decade earlier in both the retreat-reflection of the Central American Jesuit province and the many meetings of Jesuit and lay colleagues to formulate the fundamental vision and basic documents of a university for social change. The benefits of the second IDB loan were being felt—better facilities, better prepared faculty and staff: the means needed to put the UCA at the service of the country's fundamental, structural needs. But political polarization surged forward and was soon to put much of this process in abeyance.

Several political figures came to Román Mayorga early in 1979 and suggested he be open to a call to participate actively in the country's political process.[69] In late summer a high-level military official came to him and revealed specific plans for a coup to overthrow the government. Would he be interested in joining them? Mayorga was skeptical of the chances of success, but he posed three conditions for possible involvement: (1) a real cleaning out of corrupt military figures; (2) a written statement of goals; and (3) choosing at least one member of the government from the Foro Popular, which had been developing possible solutions to the profound political problems of the country. With such assurances, Mayorga joined planning meetings in the early fall.

The *ECA* editorial of September 1979 spoke in ominous tones of civil war.[70] "Furthermore, it should be presumed that any worsening or even maintenance of current levels of repression will lead to a general insurrection in which both parties in the conflict will be counting on help from abroad. This will convert this little piece of over-populated land into a lake of blood with disastrous political results" (737). How true a prediction these words turned out to be.

On the morning of October 15, 1979, the military-civilian *golpistas* took over the Government of El Salvador. The minutes of the UCA board meeting for that day state that Román Mayorga, the rector, was unable to attend the meeting "for reasons of great importance" (*por razones de fuerza mayor*): He was one of the five members of the new government. That same day a letter arrived from teachers and staff asking for a raise of 45 percent to help meet the effects of inflation. Other teachers started leaving the university to take positions in the new government—a very serious drain on UCA resources.

ECA's first reaction to the *golpe* was positive.[71] The editorial praises the beginnings of the new government—the principles in the proclamation (one of Mayorga's conditions for joining), the choice of government officials (many from the UCA), and the promise to suppress ORDEN (the paramilitary group responsible for much repression) and to respond to the urgent needs of the people.

The Jesuit provincial reported to Pedro Arrupe that "knowing about the events that were to occur, I tried to maintain complete independence, but I offered assistance as an advisor to Archbishop Romero." He said that Ellacuría, Estrada, and de Sebastián also knew about it beforehand. "The UCA had become a refuge for opposition politicians and rather honest people, and the rector and the director of research took roles in the governing junta; this explains why so many UCA people participated in the new government. . . . The people refer to it as the 'coup of the UCA' or the 'Jesuit coup.'"[72]

He went on to warn that "if this new attempt fails we will not escape the hatred and the criticism of the extreme Right and the extreme Left, and we will be in danger of being like a *sandwich*. We will try to maintain our independence. But being realistic we cannot escape the image of being participants. . . . At one point the new government thought about naming Father Estrada as minister of education, but that was soon forgotten." Other rumors suggested Luis de Sebastián to head the central bank.

Jerez continued: "The Church and the Society of Jesus should maintain a critical distance and not get 'married' to anyone." It would be easier said than done.

THE MAYORGA YEARS IN PERSPECTIVE

As we have seen, Román Mayorga made a significant contribution to the UCA, not only as its rector for four years, but even more so for his role in planning for the future and for encouraging a sense of community.

He saw the need for additional resources and a wider vision, and through his work on the loan from the Inter-American Development Bank those resources became available. He eased communication among various factions and helped the university weather the storms of opposition generated by its new thrust as an agent for social change. He strengthened the UCA by encouraging talented candidates to pursue graduate studies so that the teaching, research, and social outreach of the university might be realized effectively.

He furthered the sense of community between Jesuit and lay colleagues begun in the Achaerandio years, and encouraged wide participation in the processes that developed consensus on many programs for realization of the university's goals for social change.

With its 1979 statement of purpose, enhanced resources from the IDB loan and the planning process that led up to it, and the vibrant, collegial spirit of the university community, the UCA was poised to make significant contributions to structural changes in El Salvador. But political events put much of the process on hold.

Román Mayorga resigned from the governing junta and left for exile in early 1980, considered by some as a traitor to his own social class, but deeply admired by his Jesuit and lay colleagues for his long-lasting contribution to the university and to El Salvador.

The stage was set now for the leader of the liberationists, Ignacio Ellacuría, to become rector, a time when much would be built on the solid foundation achieved thus far, but also when opposition would become even more furious, even to the point of his assassination ten years later.

NOTES

1. ASJCA–G76/16, Vincent O'Keefe to Miguel Francisco Estrada, April 13, 1976.

2. Mayorga, 93–110.

3. Universidad Centroamericana (UCA), *Plan Quinquenal*, 1977–81 (San Salvador: UCA Editores, 1976). Hereafter page numbers for Vol. I will be cited in the text.

4. AUCA, December 10, 1976.

5. Interview with Mayorga, September, 1992.

6. See AUCA, September 19, 1975, for a lengthy discussion of the goals of the university and ways to incorporate more people into "ownership" of the UCA project. Another occasion for similar discussion was AUCA, August 14, 1978, in which the board of directors minutes expressed the desire to "achieve a stronger identification of all colleagues with the university, and to look for the best means to create "una mística" which would facilitate active participation of all personnel in the university task." In the 1980s, the UCA began to offer retreat-days off campus to look at basic issues and to renew the "*mística*." See, for example, AUCA, June 9, 1986.

7. See, for example, AUCA, October 27, 1977, when Father Miguel Francisco Estrada was asked to review the situation of unskilled laborers.

8. For example, AUCA, March 16, 1979.

9. AUCA, October 30, 1978.

10. AUCA, April 2, 1979.

11. Interview with Román Mayorga, March 21, 1994.

12. There is always a risk in mentioning names, but other lay staff and faculty members who made a considerable contribution were Héctor Oqueli Colindres, who directed and helped develop the dean of students office, and Fernando Valero Iglesias, who coordinated the extensive community service activities of the students.

Architects Juan José Rodriguez and Alberto Harth at different stages contributed to the creative architectural designs of the university, and José Jorge Simán gave valuable service in the planning office established to administer the IDB loan.

Others included Héctor Dada and Atilio Vieytez (economics), Edgar Jiménez and Fernando Flores Pinel (political science); Knut Walter (history); Freddy Villalta, Ricardo Navarro, Alberto Chiquillo, Francisco Lara Harrison, and Carlos Canessa (engineering), Giuseppe De Pilla, Gloria Bodnar, and Maricarmen Morán (psychology), Ricardo Stein (communications), Armando Oliva (philosophy), Leonel Menéndez, Rafael Rodríguez, Ana María Nafría, Carmen Alvarez, and Francisco Escobar (literature), Santiago Montes (linguistics and art), René Zelaya, Gildaberto Bonilla, Juan José Bonilla, Roberto Muyshondt and Eduardo Escapini (mathematics), Fernando Rodríguez Villalobos (administration), Mélida de Andino (librarian), Roberto Dada and Alejandro Silva (development office), David Soriano (computer center), Crista Benecke, Mario Cerna, and Wilfredo Osorio (central administration), and Rosario de Guevara and Reina Iris de López (administrative assistants).

13. "Developing a Critical Consciousness through the University Curriculum," in Hassett and Lacey, 220–42.

14. Mayorga, 116–20.

15. Mayorga, 123.

16. Mayorga, 124.

17. Mayorga, 165.

18. Interview with Knut Walter, November 1992. See also his report to the board of directors, AUCA, March 26, 1979.

19. Interview with Francisco Javier Ibisate, November 1992.

20. AUCA, meeting # 169 (late April or early May 1976; no date).

21. Correspondence with the author, July 15, 1993.

22. Mayorga, 170–1.

23. ECA 30 (October–November 1975), 713–5.

24. AUCA, January 26, 1976.

25. ECA 31 (1976), 4–5.

26. ECA 31 (March 1976), 81–6.

27. AUCA, August 19, 1976.

28. AUCA, December 20, 1976. For a summary of the issues on this land reform legislation see Ignacio Ellacuría, "The Historicization of the Concept of Poverty," in Hassett and Lacey, 105–37.

29. AUCA, February 18, 1977.

30. AUCA, June 27, 1977.

31. AUCA, August 23, 1977, and October 24, 1977.

32. AUCA, March 31, 1978.

33. AUCA, June 5, 1978.

34. For a detailed study of the reform see Lillian Moncada-Davidson, *Education and Social Change: The Case of El Salvador*, unpublished dissertation, Teachers College, Columbia University, 1990.

35. Salvador Samayoa, "Evaluación de la Reforma Educatíva Salvadoreña: Un Problema De Criterios," ECA 32 (August 1977), 589–604.

36. ECA 33 (January-February 1978), 3–5.

37. ECA 33 (August 1978), 563.

38. "Fundamentos sociopolíticos y fines de la Reforma Educatíva," *ECA* 33 (1978), 569–78.

39. "El financiamiento de la educación en El Salvador," *ECA* 33 (1978), 596–608.

40. "Valores sicopedagógicos de la Reforma Educatíva de El Salvador: Algo que debe mantenerse," *ECA* 33 (1978), 616.

41. "El Maestro según la Reforma Educatíva de 1968 (un analizador crítico de la realidad)," *ECA* 33 (1978), 619–29.

42. "Directrices para el diseño de programas de formación y actualización del magisterio nacional," *ECA* 33 (1978), 630–36.

43. This tradition continues with the cooperative study of the Salvadoran educational system by the UCA, the Harvard Institute for International Development, and the Fundación Empresarial para el Desarrollo Educativo which was cited in chapter 2.

44. ASJCA–G77/6, Pedro Arrupe to César Jerez.

45. ASJCA–G76/40, Pedro Arrupe to César Jerez, December 1, 1976.

46. ASJCA–P76/55, Jerez to Arrupe, December 29, 1976.

47. James E. Brockman, *Romero, A Life*, rev. ed. (New York: Orbis, 1989), 19, 48.

48. ASJCA–P77/7, Jerez to Arrupe, February 17, 1977.

49. See Rodolfo Cardenal, *Historia de una Esperanza: Vida de Rutilio Grande* (San Salvador: UCA Editores, 1986). Cardenal gives great importance to the impact Rutilio Grande's death had on Archbishop Romero's change of heart.

50. ASJCA–P77/20a, May 13, 1977.

51. ASJCA–P77/22, Jerez to Arrupe, May 23, 1977.

52. ASJCA–P77/30, June 15, 1977.

53. ASJCA–P77/34, July 6, 1977.

54. ASJCA–P77/43, September 2, 1977.

55. ASJCA–P77/66, December 30, 1977.

56. ASJCA–G78/17, February 28, 1978.

57. ASJCA–P78/64, October 10, 1978.

58. ASJCA–P78/11, March 3, 1978.

59. Jon Sobrino, "Los Documentos de Puebla, Serena Afirmación de Medellín," *ECA* 34 (March 1979), 125–38. For an analysis of the Puebla meeting see John Eagleson and Philip Scharper, eds., *Puebla and Beyond* (New York: Orbis, 1979).

60. AUCA, December 18, 1978.

61. *ECA* 34 (January–February 1979), 3–7.

62. Correspondence file of the Rector of the University of Central America (hereafter cited as RUCA). Ignacio Ellacuría, to Rubén Zamora, March 5, 1979.

63. AUCA, May 28, 1979.

64. Communication with the author, January 21, 1994.

65. ASJCA–P79/17.

66. RUCA, Román Mayorga to Coronel Antonio López, Director General of the National Police, May 9, 1979.

67. ASJCA–G79/13, Arrupe to Jerez, June 23, 1979.

68. In *Planteamiento Universitario, 1989*, 39–121. Page references in the text.

69. Interview with Román Mayorga, March 21, 1994.

70. "Al Borde de la Guerra Civil," *ECA* 34 (September 1979), 734–4.

71. "La Insurrección Militar del Quince de Octubre," *ECA* 34 (1979), 741–4.

72. ASJCA–P79/42, October 23, 1979.

8 THE ELLACURÍA ERA BEGINS: 1979–1981

INTRODUCTION

As we have seen, Román Mayorga left the UCA rectorship and Guillermo Ungo the research institute on October 15, 1979, to join the revolutionary government. They took with them over a dozen UCA faculty to staff government ministries and agencies. Those who stayed behind picked up some of the slack—both the temporary heads of departments, the computer center, the research institute, and also the new rector, Ignacio Ellacuría, the forty-nine-year-old Basque who had received Salvadoran citizenship, a prerequisite for the position. He had been the acknowledged leader of the UCA Jesuit liberationist wing in the early days of ideological conflict. Ellacuría thus began his rectorship, which would end ten years later in the garden at the back of the Jesuit residence.

This chapter will look mainly at the first two years of the Ellacuría decade, beginning with some reflections on Ellacuría himself, because he was so crucial for the UCA in this long period in which the model was consolidated, refined, and challenged, and during which he spent seventeen of the thirty-six months of his first term in exile.

That first year, 1980, saw the end of the revolutionary government, the exile of its leaders, and the return of some former government officials to the university. Just five months after Ellacuría began his new role, a gunman's bullet brought down Archbishop Romero as he said mass at Providencia Chapel. The country also shook with the murder of half a dozen other priests, the changing of several government juntas, and thousands of death squad victims, including the leadership of the civilian opposition forces, the Frente Democrático Revolucionario (FDR), as they met at the Jesuit high school. Then, a week later, national guardsmen murdered four American churchwomen, Maryknoll Sisters Ita Ford and Maura Clark, Ursuline Sister Dorothy Kazel, and lay missionary Jean Donovan. Ellacuría escaped to the Spanish embassy the day before the FDR massacre, and left El Salvador for exile the next morning, as the nation descended into more than a decade of civil war.

Despite the turmoil, the UCA grew to almost 7,000 students by the time of the 1989 assassination. Inflation placed UCA finances in a precarious state, especially when the IDB loan grace period ended and the money had to be paid back. Research projects increased slowly, but the UCA spent its energy on teaching, and on preparation both of articles for *ECA* and some important books that analyzed the stages through which the nation went careening during the 1980s: five elections with major parties of the right and the right-of-center replacing each other as in a game of musical chairs; major increases in United States military and economic involvement in the region; and, above all, a disastrous civil war.

Attacks at home and questions from Rome forced reexamination of the UCA model once again. In the midst of national chaos, the UCA spent much of 1981 reviewing its mission, evaluating the effectiveness of its implementation, and designing new ways to respond to the challenges of the nation and the region. This meant meetings with Ellacuría in exile, but also rallying around the team back at home, under the interim rectorship of Axel Soderberg, the academic leadership of Ignacio Martín-Baró, and the team of lay and Jesuit colleagues who had developed an esprit de corps through thick and thin since the founding of the UCA in calmer times. We will see the UCA looking realistically at its failure to do much research, but some reasons for this limitation will also be evident. That the UCA survived under such challenges, especially with the rector in exile for half the time, is no mean achievement.

Ignacio Ellacuría

Just five days after the 1979 coup, the Jesuit provincial wrote to the superior general that "under the current circumstances in El Salvador, Father Ellacuría is the most qualified Jesuit we have for this position. I believe that difficult experiences have helped Father Ellacuría to grow, even though he still has some character defects which he will bring with him to the grave."[1]

The task ahead would be enormous. "Many of the most qualified university personnel have gone to the Government to take over important posts; in total I think that about 18 have done so." Along with the letter, Jerez sent a copy of the UCA statement on the accession of the new government.

Pedro Arrupe replied in December that Ellacuría is "without doubt a capable man for this task [UCA rector], and I am sure that you will be at his side to help him in every way possible in his very delicate task and in the middle of the difficult circumstances which the country is undergoing."[2]

Arrupe goes on to say, "I have read with interest the declaration of the Higher Education Council of November 14th and I passed it on to my advisors. It is lucid in its analysis and of high quality. I agree . . . that education of the people is necessary so that the popular organizations might be true instruments of structural reform. This is a necessary condition for responsible democracy."

He urges all to "try to maintain the independence and freedom to search for truth with serenity, even in the midst of great storms, and to desire *union and collaboration for the common good* based on truth illuminated by faith. Go forward with sensitive discernment in the mission which the Lord has given you."

The difficulties the Jesuits and their colleagues faced were soon confirmed on the night of December 27, 1979, when Jerez reported that opponents "planted a bomb in the UCA computer center. It did not cause a great deal of damage. I hope we are not returning to the era of the bombs."[3]

1980: THE EXTERNAL CONTEXT

This was an important year, in which key issues bubbled to the top almost immediately: the failed political experiment of October 15, 1979, led to more drastic options from the opposition, and these in turn to repressive reactions by the government. Killings increased, civil war got closer, political positions were drawn more clearly, and the bishops of El Salvador issued a controversial pastoral letter. This is the context for Ellacuría's first year as rector, just before he went into exile.

Some forces of the left had opposed the new government, scorning it as "reformist" because of failure to get at the roots of El Salvador's problems, whose seriousness required more structural remedies. Hard-line military leaders on the right, like José Guillermo García and Jaime Abdul Gutiérrez, eased out younger officers like Adolfo Majano, and continued to govern in ways similar to the regime they had replaced.

Just after New Year's Day, 1980, Mayorga, Ungo, and the more progressive elements in the government tendered their resignations after a stormy meeting with the military in the presence of Archbishop Romero, Miguel Francisco Estrada, former vice provincial and UCA rector after the assassination, and others who had sought to hold the uneasy alliance together.[4] The military told the civilians they no longer needed them. The "reformist" solution had been found wanting; its champions fled into exile.

César Jerez informed Pedro Arrupe that "in all these events the Society of Jesus has played an important role, principally through the efforts of the UCA, and because the Archbishop of San Salvador, the humble and powerful arbiter of the situation, has counted on the Jesuits to help determine the position of the Archdiocese of San Salvador in this difficult situation."[5]

An *ECA* editorial laments that "in the face of failure for the most generous, technically qualified, and motivated effort seen in recent years, an urgent question confronts us: is not even reformism possible in El Salvador? The least we can say is that it has not been possible with these men and this political project. And it is not as if they were incapable of accomplishing it. Perhaps it does mean, however, that the reformist model is just not viable in our country, and that we need to bring about a real revolution."[6] The editorial urges unity among the opposition. "In order to avoid everything remaining just at the level of hopes and prayers, it is necessary that we all work together . . . for unity among all those forces that sincerely want profound changes, a unity which should be generous and without self-interest, a unity of all persons and groups who want to break with the current situation and struggle for a new society which is just, democratic, and peaceful."

In the pages of *ECA,* the University Higher Education Council published a statement after the resignation of UCA participants in the first junta government. "The important thing is to notice that a group of capable and honest people, after placing all their dreams and their talents at the service of profound reforms, became witnesses to the impossibility of accomplishing this goal in a society in which opponents of change hold sway, and when the process is headed by armed forces whose institutional, historical, and psychosocial characteristics have rendered them incapable of defending the real interests of the popular masses."[7] In this ringing declaration, the university "raised its voice in protest against the inhuman and savage massacre of the people. . . . We hold the Armed Forces High Command responsible for authorizing and condoning . . . the massacres of men, women and children for the sole reason that they were struggling for a dignified life and a just society." Similar words would reecho throughout the 1980s, and their accuracy would be confirmed in the Report of the United Nations Commission on the Truth, March 15, 1993.

The popular organizations united in the Coordinadora Revolucionaria de Masas (CRM) on January 11, 1980, just days after the resignations. Political leaders of the center and the left officially formed the Frente Democrático Revolucionario (FDR) on April 18, 1980. The military groups of the left, which had begun to form in the early 1970s, explored the possibility of uniting their forces, which they actually accomplished later that year as the Frente Farabundo Martí para la Liberación Nacional (FMLN).

The whole March 1980 edition of *ECA* features articles about the FDR platform, and an editorial that endorses it.

> After examining as a totality all objective and subjective conditions, those favorable and unfavorable, and in the light of the experience of the centrist solution of these past six months, it is not unreasonable to affirm that the FDR, from the political point of view, offers better prospects as a new national project which might lift the country from its current desperate situation. Even though it is not a perfect nor fully worked-out solution, nor has it incorporated all the sensible forces in the country, it does offer a solid basis on which to work to that end. But it still has grave difficulties.[8]

That same month, an assassin's bullet ended the life of the great mediator and defender of human rights, Archbishop Oscar Arnulfo Romero, after just three years as leader of the San Salvador church. The UCA felt his loss tremendously because its professors and staff had been his close collaborators.

On the fifth anniversary of his death, the UCA awarded a posthumous honorary doctorate to Archbishop Romero.[9] Ignacio Ellacuría's comments on that occasion describe well this close relationship:

> This award means we recognize the merits of the martyred archbishop, that we honor him with the best means at our disposal, and that we want his presence to remain alive and efficacious. But above all it means a commitment to do in our university way what he did in his pastoral way.
>
> It has been said with bad intentions that Archbishop Romero was manipulated by our university. It is time to say publicly and solemnly that this accusation was false. Certainly Archbishop Romero asked for our collaboration on many occasions, and this represents and will continue to represent for us a great honor, because of the person who made the request and the cause for which he did so: collaboration in political analysis, and on theological positions, especially on the occasion of his pastoral letters, and in other archdiocesan functions. But during all these consultations no one doubted who was the teacher and who was the assistant, who was the pastor setting the direction and who was the implementer, who was the prophet revealing the mystery

and who was the follower, who was the one who encouraged and who was the one encouraged, who was the voice and who was the echo. (167–8)

Rome would wait almost three years before appointing a successor to Romero, a delay which complicated the role of the apostolic administrator, Arturo Rivera Damas, the progressives' candidate in 1977 when Romero had been chosen instead, and a man who had incurred the wrath of other bishops because he supported Romero's positions. In his quiet, behind-the-scenes way, Rivera worked to alleviate the tensions and encourage dialogue, but Romero was a hard act to follow.

Controversy raged after the funeral of Archbishop Romero because United States Ambassador Robert White accepted the Salvadoran government's version of who set off the bomb that started a stampede that left almost twenty dead. Eyewitnesses such as San Francisco Archbishop John R. Quinn, president of the United States Catholic Bishops Conference, James L. Connor, president of the United States Jesuit Conference, and Simon Smith, of the Jesuit Conference staff, spoke out against the government version.

In a July 15, 1980, letter to the ambassador, Ignacio Ellacuría takes particular exception to White's comment in a letter to Simon Smith, in which the ambassador said: "As far as I can figure things out, a great number of people in El Salvador, specifically including the Jesuits, are so justifiably angry at the abuses of human rights over the last half century that they have a psychological need for a bloody revolution."[10]

Ellacuría criticizes the ambassador's affirmation "that psychologically we need a bloody revolution as a distortion and a calumny. We have expressed no such thing either in speaking or writing. Perhaps in your letter it is just a rhetorical phrase which does not mean what it actually says. I hope that is true. If not, I would ask you not to spread such wrong and dangerous ideas."

Ellacuría goes on to say that

it is one thing to affirm that armed conflict is inevitable—in which we might be mistaken, because something might occur that prevents it—and another quite different thing to say that we desire it, and even more so, that we desire it as a psychological catharsis. Our point of view is structural, not psychological. Psychologically we desire with all our strength that the bloodshed cease, that reconciliation come, and that repression be suppressed forever. We are so concerned about the bloodshed that we do not understand how the United States is supporting a regime and a government which sponsors or is incapable of stopping systematic massacre of innocent people, already about 4,000 this year. And all this is happening with no official protest on your part, with no declaration by the United States.

Ellacuría chooses this occasion to summarize for the ambassador his views on United States policy. It is worth quoting in its entirety because it gives a comprehensive overview of Ellacuría's opinions on the relationship between the United States and El Salvador in 1980.

(a) The so often proclaimed human rights policy is subordinated in El Salvador to the interests of the United States. This explains why the United States embassy has not condemned, as it ought, the most serious and constant violations of human rights we have been experiencing, especially since January. This also explains the lack of objectivity in the analysis of the various political currents in El Salvador and permits the mistaken so-called centrist solution among extremes to be considered the best one.

(b) The United States and the Christian Democrats are those most responsible for failing to impede or slow down the incredible massacre of our people. They are responsible, especially on the international plane, for why people do not see how monstrous the current situation is, and how unworkable the solution proposed by the United States. Without the support of the United States the current regime would not last.

(c) The argument that without [United States military] help we would fall into the hands of the extreme right is not valid, because there is an alternative that favors the accession to power of the Democratic Revolutionary Coalition [FDR]. Nor is the argument acceptable that says that when the reforms are implemented there will not be any need for repression. Repression is unacceptable not only as a means to an end but also as a secondary effect of something that might be necessary. The United States is responsible for this repression because it has achieved nothing in various areas, such as putting the brakes on the repressors, in the structure of the military and the security forces, and no public recognition of the inability of the official authorities to control their own repressive forces. What might benevolently be called American "permissiveness" of repression and its agents has arrived at intolerable limits.

(d) Military aid to the current regime makes the United States even more responsible for repression in the country, one of the worst in the world. It is useless to try to excuse it as non-lethal aid, or that it is used just against armed groups. It is all part of a whole, and what they save in transportation they use in killing, or they use the transportation etc. to kill with more impunity.

(e) There is room for suspicion, though it is difficult for me to prove it, that there is American support through the CIA and other agencies for the repressive campaign. In any case, American influence might be multiple, playing several cards at the same time. [CIA documents released in November 1993, confirmed United States government knowledge of extensive death squad activity at that time.]

(f) Too much time for evaluation has already passed to justify continued support of an approach which has no popular support nor generates confidence either inside or outside the country. In a new approach the United States should not intervene except indirectly by removing obstacles and effectively condemning and preventing the violation of human rights.

Through the pages of *ECA*, Ellacuría and the UCA would return to the subject of United States policy many times.

In an April 11, 1980, letter to Pedro Arrupe keeping him up to date on the ever-changing situation in El Salvador, César Jerez remarked that the UCA Jesuits "had demonstrated great capacity for work directed toward service of the country and the church in El Salvador. It has been their lot to live under threats, there have been bombs in the university, their house has been machine-gunned, and they have been judged harshly. Nevertheless, up to now none of them has asked to be transferred to another assignment. With great peace they have persevered, faithful to their vocation of service. It is not easy to take on work of this nature when one's life is in continual risk. I think that this attitude shows special vigor in their faith."[11]

In his reply, Arrupe said, "I am very much in agreement with all the good things you have said about this community and about each one of its members. I also consider that they are excellent Jesuits, and that the work they are developing, especially in the UCA, is magnificent in its totality, and in many aspects, an example for the rest of the Society of Jesus."[12]

Repression increased, however, and in June the UCA once against denounced it, especially the attacks against educators such as the Jesuit high school's four murdered lay teachers. A UCA professor had to leave the country after his brother was assassinated at about the same time as Archbishop

Romero.[13] In June, ten UCA staff members went into exile for security reasons.[14] The UCA board discussed possible use of the university campus to house refugees in an emergency.[15] The national police killed a student on the UCA campus, and right-wing terrorists dynamited the university press. The UCA declaration challenged the government to examine the reasons why so many educators were opposed to its project. "Is it because they are all subversives? Is it, rather, that they and their institutions are attacked and persecuted because they have been transformed into agents and centers of truth about the situation in the country and about the road that has to be followed to overcome this situation?"[16]

Ellacuría went to see José Napoleón Duarte, who by this time had joined the government junta. Duarte admitted national police responsibility for killing the UCA student, but he said that "reasons of state" prevented him from speaking out publicly.[17] Incidents like this cooled the relationship between the UCA and this Duarte, so different from the progressive presidential candidate of 1972.

Once again an *ECA* editorial protested, this time when the armed forces raided the University of El Salvador campus, killing about forty people and leaving hundreds wounded.[18] The military occupied the university for several years, during which time they carted off scientific equipment, damaged the library, and left the campus in ruins. The UCA protest is important not only for its strong denunciation of military atrocities but also because of what it says about the role of a university in society, and the stand it should take when forces from all sides try to subvert its mission.

> The University of El Salvador has grave problems which should not be ignored. The academic quality of its research and teaching leaves much to be desired; it has too many employees for the tasks at hand; it does not use well the many resources it enjoys, though this is not due to malfeasance. At times the university has felt obliged to take demagogic measures because of student pressure, especially on open admissions, student fees, and academic standards. At times it has been transformed into a refuge for political activities which are not strictly academic, and until recently it served as the battle ground for different student groups of the left which vied for control of the university. (650)

But with no ordinary forums available for public dialogue, it was almost inevitable that these events would gravitate toward the national university.

In a warning to the left, however, the editorial makes important points.

It is necessary to remind the revolutionary organizations that there is an autonomy and a specific nature that a university must enjoy, and that defending this reality is not a bourgeois slogan nor class-based ideologizing. . . . It is a historical necessity so that the university might be what it should be. Revolutionary organizations should demonstrate, now when they are not in power, that they are convinced supporters of university autonomy. The day a university is moved according to the dictates of a state or a political party, from whatever side they be, it will have ceased being what it is.

There should not be any confusion on this. It is one thing to say that the university should serve the people, and that it should be urged to fulfill this role by the people and their organizations, but it is something completely different to say that the university should serve and submit itself to any organization or political coalition, even if they claim to represent the people.

The UCA would not tolerate efforts from any side to twist the university to its own ends—even if it were sympathetic with the general aims of the organizations. By disagreeing with the government's suppression of the University of El Salvador, the UCA did not win favor with the government, and by warning the left to respect universities, it opened itself to criticism that its support for justice was only lukewarm. Such was the narrow path it had to tread.

Despite criticism of some University of El Salvador (UES) policies and practices, the relationship between the two institutions improved with time. The UES appreciated gestures such as the UCA's allowing the use of a large auditorium-like classroom for graduation in 1980. The two institutions sought to serve the people of El Salvador and to work for a just society, but their approaches were different.

The following year, Ignacio Martín-Baró reported to the board on a meeting with UES officials to discuss possible reopening of the national university and the effects on El Salvador with the proliferation of many "universities" of questionable quality.[19] While the UES was closed, the UCA allowed some of its classes to meet on the UCA campus, but this caused difficulties between the two institutions. Some UES officials took a general letter of support to mean that they could occupy major UCA space from September 21, 1980, until October 11, 1981. The board felt that "for political reasons and for the convenience of both universities it is not opportune to have such massive and prolonged presence of so many students on our campus, because of the various interpretations and consequences such a situation might have under current sociopolitical circumstances."[20]

Ellacuría was very careful about lending UCA facilities to groups for meetings. For example, he criticized the University of El Salvador student government organization (AGEUS) for coming on campus without permission and holding a political meeting. "We believe this is not the most opportune moment to hold meetings which might be misinterpreted and which could serve as indications of hostility toward the authorities who are looking for any pretext to intervene, as happened recently at the University of El Salvador. . . . We especially do not allow people to come armed to this university, which has no intention of attacking or defending itself with arms."[21]

He had the same reaction to the Coordinadora Revolucionaria de Masas (CRM), whose "armed members went into classrooms trying to recruit people. Such actions do not seem appropriate inside the university; instead of helping a university contribute to the people's struggles, they impede it. . . . There must always be university autonomy. If not, the university's contribution to the popular cause will not be that of a university."[22]

He also refused to let the teachers' union, ANDES 21 de Junio, use the UCA for a cultural tribute to a Salvadoran teacher.[23] However, he had no problem with giving university facilities to reflection groups of a spiritual nature.[24]

Seeing war as inevitable, a September 1980 *ECA* editorial warns all sides at least to act humanely in their struggle. It points most criticism at the government because security forces were responsible for most human rights violations. But there is also a warning for the left, which the editorial feels should be held to "an even higher requirement of humaneness. Even if their cause is fundamentally just, they should do all in their power to show themselves to have a more humane cause in both appearances and in reality."[25] The editorial calls on the government "to avoid falling into total and absolute discredit, making even more cruel the path of liberation for the people. And to the others, that they should accompany the justice of their cause with nobility in the struggle so that the path to liberation and liberation itself will contain the seeds of justice and a more durable peace."

There are no doubts where the sympathies of the journal staff lay, but the editorial states an opinion, giving reasons whose validity others could judge.

THE UCA AND THE CHURCH

After a long silence, the Salvadoran bishops finally produced a pastoral letter that came in for heavy criticism in a September 1980 *ECA* article by Jon Sobrino under a pseudonym.[26] The pastoral letter, he says,

> offers a poor diagnosis of the country's current situation, and some extremely vague and deficient theological principles that produce a poor and dangerous pastoral orientation.
>
> According to the bishops' analysis, violence is due to a polarization of two highly ideologized extremes with a "center" between them which in itself is not the cause of the violence, but is proposed, by implication, as leading toward a solution. To put it more clearly, the episcopal conference adopts the current government's point of view in analyzing the situation of violence, its causes and its solution.
>
> The bishops neither describe nor analyze the generalized repression of the people, which is the current government's direct responsibility when committed by its security forces and military, and its indirect responsibility when committed by the ultra-right paramilitary forces. A minimum of responsible analysis would identify the number of victims and the amount of violence and those responsible, and there is abundant and reliable documentation available in the country.

Sobrino characterizes the pastoral letter as irrelevant by listing a number of key issues that are indirectly the responsibility of the government but that the pastoral letter ignores: for example, the collapsing economy, abuses in the mass media, censorship, inflammatory government radio broadcasts, the state of siege, a nonfunctioning justice system, the gap between the intentions and the reality of proposed reforms, and United States intervention.

Sobrino says that the pastoral letter

> praises the current reforms offered by the government without analyzing or nuancing them, or recognizing the repression that accompanies them.
>
> The pastoral letter speaks about ideologies and it condemns them, but the bishops do nothing to discern between good and bad elements in complex ideological phenomena. They give the impression that only the church and the current government are free of ideology, and that only they offer the correct vision and practices. This is not only wrong, it is pastorally irresponsible. . . .
>
> [Its] analysis of the left's position is so simplistic, and at times so unjust, that its words of denunciation fall into a vacuum, even

when they might be correct in some criticism.

In addition to the letter's pastoral poverty, there are two eloquent silences by which the bishops provoke confusion, surprise, and indignation. The first refers to persecution of the church and the shedding of martyrs' blood. There is no mention of the priests, seminarians, catechists, and delegates of the Word who have been assassinated, nor the searches, machine-gunning, and bombs in churches, Catholic schools, and the residences of religious orders. There is not a word of consolation or encouragement, not a word of hope to maintain firm in the faith the Christians who live and work at so much risk. This silence is pastorally incomprehensible.

But even more incomprehensible is the absolute silence about Archbishop Romero. The bishops' analysis shows how the episcopal conference differs from the letter and spirit of Archbishop Romero. They do not quote him even once or in a perfunctory way. When the entire world, so many bishops of the church, so many Christians and so many church communities venerate him and proclaim him as a just and good man, as a prophet and martyr, it is simply inconceivable that the episcopal conference of El Salvador does not even mention him. The pastoral impact of this silence on the people can only mean that Archbishop Romero no longer lives within the hierarchy but must be sought elsewhere.

Sobrino makes an exception for embattled Bishop Rivera, the apostolic administrator of the archdiocese, who in his cathedral homilies on the radio and in his public statements had set himself apart from the other bishops. Needless to say, this article infuriated most bishops.

In the meantime, Jon Sobrino himself fell under theological suspicion in certain Roman quarters and his writings were reviewed for an orthodoxy check. In early 1980, César Jerez, in a letter to Pedro Arrupe, mentions that despite receiving word from Rome that there were some questions about his writings, Sobrino had "shown himself to be calm."[27] The following month, Jerez transmitted to Arrupe a copy of Sobrino's response to Cardinal Seper of the Sacred Congregation for the Doctrine of the Church, a ten-page document in which Sobrino concludes: "I have tried to present the figure of Christ as he appears in the gospels, and as presented in the fundamental dogma of the church. In this presentation I have also had in mind the pastoral situation of the church in which I work. . . . Neither in my personal intentions nor in the objectivity of my christology text do I find objective contradiction of the teaching of the church. I admit, on the other hand, that there is a certain novelty in conceptualization and terminology."[28]

In July, Arrupe sent César Jerez the response of Cardinal Seper to Sobrino, in which the cardinal maintained that some objections to Sobrino's christology "have not been clarified . . . in the explanation you have sent."[29] Seper saw the book as a monograph on the historical Jesus who can serve as a model to be followed. "But it is not, nor can it be, a 'christology' in the proper sense of that term, since you discard right from the beginning the doctrinal affirmations of the New Testament (in particular, St. Paul and St. John), leaving us, finally, with what the synoptic gospels might offer us, interpreted by methods of historical criticism, outside the margin of the faith of the church." In August, Jerez assured Arrupe that Sobrino had received the comments "with great humility" and that he would make revisions in his book. Sobrino gave fuller explanations in his *Jesus in Latin America*.[30]

But suspicions never really die. In 1992, the Austrian University of Graz offered Jon Sobrino an honorary doctorate, but the Vatican refused permission for the conferral of the degree. The university then gave Sobrino a newly minted human rights award.

Some local bishops in El Salvador continued to show hostility to the UCA. For example, Bishop Pedro Aparicio was quoted in the right-wing newspaper, *El Diario de Hoy,* that the university was permeated with Marxism.[31] Ignacio Ellacuría, Axel Soderberg, and Miguel Francisco Estrada met with Aparicio who blamed the newspapers for "misquoting" him.[32]

Two years after the Salvadoran bishops' pastoral letter that Sobrino criticized so strongly in *ECA,* Pope John Paul II wrote a letter to the local bishops about the situation in El Salvador. In it, he said

> I am perfectly aware that the discord and divisions which still disturb your country and cause new conflicts and violence find their true and deep roots in social injustice: a problem that has erupted with force on the political level, but which is above all an ethical problem.
>
> The methodology of violence has brought about a fratricidal war—placing on one side those who consider armed struggle a necessary instrument for obtaining a new social order, and on the other side those who have recourse to the principles of "national security" to legitimate brutal repressions—there is no rational justification, never mind Christian justification.[33]

The July 1982 *ECA* editorial waxes eloquent about the pope's letter to the bishops of El Salvador. The pope did not call anyone Marxist or terrorist. He criticized the "national security" school of thought as the pretext for the barbarous treatment of the population, and he called for peace and the dialogue that leads to it.

The editorial states that "from now on, no one can say that the church is going beyond its competence when it tries to help resolve the political, military, and social conflicts in El Salvador, and when it tries to do so by going beyond internal questions to open itself to the structural and public arena."[34]

The editorial urges that "the church of El Salvador put itself fully into the task of working on solutions to the country's crisis, much more so than it has done up to now, and it should do so in a different way. If it had already been doing so, then there would not have been any need for such an important and new message from the Pope." The bishops of El Salvador must not have been pleased by this implicit criticism of their pastoral letter of two years earlier.

The pope had mentioned social injustice as the root of the conflict. The editorial continues: "The policies of the United States government, the military high command, and the political right of El Salvador are based on the idea that the root of the country's evils is communism and international subversion, and Marxist-Leninist terrorism. . . . But it is important to point out that while the Pope did not hesitate to talk about 'national security' ideology, he has exercised great care in not mentioning Marxist ideology, precisely so that his main argument not be ignored because of anything that would provoke repressive action in the name of anti-communism."

The following year, on his visit to El Salvador, the pope's comments went along the same vein, emphasizing the conflict's root causes in an unjust society. The *ECA* editorial on that occasion rejoiced in this consistent message by the pope.[35]

The UCA and the FDR

On the first anniversary of the 1979 coup, *ECA* more formally endorsed the political project of the Frente Democrático Revolucionario (FDR), the civilian left. It pointed out four reasons why the 1979 experiment had failed:

(1) it had excluded the popular and revolutionary organizations as an element in the solution, even though they were the dominant class's principal enemy; (2) it had based the whole process [of reform] on the armed forces; (3) it believed in the possibility of a middle-of-the-road or centrist solution between the dominant class and the revolutionary class; and (4) its leaders were confident that it was not necessary to make a decisive break with the people and the practices that

had been put at the service of the previous socioeconomic and political order in order to bring about what was truly new.[36]

We continue to feel, as we expressed in our March–April 1980 editorial, that the solution cannot be anything other than what is presented by the FDR and supported by the FMLN. The rapid and intensive events of the past six months confirm the reasons and the prognosis we offered then. Today we can perhaps see better its defects and its strengths, and that its strengths are greater and more promising than its defects. We continue to believe that it should be supported so that it triumph and that its triumph be accomplished in the most humane and rational way possible. . . .

The left intends correctly a true revolution for the country, because this revolution is an objective need. . . . It is necessary to remove by force those who by force imposed an intolerable situation in every realm: political, military, economic, health, cultural, communication, etc. It is necessary to establish something new and this will require pressure and even some level of coercion. . . .

Joined with this democratic revolutionary left are the most sane forces, those less contaminated by the capitalistic corruption which we have always lived through in this country. . . .

It is not appropriate to close our eyes, and it is not logical to clothe ourselves in pacifism in the face of this problem with stock phrases that violence is always bad, that violence always engenders violence, and that we should condemn violence whatever its source. . . . But in affirming this truth we should not forget that the problem at its roots is really political and not just military, and it should be resolved politically and not just militarily.

This endorsement of the FDR proposal came as a result of a conviction of many at the UCA that half measures would not work. And yet the UCA preserved its independence because it fully intended to critique the FDR solution if its proponents ever came to power. This confidence in the FDR solution would last only a few months, until early in 1981, after the failure of the FMLN's "final offensive," and it would provoke hostile reaction. From that point on, especially in *ECA* editorials and articles, and pronouncements of the University Higher Education Council, there would be a ringing call for negotiations to end the struggle and to begin to put in place the ingredients for a just society—a goal not achieved for another decade.

On October 24, 1980, two bombs exploded outside the Jesuit residence, blowing a hole in the wall of Segundo Montes's room. Luckily, he had moved his bed to the other side of the room shortly before this incident, so a typewriter table got the worst of it.[37] Three days later, at 3:00 A.M., another bomb exploded at the front gate. The UCA board sent a letter of protest to the government of El Salvador. The Jesuits decided to disperse to various homes for the night, but they returned during the day to their home for meals and to work at the university.

On November 26, 1980, the same month that the FDR editorial appeared, the Jesuit community received a phone call from the Siesta Hotel, just up the road from the UCA. The caller, a military officer, said, cryptically, "The patient must be moved immediately. He is very ill." When asked if the move could be postponed a few days, the response was "If we wait, the patient will not survive." That same evening, Ellacuría left the Jesuit residence for the Spanish embassy, where he sought protection. The next day, accompanied by the Spanish ambassador, Ellacuría left for the airport and a seventeen-month exile.[38]

Later the same morning that Ellacuría escaped, 200 soldiers surrounded the campus of the Jesuit high school, Externado de San José, and twenty-five plainclothesmen entered the building and kidnapped five leaders of the FDR, the civilian opposition, who had been meeting in an office just inside the entrance. Their tortured dead bodies were found that afternoon. One week later, the United States churchwomen were captured as they came from the airport, and later violently murdered by national guardsmen.

Roberto D'Aubuisson, a central figure in the death squads, and the 1984 presidential candidate of the ARENA rightist party, blamed the left for the FDR kidnapping and slaughter. He saw it as part of the communist conspiracy.[39]

ECA ended the year on an ominous editorial note. It pointed out that 1979 had seen the bankruptcy of two models: General Romero's national security state, and the reformist efforts of the first junta, but also a coming together of many people who wanted a new model.[40] The editorial criticized the

> remnant of more conservative Christian Democrats who tried to give life once again to the political project that had been tried for two decades in our country: reformism on the foundation of a national security state. During 1980 this project has tried to project the im-

age of moderation, centrism, and opposition to the extremism of both the oligarchy and the popular organizations. Their actions, however, have constantly given the lie to their words.

And so 1980 saw itself reduced to a confrontation of forces between a project that, in its agony, offered little more than destruction and death, and an ascending movement, growing from deep within the people themselves, winning over more and more sectors, and appearing as the only viable and rational alternative for the future of El Salvador.

Then in January 1981 the FMLN launched its "final offensive," which identified it as a serious military force. But they were poorly organized, and their immediate objective of taking power met with strong resistance and prompted the renewal of United States military aid, which had been temporarily postponed after the December 2, 1980, murder of the United States churchwomen.

The UCA board noted that "the complications from political events make all academic activity impossible. [Summer school] classes would be postponed until the first available working days, with a consequent delay in the opening of the new school year in March. It would be hard to begin under conflict and with teachers not knowing whether they will be able to return to their university labors."[41] Then the national police occupied the campus from noon on Saturday, January 17, 1981, to Monday morning, January 19, "preventing the entrance of students, employees, and authorities of the university. Checkpoints continue to control the entrance of pedestrians and autos."[42] Axel Soderberg, the acting rector, and Fredy Villalta, the dean of engineering, went to discuss the matter with El Salvador's military leadership and were given assurances that the controls would be exercised outside the campus. The military claimed they were just checking for arms, but their presence was still considered a threat and a cause of great concern by students and staff.

The minutes of this same meeting report that a UCA professor wrote the board criticizing its "demonstrated complacency" during these events. He also criticized UCA officials for "establishing a channel of communication with military headquarters, that is, establishing dialogue with the assassins of the people. This contradicts the Christian spirit of this university, and it coincides with the absence of the rector, Dr. Ignacio Ellacuría, and the vice rector, Dr. Luis de Sebastián, who have had their lives threatened by the very same people who direct the military establishment." He termed the UCA administration's attitude as that of an "ostrich" and charged that "the UCA is taking a pro-government position."

What a first year as rector for Ignacio Ellacuría and for the UCA! While national events captured center stage, there was still a university to run: classes to teach, research to supervise and engage in, and the everyday involvement of the university in the community. Although we turn now to some internal matters, this momentous national context, or "national reality," as Ellacuría would have phrased it, must be kept in mind. The UCA's challenge was to be involved as a university in the national scene and, at the same time, prepare people and data for the future, while living in the present and the past, and also looking ahead to a future that had yet to be created, and in whose creation the university could play a major role—as had been the design in the staff-developed 1979 document, "Las Funciones Fundamentales de la Universidad y su Operativización."

NOTES

1. ASJCA–P79/50, César Jerez to Pedro Arrupe, November 20, 1979.
2. ASJCA–G79/46, Arrupe to Jerez, December 20, 1979.
3. ASJCA P79/62, Jerez to Arrupe, December 29, 1979.
4. Interview with Miguel Francisco Estrada, S.J., July 1992.
5. ASJCA–P80/14, January 29, 1980.
6. *ECA* (editorial) 34 (December 1979), 1038.
7. *ECA* (editorial) 35 (January–Febraury 1980), 5–18.
8. *ECA* (editorial) 35 (March 1980), 172.
9. *ECA* (editorial) 40 (March 1985), 167–76.
10. RUCA, Ignacio Ellacuría to Robert White, July 15, 1980.
11. ASJCA–P80/32, April 11, 1980.
12. ASJCA–G80/24, May 15, 1980.
13. AUCA, March 28, 1980.
14. AUCA, June 2, 1980.
15. AUCA, May 19, 1980.
16. "El Consejo Superior Universitario de la UCA condena la represión contra los educadores salvadoreños," *ECA* 35 (June 1980), 548.
17. Interview with Miguel Francisco Estrada, S.J., July 1992.
18. *ECA* (editorial) 35 (July–August 1980), 649–54.
19. AUCA, June 15, 1981.
20. AUCA, September 14, 1981.
21. RUCA, Ignacio Ellacuría to AGEUS, July 4, 1980.
22. RUCA, Ignacio Ellacuría to the Coordinadora Revolucionaria de Masas, June 17, 1980. He gave a similar response to Juan Chacón of the Bloque Popular Revolucionario, March 18, 1980.
23. RUCA, Ignacio Ellacuría to Pedro Bran, June 11, 1980.
24. RUCA, Ignacio Ellacuría to Rogelio Ponseele, March 21, 1980.
25. *ECA* (editorial) 35 (September 1980), 793–8.
26. Jon Sobrino [H.O.], "La Carta Pastoral del Episcopado Salvadoreño," *ECA* 35 (September 1980), 851–6.
27. ASJCA–P80/17, February 6, 1980.
28. ASJCA–P80/29, March 21, 1980.
29. ASJCA–G80/37, July 8, 1980.
30. ASJCA–P80/53, August 26, 1980.

31. ASJCA–G84/58, December 7, 1984.

32. AUCA, October 11, 1982.

33. AUCA editorial, October 25, 1982.

34. *ECA* 37 (1982), 633–50.

35. *ECA* 38 (March–April 1983), 225–34.

36. *ECA* 35 (October–November 1980), 929–50.

37. Segundo Montes recounted this incident to the author in July, 1981, and showed him the repaired damage to the wall.

38. Ellacuría himself recounted this story to the author in the summer of 1985.

39. *ECA*, 35 (December 1980), 1212–3. In its documentation section each month, *ECA* published the texts of important statements affecting the country.

40. *ECA* 35 (December 1980), 1125–32.

41. AUCA, January 12, 1981.

42. AUCA, January 19–20, 1981.

9 LIFE INSIDE THE UCA: 1979–1982

INTRODUCTION

In this chapter, we will try to show the UCA trajectory through this consolidating decade. We will look briefly at budget, enrollment, and faculty statistics; the university's efforts at research and its international contacts; and the development of support agencies for teaching, research, and social outreach such as the documentation, polling, and human rights centers.

With Ignacio Ellacuría, the rector, and Luis de Sebastián, the academic vice rector, in exile and the university living in the eye of a political hurricane, the staff looked more closely at itself, examining academic quality and seeking a deeper understanding of "social outreach" *(proyección social)*.

The following figures show how much the UCA grew in the 1980s after the pioneer years of the late 1960s and the 1970s.[1]

Year	Budget ($, millions)	Faculty	Students
1979	2.12	151	4,925
1980	2.27	169	4,972
1981	2.08	180	4,859
1982	2.40	186	5,890
1983	2.75	196	6,249
1984	2.83	211	6,301
1985	3.13	219	5,688
1986	3.08	233	5,674
1987	3.09	236	6,110
1988	3.10	246	6,533
1989	3.24	241	6,552
1990	2.27	264	6,677
1991	2.86	253	6,771

(continued)

Year	Budget ($, millions)	Faculty	Students
1992	3.36	287	6,864
1993	5.70	298	7,439
1994	8.06	303	7,248
1995	9.00	325	7,616

REVIEW AND CONFIRMATION OF THE UCA MISSION: 1981–1982

Ignacio Ellacuría was in exile from November 1980 until April, 1982. Although he was in regular contact with UCA personnel, in many difficult situations they had to rely on their own wits and on their history of working as a community, even though important members of that community had fled into exile. It is important to look at the issues they faced, and how they worked with Ellacuría to clarify the nature of the UCA model and to develop the practical implications of this vision.

At the request of the board, Miguel Francisco Estrada went to Costa Rica to visit Ignacio Ellacuría, who sent a message in which he expressed his concern for the difficult time the university was undergoing.[2] He was worried about the effect of the closing of the University of El Salvador and the plethora of new universities popping up all over the capital. And as for the UCA, "the departure of so many faculty members presents the problem of substitution with professionals who are not oriented to or in agreement with the mission of the UCA." He saw the need "to integrate some additional Jesuits into university tasks."

The philosophy department was particularly hard hit: "It has been deprived of most of its professors." There was also a need to find substitutes for the *ECA* board. In addition, one of the most important administrators and scholars, Luis de Sebastián, was also in exile.

Ellacuría even went so far as to say that "given the absence of several members who hold UCA administrative posts, the board should think about the advantages of accepting some already submitted resignations, and place other people in these positions either temporarily or in a more definitive way. . . . In any case," he said, "it is important to maintain contact . . . with ecclesiastical and political authorities of various points of view, and professional groups . . . who might have more influence in the search for some way out of the complex national situation, and . . . to give a sense of direction to the work of the UCA in this transitional phase."

In the spirit of Ellacuría's directives, the board met to review activities planned for the first semester of 1981 (March to July).[3] They followed an outline suggested by Ignacio Martín-Baró. Excerpts from this document can help us see the major issues to which the board and the UCA would dedicate time during this crucial year.

1.   General Orientations

    1.1   To maintain its own identity: Even though political circumstances have evolved in a notable way, and things have gotten worse for the university, this is no time to renounce its proper identity, which is characterized by:

        (a)   Maintaining ideological fidelity to the principles and ideals which have made the UCA a university that is nationally and internationally significant, especially in its explicit option for the total liberation of the Salvadoran and Central American people.

        (b)   Maintaining and reaffirming its Christian inspiration, . . . the basis for the ideological orientation of the university itself.

        (c)   Conserving and, as much as possible, increasing the academic quality of the services which the university offers, especially in teaching. . . .

    1.2   To collaborate in a university fashion with the current national process:

        (a)   To give priority to reflection on and analysis of evolving events, possible solutions, and in general, everything concerning the conflict, but also, future periods of reconstruction. [Such words would have even greater relevance during the peace process of the 1990s.]

        (b)   To conserve in whatever way possible through its academic activities the intellectual space characteristic of the UCA, and shown by its critical and independent nature. . . .

        (c)   To give a sense of direction to the efforts of the university . . . to achieve, as soon as possible, some resolution in favor of the interests of the people. Into this category would fall . . . negotiation which might serve as a way out of the current national politico-economic chaos.

It is important to notice this call for a negotiated settlement just two months after the launching of the "final offensive" of the FMLN—an early stage of the war—and more than a decade before the fighting actually stopped.

At about this same time the call for a negotiated settlement appeared in the pages of *ECA* and the author was none other than Román Mayorga, who had left the UCA rectorship to form part of the government junta on October 15, 1979, and then left for exile in early January 1980.

Mayorga calls negotiations the only sensible approach to ending the conflict.[4] His words are indeed prophetic. "Neither of the two sides in the conflict has sufficient strength to achieve a total victory over the other, even though each will be able to inflict significant damage for an indefinite period of time. This could become extraordinarily long and costly in suffering, human lives, and the economic future of El Salvador." Eleven years later, everyone would be saying the same thing, but at the time all sides considered this point of view treason or heresy.

His article suggests a number of ingredients for an eventual peace accord, and his list matches many actual agreements signed in Mexico City on January 16, 1992: disbanding the security forces, reshaping the army, socioeconomic reforms, improvements in mass communication, and reform of the justice system, to mention a few.

When Mayorga returned to El Salvador in late 1992 for his first visit since going into exile in 1980, rightist newspapers featured paid advertisements denouncing him and the Jesuits as having been behind the "terrible" peace accords right from the beginning. They cited this 1981 Mayorga article as "proof" that the UCA and the Jesuits had engineered this whole "treacherous" process.[5]

Meanwhile, back to the outline for the 1982 internal renewal of the UCA.

2.   Concrete Measures for the First Semester of 1981.

2.1   Social outreach of the UCA: . . . the principal function of the university . . . [is] analysis and reflection of the highest academic quality. [This function should be delegated by the acting rector] to the person considered competent to implement this function.

The following areas should be strengthened:

(a)   [CIDAI, the documentation center,] should be expanded to become the determining and thinking nucleus of the UCA.

(b)   Publications, especially ECA and *Proceso* (the weekly bulletin on current affairs), as well as the journals of business administration, engineering, economics, and political science/sociology are to be encouraged.

(c)   The University Press.

(d)   Communication with political and church groups in the Salvadoran community.

(e)   New financial resources for projects.

2.2   Teaching and Research:

[With all the other obligations there is not sufficient attention given to research, but] such activity would be a great UCA contribution to the current situation.

[It is important] to maintain the level of academic requirements. . . . It is a social obligation of the UCA to prepare in university fashion, and with the best quality, those students who are the principal source of funding for the global task of the university.

It is interesting that the students are seen more as university "bread and butter" rather than as agents for social change who might implement the ideas coming from the UCA.

This academic seriousness "is required by the very prestige of the UCA which is based on its scientific and Christian seriousness. It is also required because of the current level of incompetence in so many private universities. The competence issue is important, but also the . . . political intention which has influenced the founding of these universities."

The document also recognizes the importance of encouraging the staff and of revitalizing the University Higher Education Council.

2.3   The Current Economic Situation: The UCA must:

(a)   reduce costs.

(b)   firm up the budget, which is still provisional even though the school year is about to begin.

(c)   insist on getting the subsidy from the government which is already approved in the national budget.

(d)   strengthen the student loan program.

In the notes for this two-day meeting of the board, there is a memorandum from Francisco Javier Ibisate, who had been a member since 1967 (and who served until 1993 and became rector in November 1995), that Ellacuría continue as rector even in exile for at least the first semester, that the resignation of Luis de Sebastián as academic vice rector be accepted, and that Ignacio Martín-Baró be put in charge of the UCA social outreach programs with Luis Achaerandio and Segundo Montes assisting him. Miguel Francisco Estrada had already taken over as dean of students.

Two weeks later, board members Soderberg, Estrada, Martín-Baró, Cortina, and Ibisate traveled to Costa Rica for a meeting with Ellacuría. They all concluded that after looking at the Salvadoran situation from inside and outside it was clear that the UCA had an important role to play in any process of mediation, by utilizing its publications to promote the goal "above all to democratize and to create a more ample base for the democratic reform that the country needs."[6]

They state that "it is necessary to avoid being impulsive and giving the impression that we are standard bearers of the left, or that we consider ourselves the initiators of the mediated solution, only if the armed solution fails. On the contrary, our role is to show the logic of the process—the logic of why the armed conflict began in the first place, and why dialogue and previous efforts at mediation have been neglected."

They add, "If the bishop wants to write a pastoral letter on mediation, he should receive all our support." Efforts should be made to win over as many groups as possible, such as embassies now opposed to such an approach. "It is necessary to promote mediation effectively with the most radical and aggressive groups of the left, who cannot emotionally accept mediation and dialogue after so much spilled blood, and the hatred derived from the current process."

The UCA board summarizes the university's role as "to generate rationality within an atmosphere which is emotionally charged and belligerent for both sides, a task based on rationality and Christian inspiration."

At this meeting, Ignacio Martín-Baró was offered the position of acting academic vice rector; since he was not yet a Salvadoran citizen, he could not assume the position in his own right. In the midst of such discussions about a country in crisis and life and death struggles outside the campus, the board also discussed the possibility of setting up an academic major in architecture with an urban emphasis, a program that was subsequently approved in November 1986. Balancing the cosmic and the everyday dimensions of running a university had almost become routine at the UCA.

Social Outreach

As indicated in chapter 3's discussion of the UCA model, social outreach is the context and the goal of UCA teaching and research. One month after the board meeting in Costa Rica, Ellacuría sent them a draft on social outreach for discussion.[7]

It is important to remember that the primary sense of "social outreach" must be distinguished from "social outreach programs" in the narrower sense.

This Ellacuría document is important because it is the fruit of his reflections in exile and stimulated by his meetings with board members and other UCA personnel. Earlier insights on the social role of the university come together, and a separate vice rectorate for social outreach programs starts to take form. At this point, let us examine this document in some detail.

Ellacuría defines "social outreach" as

the primordial function of the UCA, that from which it receives its totality as a university, and from which all its activities receive their overall orientation. This orientation must be translated into practical measures [social outreach programs] effective in themselves and present and operative in the totality of all UCA functions. This is more urgent than ever at this moment when El Salvador is going through one of the most difficult moments in its history, and when the UCA is one of the few forces inside the country which can contribute to resolve this dramatic and decisive situation.

He sees this role as one of the principal activities of the rector. Social outreach programs should include the University Press, the documentation center, CIDAI, and *ECA*. The Social Service Center, which supervised student community service hours, should be included because it "brings the university students into practical contact with the national reality, a two-way communication intended also to be of service to the community's most needy." Social outreach should also be realized in public events such as roundtables, conferences, and congresses, and in the "development and implementation of those contacts with relevant sectors of society (politicians, economists, religious and military leaders) so as to facilitate, sponsor, and bring to completion solutions proposed by the UCA, and at the same time, to communicate information and UCA opinions on the national reality." If possible, a radio station and a weekly newspaper might be added.

Though he states, "Social outreach should be focused now on a political solution and mediation of the civil war," Ellacuría admits a certain amount of ambiguity in working for a political solution to the conflict because it could appear that "we are sponsoring solutions that might bolster the current situation, but which do not advance the requirements of the process itself." He seems to imply that by encouraging dialogue, the UCA might get both sides to stop fighting and agree on a solution. Such a solution, however, could turn out to be a half-measure that does not get at the roots of the problem—an unjust society. This would be the accusation of some from the left. Of course, the right would also oppose such a solution because it would fear that concessions at any level might be just a prelude to the eventual collapse of the system within which it was thriving. In any case, all should be done "in a university fashion, which might result in the possibility that the right would stop attacking us and the left might not ask of us things which would not be appropriate for a university to do." Ellacuría exhibits a certain amount of wishful thinking there.

He stresses the unique potential of the UCA to serve the country through its social outreach: "the ideological pluralism of UCA members and the combination of its multiple relationships should be put to maximum advantage. All this requires caution, but even more importantly, it requires at its head a programming center that sends, receives, and processes messages."

These tasks might require setting up a permanent seminar on national reality, which could be developed in conjunction with *ECA*, but eventually expanded so that qualified persons from inside and outside the UCA would be invited. In germ this was the Cátedra Universitaria de la Realidad Nacional, the National Seminar on the National Reality, which started in 1984. Whatever the format, Ellacuría sees the importance of getting the results "processed and interpreted" for "neuralgic points in society and the general public."

There should be

> special contact with the church-sector of the community:
> (a) Bishop Rivera and the papal nuncio [no mention of other bishops by name]
> (b) Clergy in their monthly meetings, the priests' senate, and other groups
> (c) Men and women in religious orders through their organization, CONFRES
> (d) Catholic high schools [an interesting addition in the light of his generally dim view of these institutions on other occasions].

There were other formats in which Ellacuría feels this social outreach could take shape, especially processes to encourage mediation of the conflict:

> 1. Attention toward professionals, encouraging contacts with them through their regular organizations.
> 2. Conversations and discussions with owners of small and middle-sized businesses and similar groups.
> 3. Approaches to some universities and attention to the problem of the National University.

4. Approaches to labor unions, which are adherents of the revolutionary movement, [and the popular organizations].

5. Establishment of personal contacts with qualified political and military personnel open to a political solution.

6. Contacts with the FMLN-FDR to be critical and encouraging of their efforts toward a political solution.

7. Helping student organizations make their own contribution toward opening politico-democratic spaces, and distancing themselves from militarization.

> (a)   It is probable that student activism will once again be on the rise, and it would be helpful to give it an appropriate channel so that it not become a threat against academic activity or a form of external aggression.

> (b)   On the positive side we should reinforce democratic-revolutionary opportunities, helping the students to see in the practical order that revolutionary activity and military action are not identical.

8. There should be provisional establishment of a social outreach council which would supervise policy and encourage and orient activities; it could serve as a permanent mechanism for evaluation.

He proposes a meeting of all staff involved in social outreach activities, and he specifically mentions Rogelio Pedráz, Italo López Vallecillo, Segundo Montes, Ricardo Stein of CIDAI, Ignacio Martín-Baró, Miguel Francisco Estrada, and Crista Benecke.

In its May 15, 1981, meeting, the board "reiterated the priority that social outreach should occupy in the university task, giving a sense of direction to research and teaching." The board "gave general approval to the content of the Ellacuría document" and observed that it would "get translated in a reorganization of the vice rectorates, and result in the establishment of a separate vice rectorate for social outreach activities held by the rector himself." The social outreach council was set up and it included representatives from CIDAI, the University Press, the secretary of communication and production, and *ECA*. Jon Sobrino was the interim coordinator. On September 6, 1982, the board established the vice rectorate, and Ellacuría was appointed to the position, in addition to his post as rector.

While social outreach activities were to be rooted in solid teaching and research, these functions seem to be taken for granted in the Ellacuría document, which gives more space to social outreach activities that would be examples of, but not identified with, the social orientation of the university in the wider sense. There is also great emphasis given to supporting a mediation/negotiation process to end the war. But there was still the problem of exiled faculty to be dealt with. What would be the basis for these social outreach activities after the exodus of so many talented personnel as a result of the 1979 coup and repression in 1980 and 1981?

In June Ellacuría wrote to acting rector Axel Soderberg,

> I see the UCA as an oasis . . . doing useful things in carefully preparing some professionals, who we hope will respond professionally and politically even under difficult circumstances, and who will try to advance the process that leads to a solution to end the hell in which the majority of the people in this country lives, a situation aggravated by war, repression, insecurity and the most profound economic crisis.
>
> I see things as rather bleak. It seems to me that in the short run of the next months there will be no solution. The left is not going to defeat the government, nor will the government achieve a victory over the left. As a result, social and economic disaster is going to continue and get worse. Will this worsening bring about a new situation that will require a negotiated political solution? At the present time such a scenario seems difficult to accomplish, because the United States and the military believe, or want to believe, that they can accomplish a definitive military victory relatively soon. It is said that by August–September, people will be convinced that this is not going to be easy or soon. All the other groups, including the Christian Democrats, both inside and outside the country, are pushing for a negotiated agreement despite the difficulty in achieving it and that the possibilities are not very clear. But it would be something. On the other hand, the solution that involves elections will not resolve anything, but it will oblige the government to present a more democratic appearance, and that is something that would be favorable to the UCA.
>
> For all these reasons I would like you all to think about what I should do. If I should come back soon or not, if I should come back for a period of time or definitively. In the case of not coming back, what should I continue to do? What I am doing now gives me plenty of work and I am busy all day; I spend all day on UCA affairs, directly or indirectly. But it is important to consider whether I should continue as rector, if it looks as if my absence is going to last much longer. . . . I think everything depends on the probability of my coming back into the country. Perhaps through the United States ambas-

sador—via Paco [Estrada]—I could make a provisional entry, and later it could be extended. Or perhaps through Bishop Rivera or the nuncio with whom I spoke at great length in San José.[8]

But Ellacuría did not return at that time.

In July 1981 the UCA board decided to form an ad hoc advisory committee of all UCA officials and department heads, and the Jesuit provincial.[9] In addition, they listed persons who could substitute for board members who might become incapacitated in one way or another—an indication of realism about their precarious situation: Jon Sobrino, José María Gondra, Luis Achaerandio, Segundo Montes, Fredy Villalta, Mario Cerna, Crista Benecke, Italo López Vallecillo, Ricardo Stein, and Orlando Menjívar. If Axel Soderberg could not function as acting rector, this post would pass to Ibisate, and then to Gondra, and then to Villalta.

THE ACADEMIC LIFE OF THE UCA

At the end of this crucial first semester of 1981, Ignacio Martín-Baró, the acting academic vice rector, gave a report to the board.[10] It is important to look at this report in detail because it covers internal academic conditions rather comprehensively.

Martín-Baró reminds the board that any evaluation of the semester's work had to keep in mind

> martial law and the curfew imposed on the country since January 11 [which had eliminated must of the evening program], and add to that the current climate of violence and the official state of siege, which has been prolonged without interruption since March 1980. . . .
>
> In general, the climate of insecurity has been constant, especially from January to April. Holding the UCA hostage and the occupation of the campus at the end of January, the rumor campaigns of possible searches, the uncertainty of sporadic confrontations, and bombs exploding right on the university campus—all this has kept the university population in a constant state of alert, more or less noticeable, and unpropitious for intellectual concentration and for teaching and learning.
>
> [Although problems are many,] it is possible that the very gravity of the situation has contributed to generate a spirit of seriousness and responsibility leading to the achievement of essential objectives, and this has helped overcome those difficult moments.

He felt the UCA was thriving on adversity.

Martín-Baró sees the most serious problems as (1) the absence and/or loss of administrators and academics, among them the most valuable and most identified with the UCA; (2) the departure of good students, especially in the upper years of the various majors; (3) the unavoidable cancellation of the preparatory course for admitted students; and (4) the lower admissions requirements for the UCA. The academic vice rectorate (de Sebastián's position) had been vacant for eight months, and the director of the research institute (Ungo) was in exile.

There were 4,859 students enrolled; 1,526 were new students. The overall numbers would have dropped considerably if there had not been so many new students.

> In general, the professors agreed that the new students were academically less prepared, but more motivated and dedicated to work than those of previous years. The lower admission level was attributed both to more lax UCA standards, and to the more deficient academic preparation that the students bring from secondary school each succeeding year. To this one has to add the fact that the student body that arrived at the UCA this year generally comes from lower socio-economic levels (lower-middle sectors from the outskirts of the city, e.g., from Mexicanos, Soyapango, Cuscatancingo, etc.) and they have completed high school studies in centers of poor quality.

Because of the political turmoil and personal security issues, there were more part-time teachers who generally had less commitment to the UCA, but Martín-Baró observes that "there was a positive response by all personnel to the call for extra effort to put up with the difficult economic and social circumstances, that we were confronting." Despite these circumstances 227 courses were taught in 315 sections with an average of over fifteen students per section—large groups at the more basic levels and sometimes fewer than ten in the more advanced courses. He concludes that despite all the problems, "the quality of teaching had not dropped at the UCA," but he does not give any specific data on which to base this optimistic judgment. He does recognize that there are student complaints, ranging from dissatisfaction with the psychology department; to not enough teachers in philosophy, literature, sociology, and political science; furthermore, industrial engineering was without a single full-time teacher.

He draws attention to the thesis requirement as an obstacle to graduation: "Some students have been absorbed into other private universities which are so anxious for students that they are willing to offer all sorts of opportunities for graduation." There were temporal and financial constraints which the students felt they could not tolerate, so they took the line of least resistance, completing all or most of the coursework at the UCA, and then graduating from the another university after throwing together something that passed for a thesis.

Martín-Baró states that there is not much research going on. CIDAI, the documentation center, was channeling what did happen in this area—especially analyses of the current situation. "Certainly the UCA research panorama is grim and desolate, especially if one examines it with a critical eye. Some are purely library projects of minimum significance, and scarcely any time and effort has been expended on them." There was some research in the licentiate theses, and a good number of faculty had helped with the journals and the work of CIDAI. There were improvements in the library, a new Hewlett Packard 3000 computer, and the purchase of statistics software for the social sciences. An outside observer would probably say, however, that given the circumstances, it was amazing that they were able to survive at all, never mind accomplish anything. But the ambitious goals of the 1979 document were on hold.

This grim overview of research and teaching quality identifies a UCA structural problem, one that would grow even more serious in the later 1980s—a fundamental weakness in those areas that were expected to anchor social outreach in the wider sense of social transformation.

1982: Taking Stock

With Ellacuría still in exile, the substitute and permanent board members Soderberg, Estrada, Martín-Baró, Cortina, and Ibisate traveled once again to Costa Rica for meetings from January 9 to 11, 1982. They cited as their objective for the new year "to reinforce the university in its structure, organization, and functioning," and to "try to understand and help others understand what was objectively going on in the country, and to inform those people who are determining factors in the process. "They sought to combine objectivity and university independence. In this way, they would make a contribution toward "'the day after tomorrow' and the political, social and economic reconstruction of the country"—a goal even more relevant in the 1990s with the signing, and halting efforts toward implementation, of the peace agreements.

This would require "a qualitative leap forward within the UCA, once previous plans were completed"—the results of the major planning process of 1976–1981, described in the last chapter. In the next stage, there would be fewer expenditures for building and more to improve what already existed. This new stage would involve "organizing a flexible planning process adapted to the [national] process, letting some personnel go, and strengthening others according to specific cases and needs, and an effort to reinforce research." With so many new universities, they saw the need to keep UCA academic standards high.

There was an interesting note that showed the breadth of the UCA's understanding of its mission. "The function of critical awareness should also include the conduct of groups from the left. It seems that they have committed errors in interpreting the positions taken in some of our publications, . . . In the long run they will be grateful for our objective critical judgment."

When looking at the UCA financial situation, the board concluded that there was need to seek outside funding for the social projects. There was no mention of regular expenses such as salaries, a problem that would become even more acute in the future, but someone did raise the possibility of a third loan from the Inter-American Development Bank—a thought that would have solicited groans from those who had to face the problems of paying back the second IDB loan after the assassination.

With the country in chaos and the rector in exile, it is quite remarkable that board members had the foresight to dedicate so much energy and concern to plans for internal institutional strengthening. For example, they recognized "the need to give considerable follow-up to what the teachers are actually teaching; some department heads do not seem to know very much about their professors." Evaluation of professors seemed limited to student questionnaires. Importance had to be given to "careful faculty selection so as not to mortgage the future of the UCA with teachers who are deficient in academics and vision." They called for "an academic reform" and revision of the curriculum and study plans. And thinking ahead to the future, they decided "to analyze the opportunity to open some master's degree programs which would meet the circumstances of the students and country." Engineering was mentioned specifically, though judging by the strength of the faculty, this would be some time in the distant future.

As mentioned in Martín-Baró's 1981 evaluation, the board recognized that research "had deteriorated notably, owing in part to the departure of many competent academics and the heavy teaching loads and administrative tasks of those who stayed behind." They saw the need for "research that would be directed toward understanding the national reality in order to improve it—eminently practical research rather than pure research or studies of the past."

Ellacuría urged them to visualize what El Salvador would need in the coming months, and to see what they could do "to help whatever government was in power."

The board recognized that "there were certain defects in the current organization of the university and excessive concentration of functions in a few positions," and they decided to take advantage of Miguel Francisco Estrada's business administration thesis to bring the organization up to date. But it did not change substantially, and the concentration of major responsibilities on a few Jesuits would come to haunt the UCA after the assassination.

At this Costa Rica meeting, the board also approved the plan of Isidro Pérez, S.J., for a pastoral center.[11] Right from the beginning there had been a Center for Advanced Religious Culture, which later became the Institute of Theology, which offered individual courses. UCA professors had published articles in theology and on pastoral questions in regular UCA periodicals, and a master's in theology had been offered since 1978.

Pérez mentioned in his report, however, that "Archbishop Oscar A. Romero had requested on various occasions more explicitly religious activities at the UCA so that the Christian inspiration of the university might be made more concrete and fully developed." Pérez suggested the preparation of an overall university pastoral project, which would include:

1. Christian formation: courses, conferences, retreats
2. Spiritual renewal and spiritual direction
3. Different forms of Christian expression: eucharist, sacraments, and prayer
4. Research and distribution of information on religious themes
5. Preparation of pastoral ministers

In a later petition for financial support, Jon Sobrino gave additional details about the nature of the center.[12] "Its ultimate finality is to produce theological thinking which will help pastoral activities in the social context of oppression." It would include:

1. A center for theological reflection
2. An associate's degree (*profesorado*) in religious and moral sciences
3. Theological publications
4. Pastoral attention
5. A university chapel
6. A library specialized in religious themes

This center would be considered a work of the Society of Jesus—not of the UCA as such. "Even though the center is visualized as being in close relationship with the university, the UCA is a separate juridical entity which cannot legally have any religious affiliation. Thus, it would be difficult for the university to run a pastoral center."

The Costa Rica board meeting ended with some discussion of whether Ellacuría should continue as rector if his exile were to be prolonged indefinitely, or whether it was advisable for him to return. The answers were not clear at that point. At the March 1, 1982, board meeting they voted three to two to recommend that Ellacuría return to El Salvador. They planned a third meeting in Costa Rica for April, but Ellacuría had returned by then.

All was not serene. In October 1982 the board took notice of negative comments against the UCA by the minister of defense and rumors of possible removal of Ellacuría's citizenship. Such a step would have forced his resignation as rector because Salvadoran citizenship was a prerequisite.[13] Another attempt to remove Ellacuría's citizenship was voiced in 1986.[14]

But shortly after his return from exile, Ellacuría took out time to praise the American Chamber of Commerce speech by United States Ambassador Deane Hinton, and his "courage in saying things that few dare to proclaim in public, even though many are aware of them."[15] He adds,

> Good, very good was your speech of October 29 in which you expressed with clarity and firmness positions which were very similar to those which the late Archbishop Romero, the church and our university have been repeating in thousands of ways, and for which we have been accused of being demagogues when they were not accusing us of being communists. This means that I am personally in agreement not only with your principal message which referred to the great need to improve the justice system, but also with many concrete accusations you made about assassinations committed in this country over the past three years. . . .
>
> Those who are asking every day for North American military and economic presence have no moral authority to complain when the representative of the United States reminds them of the conditions under which the people and the government of the United States have committed themselves to give this assistance.

RESEARCH FOR SOCIAL OUTREACH

Despite all the obstacles, with competent investigators forced into exile and the need for the remaining staff to analyze rapidly changing events in the country and the region, there were still important efforts toward research.

A brief look at some of the projects will illustrate the point.

In the midst of the country's turmoil, the UCA tried to chip away at the research agenda identified by Román Mayorga in 1976. Projects varied in size and importance. At times external agents commissioned research; at other times they were generated by the UCA. A small cadre of personnel, academically prepared at the graduate level and supplemented by others with less training but high native ability and motivation, made a start toward the realization of the university's research and social outreach goals, as the following examples will illustrate. (The date the project was discussed or approved by the board is included after each item rather than in separate notes.)

Just weeks after he had left the ruling junta, Román Mayorga spoke in Washington with Ignacio Ellacuría about the UCA's participating in a cooperative study with the Colegio de Mexico on Central America (January 28, 1980). Ricardo Navarro proposed that the UCA start a Center for Appropriate Technology that would have the "character of an independent university within the UCA." The board gave permission for a feasibility study but determined that if such a center were established (and it was not) it would come under the jurisdiction of the academic vice rector (May 25, 1980). There was an entire issue of *ECA* dedicated to the topic of appropriate technology in April 1979.

The minutes for the November 17, 1980, board meeting list some of the projects then under way at the UCA; it gives an idea of the university's research agenda scope at that time. Keep in mind all the rest that was going on at the same time in 1980, as recounted earlier:

A linguistic atlas of El Salvador
Popular culture: a study of Salvadoran traditional oral literature
Financial sector strategy
History of philosophy in El Salvador: Nineteenth century
Personal values of groups in El Salvador
Aspiration levels of the middle sectors in El Salvador
Salvadoran agriculture and its social implications
Current problems of the church
How malnutrition, the lack of early stimulation, and other social variables affect the development of children
Pre-Colombian musical instruments
Indigo industrialization

Ten principal investigators are listed; five were Jesuits, and one of the Jesuits (Martín-Baró) was directing two studies. In the September 13, 1982, meeting, Ignacio Martín Baró reported to the board how difficult it was to engage in research with all the teaching obligations, the scarcity of personnel trained in research methodology, and the poor quality of some departments, such as business administration.

In 1983, the University of Wisconsin Land Tenure Center sought out links with the UCA for mutual research projects. This opportunity brought up the touchy issue of accepting funds from US-AID, but the UCA got around it by dealing exclusively with the University of Wisconsin even though funds for the program came from that university's arrangement with the government agency. The project was approved the following month (December 5, 1983).

In 1984, Jon Cortina, S.J., proposed a meteorological station at the UCA. The university took the project under consideration but it never developed. The recently elected Duarte government's planning board (MIP-LAN), through Fidel Chávez Mena, a high official in the Christian Democratic Party, proposed funding a sociological study by Segundo Montes. There was concern about potential political commitments in such a contract, but the possibility was taken under study (November 14, 1984).

A link from the early days of the UCA was picked up again when FUNDASAL, the agency for construction of low-cost housing, which had been started with cooperation of the UCA as *vivienda mínima*, explored research contracts with the university (February 18, 1985).

With the departure of its director, Guillermo Manuel Ungo, to join the 1979 provisional government, the research institute failed to flourish. Therefore, in 1985, Ignacio Ellacuría proposed a new structure with two divisions: one in technological areas of science and engineering, and another that would encompass all the rest. By the assassination, the technological council had begun to review research proposals under the direction of Juan Ricardo Salazar-Simpson, S.J., but the other council never left the drawing board. Once again, the lack of trained personnel made such structures difficult to implement (March 8, 1985).

Axel Soderberg, acting rector during the Ellacuría exile, former engineering dean, and later financial vice rector, launched a major study of electrical power alternatives in which researchers measured rainfall patterns and river current in an effort to identify appropriate technological resources for rural areas (October 18, 1985). This six-year study served as the basis for proposals to provide El Salvador with energy sources that would make the country less dependent on a few facilities. The eight-hour blackouts of 1992 were an indication of the need for such alternate sources of energy.

In 1987, Ignacio Martín-Baró presented a proposal to the board for cooperation with the organization of national universities in Central America (CSUCA) in a study of "the nature of the processes of democratization in Central America" (September 7, 1987). There was concern about which faculty members would have the qualifications to do such studies—a perennial problem for the UCA—and what the financial implications might be.

In 1988, the UCA made an agreement with IBM to buy a mainframe computer at a reduced rate so that the staff and students could produce software for educational purposes and commercial use (November 14, 1988). A combination of unrealistic IBM promises and UCA computer center staff weaknesses turned this project into a several hundred-thousand-dollar mistake that the post-assassination team had to deal with in 1990 and 1991. But engaging in an agreement of that scope indicated that the UCA was thinking both in national terms and about making a significant contribution to technological changes in El Salvador. Such an enterprise would be a major undertaking with risks under the best of circumstances. It is even more remarkable when one considers all the other events occurring in the country at the same time, as indicated earlier in this chapter.

The First Ellacuría Term as Rector

On October 25, 1982, the board elected Ignacio Ellacuría to a second term as rector. Even though he had spent almost half the first term in exile, he helped advance the university's sense of direction and he articulated key dimensions of the mission, such as social outreach. There was much yet to do, and he would serve the UCA seven more years as rector. But his own reflections on his first term are worth noting before we move on to the remaining period.

"I began the rectorate under special circumstances, when after October 15, 1979, it appeared that the country was about to enter a new era during which a capable and progressive government was going to be able to start to bring about many goals of justice and social change which had motivated the UCA ever since its early days." In the 1980s there would be new opportunities for the UCA to realize its "political" mission in the special way the university defined that word—a concern for the needs of the people.

Despite the crisis of 1980, however, "it did not seem legitimate for the UCA to retire from the fierce conflict that was developing; it was necessary to strengthen its university presence in the conflict. Therefore, once we were assured that the academic and organizational sides of the UCA were functioning sufficiently well, we sought to make the conflict rational by looking for and sponsoring solutions which were more just for El

Salvador, regardless of how difficult this would be."

With the closing of the University of El Salvador, there was increased pressure from organizations to set up a refuge inside the UCA. "The situation was delicate, but not without a struggle we managed to maintain an acceptable equilibrium. Up to a certain point we were able to control this presence, reducing as much as possible its negative effects. This situation obliged us and made it possible for us to come into contact with the left, which for the first time in its history got to the point of respecting us for our uniqueness as a university and our type of service on behalf of the country."

"There is always the lingering doubt as to whether we were too involved. Because of the direction and the speed of the process we were a bit idealistic," but basically, he concludes: "We acted with prudence and we did not go outside university boundaries." He looks back at internal reviews of the university and the reorganization that came of it. Referring to his forced exile in November, 1980, he says that "from outside what encouraged me was the 'social outreach' of the UCA, which is what had grown the most in quality."

Looking at the negative side, he feels that he was very busy and that he did not have sufficient contact with personnel and students "because of the need to stay out of the public eye, and the shortage of time taken up with so many tasks. . . . The result is a certain amount of bureaucracy and verticalism, so that the UCA could appear at times to be governed from a higher center which is inaccessible and considerably unknown." He also questions whether his own involvement in the national process is bringing added pressure on the UCA. Ellacuría seems content with his first term, his own performance, and especially that of the UCA.

Structural problems—the poor quality of much teaching and research, and highly centralized responsibility in the hands of a few, especially Jesuits—were recognized early in this first Ellacuría term. But would sufficient steps be taken to remedy this situation? We will return to this question in the next two chapters.

NOTES

1. The budget is calculated from 1979 to 1989 at 2.5 *colones* to the dollar even though one could get more *colones* for the dollar through other sources. From 1990 on, it is calculated at 5 colones to the dollar.
2. AUCA, February 16, 1981.
3. AUCA, March 11–12, 1981.
4. *ECA* 36 (1981), 367–82.
5. For example, *El Mundo*, September 28 and 29, 1992; and also *El Mundo*, March 8, 1993, and *La Prensa Gráfica*, March 15, 1993, when the truth commission

report was published.

6. AUCA, March 28–29, 1981.

7. AUCA, April 27, 1981.

8. Copy in AUCA, June 23, 1981.

9. AUCA, July 13, 1981.

10. AUCA, July 29, 1981.

11. ASJCA. There is a copy of this plan in the archives in a folder entitled "Plan de Pastoral," but there is no date on it.

12. ASJCA, August 20, 1982.

13. AUCA, October 18, 1982.

14. Doggett, 29.

15. RUCA, Ignacio Ellacuría to Deanne [sic] Hinton, November 8, 1982.

10 CONSOLIDATION: 1982–1984

The previous two chapters accompanied Ignacio Ellacuría and the UCA during his first turbulent term as rector, which included almost a year and a half in exile. We saw a UCA growing internally by careful reflection on its goals and the development of concrete steps to bring these goals to fruition. Despite attacks and scarce resources, financial uncertainty, and the loss of key personnel for security reasons, the UCA managed to play a major role in the country's rapidly changing events. But the crisis-management atmosphere left important structural areas less attended to.

In this chapter and the next, we will examine consolidation of the model and ongoing dialogue on the nature of the university, internal developments, and UCA analyses of key issues facing the country, especially through the pages of *ECA*. We will discuss the UCA's relationship with succeeding governments, especially the Duarte presidency and what government critics would call "reforms with repression," and then the tortuous ups and downs of peace negotiations, until so much changed with the UCA assassination, the peace talks, and a new era for El Salvador after the agreements of 1992.

Ongoing Dialogue on the Nature of the UCA

The October 1, 1982, board meeting reopened discussion on the juridical nature of the UCA sparked by questions from Jesuit superiors. A new working document, "Sobre la Fundación de la Universidad 'José Simeón Cañas,'" refers back to the texts prepared for Rome after the tenth anniversary articles by Ellacuría and Mayorga, which had raised eyebrows, especially with their statements about UCA independence from ecclesiastical authorities. Some citations from this document help illustrate the issues:

From all that has been said, one can conclude that the UCA was founded by a group of Jesuits, helped by a group of laypeople, at the request of the hierarchy and by petition from certain social forces in El Salvador. The university that was actually founded, however, could not be made subject to the will of the hierarchy, nor even the Society of Jesus. It had to be administered in accordance with the objective experiences of what was the university and political reality at that moment, and in conformity with requirements of the Salvadoran Assembly, and regulations which the founders freely accepted, and are obliged to fulfill, not only for legal but also for ethical reasons.

. . . This law and these regulations contain two essential characteristics: university autonomy in teaching, funding, and administration, and its nature as a "corporación de utilidad pública" [special kind of public not-for-profit institution]. Both characteristics prevent it from being a Catholic university either in law or in reality, because such an institution would be defined as church property and responsible to authorities who could impose their will on teaching, funding, and administration. The board of directors, as the principal and definitive party responsible for all university activity, is obliged to protect the good of the university, and to be in compliance with the law by implementing the regulations and statutes which govern it.

This real and legal character of the UCA does not preclude the university's Christian inspiration nor excellent relations with the hierarchy of both the church and the Society of Jesus. The UCA is not a university that has gradually become more secularized or independent; it is rather a private university which has tried to function in keeping with a Christian spirit, which takes form in what the reality of the university and the nation require.[1]

This document seems to suggest that the UCA had no choice but to obey the 1965 private school law, but one should recall that UCA staff members had a major role in formulating the law in the first place.[2]

On February 13, 1983, Paolo Dezza, then the personal delegate chosen by Pope John Paul II to run the Jesuit order and the original proponent of the "one university/several campuses" UCA model, wrote Ignacio Ellacuría to urge greater cooperation with the Salvadoran bishops.[3]

It is certain that the expressed will of the Holy See, the bishops, and the Society of Jesus with respect to the university was to give life to a university *officially* Catholic, and therefore canonically erected. Circumstances have brought us to the conclusion that the university has not been canonically erected, and is not, therefore, *officially* Catholic, but this does not prevent it from being, and it should be, de facto, as is the case in other countries where universities of the Society of Jesus or entrusted to the order cannot be officially Catholic, but which are de facto Catholic.

The very statutes of the Universidad JSC [José Simeón Cañas] were composed in such a way that the board of directors would remain in the hands of the Society of Jesus, and that the priests who direct it have received from the Society the mission of running a de facto Catholic university without violating the laws of the nation.

The Society of Jesus, by its very nature and because of particular links that unite it to the Holy See, wants faithful implementation of this mission entrusted to the priests assigned to the university. The Society is ready to help, if difficulties present themselves, so as to resolve them in the best way possible, always trying to safeguard this de facto Catholic character of the university.

Therefore, dear Father Ellacuría, I am confident that with your cooperation and that of the other Jesuits who work in the university, we can overcome difficulties that impede it from fulfilling the great and beautiful mission it has undertaken for the true welfare of all El Salvador.

Dezza ends the letter with friendly words and best wishes to all for the difficult task they have "in the middle of so many conflicts."

Ellacuría traveled to Rome and reported back to the board on February 18, 1983: "There were strong criticisms against the UCA in the Vatican and, as a result, in the Jesuit curia."[4] The nuncio in El Salvador had sent an eighteen-page document to Rome in which he alleged that "the UCA had deviated from its foundational purpose in the positions it was taking, but especially in its independence from the hierarchy." The bishops wanted to form their own university because they saw coming to an agreement with the UCA as an impossibility. Consequently, the Vatican put pressure on Paolo Dezza to insist that the UCA function as a Catholic university in terms satisfactory to the local bishops. The nuncio had visited Dezza in Rome to urge dialogue by all sides, and he petitioned the Sacred Congregation for Catholic Education and the Jesuit curia "to remove from the UCA some rather radical Jesuits."

Ellacuría had spent three hours in discussion with Dezza in Rome and three days more with his staff. He reported that

the thesis of P. Dezza is that the UCA should be oriented as a Catholic university in what it teaches and does, and in indirect dependence on the Jesuit superiors. As a consequence, he sustains the opinion that even though we do not depend directly on the bishops of El Salvador, but rather, directly on the Pope through the Jesuit chain of command, we should seek to achieve dialogue and good relations with them, but avoiding inopportune interference. I explained to him in what sense this might be accomplished, and the objective difficulties, both of a legal and real nature, which would prevent the UCA from functioning as a work completely run by the Society of Jesus. There was understanding and acceptance of the position presented. There was no pressure to change any Jesuits, but he asked that we not insist in public on UCA autonomy, for example, by saying that we do not answer to anyone. He recommended dialogue with the bishops.

These discussions alleviated some tensions for a while, but the issues would again bubble to the surface.

A year later, on February 20, 1984, Ignacio Martín-Baró reported to the board on his attendance at the meeting of Jesuit university rectors in Mexico City, where he substituted for Ellacuría. The group was exploring the formation of an association comparable to the Association of Jesuit Colleges and Universities (AJCU) in the United States. He said that "in general, the participants fled from any discussion of touchy issues. For example, someone mentioned the irrationality of the Universidad Ibero-Americana of Mexico proliferating new [campuses] at the precise moment when the Mexican Jesuit province was studying whether it could administer the two universities they already had."

When the subject changed to Christian inspiration of the universities,

in general the predominant idea was that university identity should come from the Jesuit community and its priestly work. I mentioned the necessity of university identity having an effect on each person at the institution [and adopting] . . . the preferential option for the poor, and that this should not be something accidental nor just an accessory to the specifically university task. Judging by the questions this observation stirred up, the presentation was either not understood or not accepted. There was little response to nor admiration for the publications of the Salvadoran UCA, and the social outreach programs of the UCA in Nicaragua got the same reaction. The discussion was made up of positions that were somewhat spiritualistic . . . and which boiled down to a general affirmation of the importance of the Society's university apostolate.

Meetings like this one did not encourage the UCA Jesuits to try to strengthen links with other Jesuit universities in Latin America. They were on different wavelengths, and for this reason, it is no surprise that the university was encountering confusion and opposition in some Roman quarters, though not generally with Jesuit superiors, who were more appreciative of the uniqueness of the UCA.

At the July 1, 1985, board meeting, Ellacuría tells the UCA board that he was "too busy" to go to the Rome meeting of Jesuit university presidents.[5] He mentions sensitivity to possibly giving the impression the UCA is a Jesuit university in the more technical sense of the term, and that it might put in jeopardy the autonomy which he is always trying to defend.

THE CHRISTIAN INSPIRATION OF THE UCA REVISITED

At the same time as discussion of the nature of the UCA, Jon Sobrino gave a talk in Spain on June 4, 1987, at the University of Deusto's 100th anniversary. He caused quite a stir with the speech because the listeners were expecting something more along the lines of joyous celebration rather than serious questioning of the traditional model of the Catholic university.[6]

Sobrino develops the theme of the university inspired by a Christian vision as one which "places itself at the service of the Kingdom of God with an option for the poor" (152). He criticizes so-called Christian universities that "have not questioned society's unjust structures, nor used their social weight to denounce them, nor have they made central to their work the research and planning of new society models. . . . In Latin America, Christian universities have not distinguished themselves by their opposition to dictatorships and national security regimes roundly condemned later by everyone, once they have fallen" (154). Instead these universities have sometimes aligned themselves with "ecclesiastical forces that are conservative or even reactionary, distancing themselves from the church's more open and Gospel forces" (154).

Sobrino stresses the importance of the kingdom of God and its realization through a serious commitment to God's people as they suffer. He describes the prime problem as poverty, which he defines as: "real nearness to death, to the slow death imposed by unjust and oppressive economic structures . . . and to sudden and violent death, when repression or the wars spawned by poverty produce numerous victims" (159).

Far from being the creation that God wishes, ours "is a world of death, of sin" (159). The Christian's vocation is to create a world consistent with the Gospel. This means an option for the poor that comes first; then the Christian university can engage in teaching, research, and social involvement because it has made this previous commitment, which will give flavor to all else it does.

The university inspired by a Christian vision must prepare its students theologically and spiritually so that their Christian commitment has deep roots. It must emphasize theological reflection on social reality so as to offer Gospel-based criteria for whether social structures are just and are contributing to fostering the kingdom of God.

Once again we see a consistent message from the UCA on the nature of its role, an important and a dangerous one. Back at home, trouble mounted; death threats arose against the UCA Jesuits.

Jesuits at the UCA have mentioned over the past decade that every time a new papal nuncio arrives in the country, he suggests that the UCA apply for designation as a pontifical university. But the UCA has clung to its autonomy. Controversy in the United States during 1993 and 1994 on the formulation of specific legislation to implement the apostolic constitution on the Catholic university, "*Ex Corde Ecclesiae*" (reviewed in chapter 2), gives more weight to the arguments for considerable autonomy, especially if the regulations give more authority to the local bishops to determine the "fidelity" of a "Catholic" university.

The autonomy issue was never definitively resolved before the assassination, and it would come up again in the post-Ellacuría period.

SOCIAL OUTREACH: NEW CREATIVITY

Ignacio Ellacuría was the main source of inspiration for most UCA structures for the transmission of the university's work to the general public and to decision makers—its social outreach programs. For example, under his direction the resources of the original documentation center were expanded until CIDAI became the best source of material on El Salvador.

He felt that elections gave little insight into the desires of the Salvadoran population. So he developed with Ignacio Martín-Baró the idea of the Instituto Universitario de Opinión Pública (IUDOP) to gather public opinion on crucial issues facing the nation—election polls and reactions to economic measures and to the various civil war "solutions." For example, in a report on three surveys, entitled "Social Polarization in El Salvador," Matín-Baró concludes that "the data seem to indicate that a large sector of the Salvadoran population does not identify psychologically with any armed contestants in the conflict, and that they prefer a political solution."[7]

With no forum in which participants might feel safe enough to discuss their views on national problems, Ellacuría began the Cátedra Universitaria Realidad Nacional (University Forum on the State of the Nation) in 1984.

Violations of human rights seemed to have no limits in El Salvador. With the assistance of Segundo Montes and Ford Foundation funding, the UCA established the Human Rights Center (IDHUCA) for research and information in this important area. Montes and his colleagues dedicated the early years of the institute to study and analyze problems of refugees and displaced persons.

Ignacio Ellacuría and Jon Sobrino founded the journal *Revista Latinoamericana de Teología* so that liberation theologians might make their writings available to the church. It featured articles from major writers such as the Boff brothers, Brazilian priests; and Jesuits José Gonzalez Faus, Rafael de Sivatte, and Javier Alegre.

These social outreach programs were of central importance, but it is necessary to look also at another important facet of the university, its curriculum.

THE CURRICULUM

First of all, one should remember that the Salvadoran higher educational system differs from the usual United States division of a more general liberal arts or broadly based foundation, with some concentration on a major or specialization, and then more specialized programs in graduate school. For example, a student contemplating a career as a lawyer in El Salvador would begin a law program upon graduation from high school right at the start of university studies—usually a six-year program with a thesis for the licentiate degree.

Scarce resources and the urgency of preparing professionals in a developing nation are the usual justification for such an approach, and there is much to be said for it. But it results in a narrow view of education that mainly emphasizes professional specialization and little exposure to social studies, philosophy, history, and literature. Some say these subjects are covered adequately at the secondary school level. If and when offered, these subjects are usually covered in survey courses. Even elective courses tend to be within the area of specialization.

Sample programs from the 1990 UCA catalog in psychology, law, business administration, and electrical engineering illustrate this point.[8]

Psychology (58)

1st Year	2nd Year	3rd Year
Intro. to psychology I, II	Psych. currents I, II	Learning theory
History of culture I, II	Statistics I, II	Psychometrics I, II
Linguistics I, II	Evolutional psych. I, II	Psych. dynamics I, II
Philosophy I, II	Psychobiology	Adv. educ. psych.
Mathematics	Psychophysiology	Experimental psychology
Scientific visions	Sociology	Child psychopathology
	Research methods	Experimental analysis
	Evaluation methods I	in education
	Seminar: Interview	
	techniques	

4th Year	5th Year	6th Year
Social psychology I, II	Therapeutic counseling	Thesis
Evaluation methods II	II	
Adult psychopathology	Clinical practica I, II	
Psychological work I, II	Professional orientation	
School practica I, II	Professional ethics	
Therapeutic counseling I	Family counseling	
Elective	Group social psychology	
	Elective (2)	

Law (88)

1st Year	2nd Year	3rd Year
Intro. to economics I, II	Statistics I	Civil law process I, II
Sociology I	State theory I, II	Constitutional law I, II
Roman law I, II	Civil law I, II	Civil law III, IV
Intro. to study of law I, II	Criminal law I, II	Criminal law III
Law research techniques	General process theory	Criminal law process I, II
Elective (2)	Juridical logic	Sociology of law
	& methods	
	Public finance	

4th Year	5th Year	6th Year: thesis
Commercial law I, II	Finance law	Labor process law
Administrative law I, II	International private	Agrarian law
Labor law I, II	law	Legal ethics
Civil law V	Human rights	Contemporary law
Political philosophy	International public	problems
Philosophy of law	law II	
International public law I	Notary law	
	Tax law	

Business Administration (71)

1st Year
Mathematics I, II
Accounting I, II
Intro. to economics I, II
Sociology I, II

2nd Year
Mathematics III
Finance Mathematics
Cost accounting I, II
Microeconomics I, II
Administration theory
History of economics I, II
Philosophy I, II

3rd Year
Operations research I
Quantitative methods I, II
Intro. to marketing
Macroeconomics I, II
Psychology I
Business Law I
Management
Adminstration—sales
& publicity
Business psychology
Fiscal labor law

4th year
Industrial Relations I, II
Market research
Production adminstration
I, II
Financial adminstration,
I, II
Intro. to information
systems
Process control
Marketing administration
Research seminar

5th year
Financial admin. III
Project formulation & evaluation I, II
Business policy I, II
Economic development I, II
Ethics
Thesis

Electrical Engineering (94)

1st Year
Mathematics I, II
Chemistry I, II
Advanced algebra
Engineering graphics I, II
Physics I

2nd Year
Mathematics III, IV
Physics II, III
Metals
Material resistance
Statics
Dynamics
Numerical analysis
& digital computation
Humanities elective I

3rd Year
Fluid mechanics I, II
Analogical computation
Thermodynamics I
Linear electrical systems
I, II
Statistics I
Laboratories & measure-
ment
Electronics I
Conversion—electrical
energy I
Engineering economics
Social elective I

4th year	5th year
Electromagnetic theory	Electronics IV
Hydraulic machinery	Industrial installations
Electronics II, III	Technical elective (2)
Conversion—electrical	Humanities elective IV
energy II	Social elective IV
Anal. potential systems	Thesis
I, II	
Automatic controls I, II	
Electrical communication	
Social elective II	
Humanities elective II	

Now that the peace accords have given the UCA some breathing space in the mid-1990s, the university community intends to take a closer look at the coherence of the curriculum and the effectiveness of teaching methods. The UCA major documents developed over the past two decades will offer clear criteria by which to complete this evaluation.

THE NATIONAL REALITY IN *Estudios Centroamericanos*

Although it is important to remember that *ECA* was not the only medium through which the UCA accomplished its social outreach goals, it is a convenient way to show how the university tackled national problems as they came up in the final years of the Ellacuría era; for example, several elections, the Duarte presidency, United States policy, and negotiations for peace. These topics will be treated chronologically rather than separately, because they frequently intersected with each other. Such a presentation will help give a better sense of the sweep of events and the UCA's reaction to them. When possible, they will be presented in the words of the UCA authors.[9]

1983

The military-civilian junta scheduled elections in 1983 to choose a constitutive assembly to write a new constitution for the republic. *ECA* wondered about this step, taken

> without even minimal consolidation of the reforms attempted so far, and in a climate of generalized terror due to systematic repression of all dissidents, and in the middle of a civil war which has worsened

the economic crisis to intolerable limits, and contributed to the dismantling of society.

It is difficult to understand the democratic value of elections from which the largest and most significant opposition forces will be excluded. And it is obvious to everyone that even if the FDR or another party . . . should decide to enter the electoral contest and should win the elections, it is unlikely that the military government would ever turn over to them constitutive power. It did not do so years ago, and it seems even less likely in 1983. . . .[10]

After the elections, *ECA* carried a more detailed analysis of the process in ten critical theses; two of them summarize the main point of the editorial.[11]

Thesis 1 states that "the Constitutive Assembly electoral process was not a proposal that arose out of real current needs of the country, nor from the Salvadoran people. It was initially a United States imposition, and not an effort to discover the national will but instead to advance the United States project to end the Salvadoran conflict.

"Then, confronted with the FDR-FMLN political offer of negotiations, the United States proposed and then imposed the elections option." Agreeing to negotiations might have given a modicum of power or leverage to the left; elections, however, would insure that the left would not be in the official picture. The United States and the Christian Democrats thought the latter would win the elections since that party supported reforms and free elections. But the people rejected this proposition and elected the right—just to have a change. In Salvadoran elections of the 1980s, the incumbents were consistently thrown out of office and their major opponents elected, not necessarily as a vote of confidence in the winner but rather as a turning to other alternatives made available in these limited elections that had systematically excluded the real opposition.

Thesis 6 states that "the event of March 28 gave victory to the coalition of the right, and the will of the winners was not respected by the powers that had programmed the electoral project." In other words, the United States expected the Christian Democrats to triumph. But when the party of the right, ARENA, won the elections, the United States would not tolerate its leader, Roberto D'Aubuisson, as the new president of El Salvador because of his sordid death-squad reputation. Congress might not continue to send military aid once the Christian Democratic facade was removed to reveal the real character of the government run by the military.

The Reagan government sent special envoy General Vernon Walters for consultation with the Salvadoran government. As a result, a substitute president was found, Alvaro Magaña, and vice presidencies were established in the assembly from the three participating parties: ARENA, the Christian Democrats, and the old military party, the PCN. Roberto D'Aubuisson became president of the assembly that would write the constitution.

Then *ECA* turned to United States policy and its impact on El Salvador.[12] "In effect United States assistance is an essential part of the war of which terrorism is a strategic element; also the killing of civilians, the illegal actions of the security forces, and everything perpetrated with the advice or permission of the United States."

This is an important and devastating point. The Americans should have known what was going on as a result of their assistance. There was a steady stream of information, especially from the rural communities, the church, and other international sources. Yet the embassy chose to look the other way, putting the best face possible on what they were told by their Salvadoran allies. Critics felt that this was the same kind of "blindness" shown in Vietnam, when United States military forces accepted casualty figures, supposedly not noticing that these included women and children and many civilians swept up in a misguided notion that everyone is the enemy. The 1993 Report of the United Nations Commission on the Truth raised the same issues, as did the United States government documents released in 1993 and 1994.

> From this point of view there is not only absolute and abusive violation of El Salvador's sovereignty, but also the United States has converted itself into the principal party responsible for the tragedy inflicted on El Salvador. That we Salvadorans tolerate this trampling on our sovereignty is already a national disgrace. But this conduct should make the people in the United States feel ashamed, too, because they have been deceived. They contribute indirectly to its happening. The Reagan administration is wreaking terrible evil on the Salvadoran people and it is fooling the American people.
>
> The [U.S.] president gave an address to the Congress about the situation in this area and he grossly distorted the data. . . .
>
> [In El Salvador United States government officials] have nothing to say about crimes that have now reached 40,000 dead; they hide the nature of these assassinations with false appearances. They tolerate the failure to prosecute and convict obvious assassins even of United States citizens so as to avoid exposing their closest collaborators in the war, and they certify significant improvements in respect

for human rights just so they can advance the political and military plan they have mapped out, and which they will implement whether or not there is improvement in human rights.

How prophetic were these words in the light of the March 1993 Report of the UN Commission on the Truth, and the other released United States documents.

The article seems to presume that a United States military invasion of Nicaragua and El Salvador was inevitable.[13] "In any case, it is high time that the United States learn to treat its neighbors with dignity. Given their own development and history, the United States should be more sympathetic to political and economic models which might not be those of their own country, but these models should not be considered as necessarily in opposition to them."

Another section of this article urges the FMLN to tone down the rhetoric, to be flexible, and to reexamine the dogmatic tenets of its position. *ECA* reminds the FMLN that it does not represent all of El Salvador, and that it should be careful of the potential use the USSR might want to make of them to get back at the United States. There were valid security concerns of the United States which should be recognized and respected. The article calls on the FMLN to be "open to honest cooperation with other social forces in the country which are not less patriotic, nor less interested in searching for justice and liberty of the majority of the people."

1984

ECA began 1984 with an editorial entitled "Agony of a People: The Urgency for Solutions," a telling description of the state of the country with an overview of the war, the economy, violations of human rights, and the stubbornness of the United States in refusing to allow negotiations.[14]

> Not only are thousands of individual Salvadorans dying; it is an entire people that is dying, and its leaders are the ones who are digging the graves where their lives, their projects and their possibilities will be buried . . . without much hope of resurrection.
>
> War will continue to be the determining element in national reality and public life. And now the elections promise only to legitimate the war and in no way to legitimate a process of dialogue and negotiation, which the parties do not dare to propose in the election campaigns. They actually deny any connection with such a way out. When they talk about peace they do not hide their views on the necessity of war, the military solution.

Some observers were convinced that without United States military aid, the FMLN would probably have defeated the Salvadoran military by that time.

> Even the nationalistic jingoists are not willing to have their military-age sons offering service to the armed struggle; this is left to the country people, to those who live in slums, to those who do not understand why they, and only they, have to fight against their brothers and shed their blood in a war that is not theirs. . . .
>
> The United States is one determining element as to what has happened, is happening, and will happen in El Salvador. . . .
>
> Just comparing the difference between the fundamental position of the Contadora group—a pluralist and moderate group of Latin Americans—and the fundamental position of the Kissinger Report serves as an argument to demonstrate how wearisome it is to find real solutions for Latin Americans projected by the United States.

There is almost a tone of pleading that the United States government stop blocking the negotiations. Later, when the peace agreements were finally signed, the then assistant secretary of state, Bernard Aronson, stated on the CBS national television network on January 31, 1992, that the United States had been in favor of negotiations all along!

In 1984, José Napoleón Duarte, the Christian Democratic candidate, defeated Roberto D'Aubuisson for the presidency. Once again, in a series of articles, *ECA* called the election a substitute for negotiations between the government and the FDR-FMLN.[15]

The June editorial, "Does El Salvador Have a Solution with President Duarte?" answers its own question with "no."[16] Duarte, *ECA* says, blames the international communist conspiracy for the war, he presents no concrete economic plans, and he used a belligerent tone in his inaugural address. "It seems that his party was more preoccupied with gaining power during the two previous years than in studying strategies and tactics, so that when they gained power they could resolve national problems." In the inaugural, his diagnosis of the problem was similar to that of Reagan: "with the help of Marxist governments such as Nicaragua, Cuba, and the Soviet Union, an army has been trained and armed which has invaded our country and its actions are directed from outside." Duarte believed in the military solution, and in his pre-inaugural trip to the United States, he requested more military assistance.

"As for the possibility of immediate negotiations as a means to end the war, it was not even mentioned." As for the economic challenge, "he does not offer concrete solutions, just general directives."

On June 5, 1984, Ignacio Ellacuría began to keep a schematic diary on his meetings with political figures to discuss problems in El Salvador.[17] In the first year, for example, he left an outline of forty-eight meetings: eleven with Duarte government officials, including Fidel Chávez Mena (Planning), José Morales Erlich (vice president), Abraham Rodríguez (Christian Democratic party founder and close friend of President Duarte), and Colonel López Nuila; seven with United States Ambassador Thomas Pickering and his staff; eleven with the FMLN-FDR leadership; seven with Archbishop Arturo Rivera Damas and five with other ambassadors; and two with the leadership of the Partido Conciliación Nacional (PCN). He summarized the main points they made, and occasionally he indicated that the conclusions were not his own. There is a high level of specific details in many of these conversations, which shows the trust these persons put in Ellacuría, and the respect he showed each of them.[18]

Ellacuría saw these interventions as an essential part of the UCA social outreach and his role as rector, and what he meant by acting "in a university fashion." He tried to state his understanding of the various viewpoints objectively, and not try to manipulate one group or another, even though, at times, his sympathies were clear.

The topics covered the inevitable devaluation of Salvadoran currency, Duarte government efforts to exercise control over the armed forces, secret meetings in preparation for and supplementary to the public dialogue between the government and the FMLN, the reaction of each party after negotiations, rival assessments of the relative military strengths of the Salvadoran army and the FMLN, and the role of the United States in the conflict.

It would take the UCA story too far afield to recount the fascinating details of these meetings; we leave that to another study that recounts the history of this period. The abovementioned details are sufficient to indicate the quality of Ellacuría's sources for the analyses that appeared in *ECA* editorials and articles throughout the 1980s.

This chapter has explained in some detail consolidation of the model and has given examples of how the UCA confronted a series of issues in the light of its basic vision. The next chapter recounts the final five years of the Ellacuría rectorate, which ended with the assassination.

NOTES

1. "Sobre La Fundación de la Universidad 'José Simeón Cañas,'" September 30, 1982, 7. Copy in AUCA, October 1, 1982.

2. Conversations with Luis Achaerandio, December 1990.

3. ASJCA file on UCA.

4. AUCA, February 18, 1983.

5. AUCA, July 1, 1985.

6. Jon Sobrino, "Inspiración Cristiana en la Universidad," *ECA* 42 (1987), 695–705. Also in Jon Sobrino, et al. *Companions of Jesus: The Jesuit Martyrs of El Salvador*, trans. Sally Hanlon (New York: Orbis, 1990), 152–73.

7. *ECA* 38 (1983), 129–42.

8. *Catálogo General: Universidad Centroamericana, José Simeón Cañas, San Salvador, El Salvador, 1990.* Page numbers indicated in the text.

9. For a more detailed presentation of contemporary events in the country, especially Ellacuría's relationship with them, see chapters 10 and 11 of Whitfield, 291 ff.

10. *ECA* 36 (1981), 835–44.

11. *ECA* 37 (1982), 233–58.

12. *ECA* 38 (1983), 391–407.

13. The author recalls conversations with the UCA Jesuits in 1983 in which they were quite convinced of the possibility of an invasion by the United States, especially in Nicaragua. Although it seemed unlikely to the author at the time, one only had to recall the history of many invasions of Central America by United States troops earlier in the present century, and the invasions of Grenada and Panama, to begin to understand why this scenario was not just a figment of their imaginations.

14. *ECA* 39 (1984), 1–12.

15. *ECA* 39 (1984).

16. *ECA* 39 (1984), 378.

17. There are a good number of details from this diary in Whitfield's analysis of contemporary events. The diary is in the archives of the "Centro Monseñor Romero."

18. The author recalls a conversation with Ellacuría in mid-1985 in which he indicated his respect for Thomas Pickering as a serious diplomat with whom one could talk, even though they agreed to disagree on most analyses of the Salvadoran situation. The author is particularly grateful to Rosario de Guevara, long-time secretary of the UCA rectors, who has transcribed the text from Father Ellacuría's handwritten diaries—not an easy task.

11 CHALLENGES AND ATTACKS: 1985–1989

This chapter covers the second half of the Ellacuría rectorate and gives more examples of how the UCA model took form in the middle of the civil war. In the correspondence and in the pages of *Estudios Centroamericanos (ECA)*, we will see the interplay of external and internal events, and eventually the assassination and its aftermath.

1985

The first *ECA* editorial of the new year listed six major tasks that were spelled out in detail: (1) humanization of the war; (2) improvement in respect for human rights; (3) reactivation of the economy; (4) special attention for displaced persons; (5) recuperation of national sovereignty; and (6) serious advances in national dialogue.[1]

An *ECA* editorial in April on the 1985 local elections presented the same type of criticism of the process as in the previous year's presidential elections.[2]

Then the May–June edition evaluated the Duarte presidency's first year in an editorial entitled, ominously "Grave Concern after the First Year of Duarte."[3]

"In judging the first year of the Christian Democrats one would fall into great error if one were to think that it is the president who in a real sense is directing the country's political path, and that therefore it is to him that one should attribute ultimate responsibility." According to the editorial, those who direct El Salvador are the Reagan administration and the military, and in the economy it is the wealthy.

"The Duarte government has been more efficacious in taking care of North American business than Salvadoran interests. When these two coincide all goes well; when they do not, things stand still or get worse." Duarte had announced at the United Nations General Assembly in New York his intention to engage in dialogue with the rebels. The armed forces and the oligarchy put pressure on him after the UN speech to go more slowly, and after the initial meeting at La Palma, he followed their advice. As a result, the next meeting at Ayagualo failed. Duarte continued to speak of the FMLN as subversives and terrorists, a practice not conducive to dialogue.

The editorial points out some positive accomplishments: Duarte's army had not been defeated, he won a popular majority in the elections, there was less hostility from the right, and there were some slight improvements in human rights. "All of this, taken as a whole, does not appear slight, and even though it is partly a result of the process launched by the 1982 elections, a process controlled by the United States, it has been consolidating more and more during these twelve months of government by the Christian Democrats."

On the negative side is the hopeless war itself, failure in the peace talks, and still many violations of human rights. "The basic needs of the majority of the people are every day more difficult to satisfy with the dramatic increase in prices and the loss of jobs, all of which is due principally to a war economy which destroys a lot more than it constructs."

In summary, "a year is not sufficient time to do anything of importance. Therefore it cannot be said that Duarte has failed. But if he does not consolidate the good he has accomplished, and above all, if he does not eliminate the evil that continues in existence, the Duarte presidency will be a failure."

Ignacio Martín-Baró also wrote an article on the first Duarte year which is much more critical, a grim assessment of what to expect for the future. He says Duarte's words have little content and that as of yet there are few particulars in his programs.[4]

Toward the end of 1985, Archbishop Arturo Rivera Damas and Ignacio Ellacuría played major roles in arranging the release of President Duarte's kidnapped daughter and an exchange of government and insurgent prisoners.[5] Ellacuría sent a memorandum to the university community describing the event.[6]

To determine who was responsible for the kidnappings, he and Archbishop Rivera traveled to El Zapotal in Chalatenango and to Aguacayo in the Guazapa battle zone to interview FMLN leaders. "We tried to identify their expectations and we communicated the proposals of the government. . . .

"[Our efforts] were motivated by humanitarian, political, and ethical considerations. Involved in all this were the lives of 150 persons for whose benefit we labored; also involved was the political process of the country, because a poor solution to this immediate problem could have brought us back to 1980–1981."

Ellacuría cited the larger context for UCA involvement. "On this occasion the UCA received many petitions to help in a humanization of the conflict and promotion of dialogue," to which Ellacuría had agreed. The people in Guazapa mentioned specifically "indiscriminate bombing, killing, people disappearing or being captured for political reasons."

It was well known that the participation of Father Ellacuría in the liberation of President Duarte's daughter was quite decisive. It is interesting to note that Duarte never thanked Ellacuría for his intervention.[7]

1986

The UCA was not content simply to criticize the efforts of the government; the whole January–February 1986 issue of *ECA* contained suggestions on solutions to the country's problems: The economics department covered a gamut of options, Lara Velado discussed juridical issues, Montes explained the problem of displaced persons and their needs, and Ellacuría and Sobrino reviewed the role of the church in the conflict. It is important to emphasize the importance of this positive approach in light of the UCA self-definition as a critical and creative conscience for the nation. The UCA saw that it was insufficient just to denounce violations.

In March, *ECA* carried a lengthy article by a principal FMLN leader, Joaquín Villalobos. In April, United States policy was again the main topic, with a reexamination of the same basic issues. And then in May–June, Duarte's second year as president came under review.[8]

"When all is said and done, the militaristic option imposed by the United States constitutes the great trap into which the Duarte government has fallen, and if he does not make a prompt and radical change of the rudder, it will carry him to the end of his constitutional mandate without being able to achieve what he himself has fixed as his highest priority: peace."

The editorial says that Duarte has made some progress in lessening "state terrorism," and some mass media comments get through the web of censorship and control by the right, but there are increased detentions, threats against labor groups not in sympathy with the government, attacks on human rights groups, and indiscriminate bombing of civilian villages in remote rural areas; the military continue to act arbitrarily, and the courts do nothing to change this. "It is almost ridiculous if not offensive to hear Duarte talk about the 'impressive social accomplishments' of the current government, when we see the concrete situation in which the Salvadoran people find themselves." But, the editorial adds, "it would be unjust, if not erroneous, to blame the Duarte government as the cause of all the evils which overburden the Salvadoran people, just as it would be unjust or erroneous to exonerate them from their part in the responsibility, or justify their ineffectiveness by the magnitude of the problems they confront."

"The fundamental problem of El Salvador, as with all the peoples of Central America and of all Latin America, is not one of formal democracy, but of social democracy, that is, of development and justice." In summary, "After two years, Duarte's government has not been able to advance toward a solution of crucial problems of the country: the basic conditions of misery and injustice at the root of the conflict have deteriorated. He has not been able to establish a regime of freedom and sufficient guarantees so that the Salvadorans who are not in agreement with the established power can participate effectively in public life." The editorial paints a grim picture.

But *ECA* kept insisting on the importance of dialogue. The August–September issue was dedicated to this question, with articles by a wide spectrum of authors: Hugo Carrillo, head of the PCN, the old party of the military; Jose Antonio Morales Erlich, a major leader of the Christian Democrats, former mayor of San Salvador, and a vice presidential candidate in 1977; four labor groups; San Salvador Archbishop Arturo Rivera Damas; leaders of basic Christian communities; and the following UCA departments and units: economics, business administration, law, IDHUCA (the Human Rights Institute), psychology-education, the CRT (Center for Theological Reflection), and Ignacio Ellacuría.

There was also an opinion poll report by Martín-Baró, a lengthy chronology of dialogue efforts for the previous years, and a bibliography of *ECA* contributions that included twenty-nine editorials, twenty-five articles, and the complete texts of sixty-seven separate documents from 1979 to 1986—an amazing tour de force, and typical of *ECA* issue after issue right up to the assassination in 1989.

Meanwhile, social psychologist Ignacio Martín-Baró was breaking ground in his own area of expertise. He challenged fellow psychologists in Latin America to shake off foreign models and to look at the day-to-day reality of people for relevant analytical categories.[9] "Latin American psychology, save for a few exceptions, has not only remained servilely dependent when it needed to lay out problems and seek solutions, but has stayed on the sidelines of the great movements and away from the distress of people in Latin America" (319). He praises his psychology colleagues, however, for their contribution to Paolo Freire's theories on "consciousness raising" and the educational methodologies that make students become the driving force of their own learning, and take active responsibility for their own and the community's progress. He reviews a series of paradigms he considered faulty because of their "scientific mimicry," "inadequate epistemology" or "false dilemmas" (321–6). He tells his fellow psychologists "we have to re-think our theoretical and practical techniques, but re-think them from the standpoint of the lives of our own people; from their sufferings, their aspirations, and their struggles" (327).

To create a liberation psychology is "not simply a theoretical task; first and fundamentally it is a practical task. . . . It must break out of its own enslavement. . . . Psychology must be liberated" (326). It needs "a new horizon, a new epistemology, and a new praxis" (327).

As for horizon, "at the present time the most important problem faced by the vast majority of Latin Americans is their situation of oppressive misery, their marginalized dependency that is forcing upon them an inhuman existence and snatching away their ability to define their own lives" (328). Psychology must help in "overcoming their existential fatalism (which some people modestly or ideologically prefer to call 'external control' or 'learned helplessness' as if it were a purely intra-individual problem). For the Salvadoran people it entails direct confrontation with structural forces that oppress them, deprive them of control over their own existence, and force them to learn submission and expect nothing from life" (328).

As for epistemology, we must "relativize that knowledge and critically revise it from the perspective of the popular majorities. Only then will the theories and models show validity or deficiency, utility or the lack thereof, their universality or their provincialism. Only then will the techniques we have learned display liberating potential or the seeds of subjugation" (329).

The new praxis would mean deep involvement in everyday problems of the people, as was Ignacio Martín-Baró's own experience during his weekend pastoral work in the rural town of Jayaque.

He calls for completion of several tasks: recovery of historical memory ("reconstruction of some models of identification that, instead of chaining and caging the people, open up horizons for them, toward their liberation and fulfillment"), de-ideologizing everyday experience ("to retrieve the original experience of groups and persons and return it to them as objective data. People can then use the data to formalize a consciousness of their own reality, and by doing so, verify the validity of acquired knowledge"), and using people's virtues (331).

In September, there were increased attacks against Ellacuría: a television program on the dialogue between the government and the guerrilla that raised much comment. The storm raged because some Ellacuría comments in Washington were poorly reported by the UPI. When he criticized the dependence of El Salvador's foreign policy on the United States (which was just a parenthesis on a televised interview) the Salvadoran foreign minister made public statements along with a whole group of personages such as the infamous ex-Major D'Aubuisson. They spoke of removing his citizenship and throwing him out of the country.

But Ellacuría continued to involve himself and the UCA in national problems. He wrote to Congressman J. Joseph Moakley in September to thank him for efforts on behalf of Salvadoran refugees in the United States, and he urged him to continue to insist on political asylum for these people who would be killed if they were returned to El Salvador.[10] Congressman Moakley and his staff were to play a major role in bringing to justice the assassins of the UCA Jesuits and the two women.

In the October 1986 edition, *ECA* kept up the pressure with a twenty-two-page article by Ellacuría, with the assistance of CIDAI, on "Endogenous Factors in the Central American Conflict: Economic Crisis and Social Disequilibriums," a piece that was full of charts, statistics, and analyses. In that same issue was an article by the famous social scientist Edelberto Torres Rivas on the bigger picture of Central America.

Opposition to and threats against the UCA continued.

The December issue featured a joint statement by the UCA and the University of El Salvador on the occasion of the October 10, 1986, earthquake that devastated the capital, as if there were not sufficient problems to handle. The two universities committed themselves to improve the quality of their common work on behalf of El Salvador—a far cry from the early days of hostility at the 1965 founding of the UCA. Both universities called for:

1. A negotiated settlement of the war
2. Genuine democratic processes
3. Recovery of national sovereignty
4. Adjustment of the national budget according to national priorities, not those of the war
5. Improvement of education
6. Repair of earthquake damage

In this same December issue, Francisco Javier Ibisate of the UCA board described an economic model for national reconstruction. There was no letup in getting into print the research and analytical efforts of the UCA staff and faculty, despite so many limitations on resources.

1987

Many of the same themes fill the pages of *ECA* in 1987, and they center on the war and its structural causes, which was one subject of an open letter to the Central American presidents gathered in a summit meeting.[11] It points out the great damage done to the region by making it a battleground for the East-West conflict, which had so little to do with the region's problems. The letter adds nuances to some parts of the Arias plan for peace and the initiative from Costa Rican president and Nobelist Oscar Arias, by showing that the armed conflicts in various countries had significant differences. It cites the contra war in Nicaragua, which is based largely outside the country, and the FMLN struggle in El Salvador, which was seen as a more grass roots movement.

That same edition reported another IUDOP poll and offered an article on political participation by Segundo Montes—a steady flow of social outreach production.

In July, the provincial reported frequent attacks in the newspaper against the UCA, specifically against Father Ellacuría.[12] There were also phone calls with death threats for all the priests. The provincial told the superior general that this dangerous situation suggested a possible move of the UCA II Jesuits to the house then occupied by the UCA I community, and eventually to a residence next to the Romero Pastoral Center inside the campus. These moves were actually made, but, as later events proved, security was not improved significantly.

The September edition returned to the topic of negotiations and dedicated a whole issue to the latest meeting, Esquipulas II. The editorial praises the Central Americanization of the dialogue and resistance to outside interference. Again, it adds nuances to the differences in each nation's conflict, and cautions against broad amnesty measures that might allow criminals to stay in business. It recognizes the need to firm up justice systems and to punish the perpetrators of crimes against the people.

An editorial in the October *ECA* returns to Esquipulas II and points out that "the principal difficulty in arriving at a regional peace accord is the United States, though not so much the congress as the administration. . . . The Reagan administration is to blame for the belligerency of the contras [in Nicaragua], the violation of Honduran sovereignty by the contra presence in its territory, and El Salvador looking for a military solution in the middle of a counterinsurgency project in a low intensity war."[13] The November–December *ECA* was totally dedicated to a Cátedra Universitaria Realidad Nacional (University Forum on the State of the Nation) on Esquipulas II, with comments from many labor groups, Archbishop Rivera, and all political leaders except ARENA.

1988

But hopes for the Esquipulas II peace proposals were dashed, and the *ECA* editorial for January–February laments a "missed opportunity."

The FMLN felt optimistic about the potential balance of forces, which they thought to be in their favor during 1988. But the *ECA* editorial cautions them that "without putting aside the analyses of the situation which the FMLN has made, not even the theoretical possibilities of their new presentations of their situation can guarantee an objective basis for the conclusion that in 1988 the correlation of forces will change substantially, nor that the process will accelerate."[14]

The editorial also notes some positive changes in ARENA rhetoric—more moderation and realism.

In a conference of psychologists outside San Francisco in early 1988, Ignacio Martín-Baró shared with colleagues some research about the effects of war on the Salvadoran population—another example of scholarship applied to a concrete problem facing the people.[15] Woven throughout the article are references to international scholars, an indication of the breadth and the depth of Martín-Baró's scholarship. He analyzes the "dirty war" and "psychological warfare" intended to bring struggles against oppression to an end—torture, bombing, disappearances, and the more subtle isolation of people by military blockades, preventing even relief workers and food supplies from getting to people in the insurgent-occupied areas. Martín-Baró explains the effects of the war—"particular traumatic acts as well as those generated by a permanent atmosphere of harassment and insecurity." Such was the atmosphere that grew even more serious in El Salvador.

After the ARENA victory in the March 20, 1988, elections, the *UCA* March–April editorial sounds a more positive note than on previous occasions. While the elections should not be seen as a cure-all, the editorial sees as significant the participation of over a million people. It shows some faith in elections on the part of many—and all this despite FMLN pressure not to participate. Many did not vote, however, because of obstacles at those polling places where the opposition was expected to be stronger—a phenomenon also experienced in the March and April 1994 elections. One should not identify, the editorial says, democratic process and elections.

"In the chain of elections that of 1988 has significance. . . . It has raised the political awareness of a large part of the population, and brought into the open important disagreement with the direction the process is taking, especially as managed by the executive, the legislature and the dominant power."[16]

The editorial calls the FMLN to task on its attitude toward the elections: "The absolute rejection of elections, especially by violent and even threatening tactics, as the FMLN has done, is a mistake, and it brings along

with it more evils than good for the country, and for the FMLN image before the national population, and before international public opinion." But,
on the other hand, the editorial says, "it is without foundation and decep-
tive to conclude that the election has shown enthusiasm of the majority of
the people for electoral processes in themselves and even less so as the principal means to get out of the crisis. . . . Election results signify neither popular
rejection of the counterinsurgency project nor its approval."

The editorial feels that "the Christian Democrat loss of the popular
vote to ARENA could be explained as a form of punishment for their record,
for the party as a whole, and as a vote of support for a new direction."

Moving away from the two major contenders, the editorial suggests
that "there are sufficient indications that the proposal of a project from new
political parties, as could be the case with the Democratic Convergence [a
coalition of center and center left parties] could in time attract a good number
of votes, and that would give a certain weight to that coalition." On a pessimistic note, however, "the many escapades connected with the election,
such as the electoral campaigns themselves, show that the parties have not
yet overcome the temptation of fraud." A final note is the optimistic statement that "there is no proof that the results were transmitted from the United
States Embassy."

This same *ECA* issue carried an article by Segundo Montes on the
elections and more IUDOP polling results.

Attacks against the UCA continued. Colonel Sigifredo Ochoa Pérez
claimed the UCA was training revolutionary fighters on campus. Ellacuría
wrote a letter to the editor of a newspaper that had reported the charges.[17]
He terms Ochoa's declaration "completely false and irresponsible. In case
the colonel has proof to the contrary I ask him to make it public and to communicate it to the UCA authorities in order to rescue them from their igno-
rance. The UCA does not prepare people for war. . . . It prepares for peace
and for justice that would come as a result. . . . We accept any type of criticism but not condemnations and calumny which do more harm to those who
utter them than to those who are their object."

In October, Bishop Marco René Revelo, president of the Salvadoran
Episcopal Conference, accused the UCA of being a "facade" for the FMLN,
a charge that was generally seen as very serious and dangerous since it was
made by a bishop.

A few days later a bomb exploded at the Jesuit university in Guatemala, the Rafael Landívar, just days before UCA theologian Jon Sobrino was
scheduled to speak there.

One sign of cooperation was the UCA's proposals for the Debate

Nacional, sponsored at the time by the Archdiocese of San Salvador.[18] "No fewer than ten different departments with more than eighty professors were working on it conscientiously for various weeks. They also used studies that had been developed in the past. Their final document was discussed for two sessions of two hours each and approved by the University Higher Education Council. . . . We are sending the document with an appendix which gives bibliographical references that support and expand on the proposals made in the text."

1989

This fatal year began with an optimistic editorial in *ECA* that commends the new atmosphere in the country and the willingness of both ARENA and the FMLN to be more flexible. But attacks against the UCA began to increase.

In the March *ECA* editorial, Ellacuría summarized in a strong indictment so much of what had happened, and so much of what was to come:[19]

> With the October 1979 coup the process that had begun with the previous coup of 1961 was broken. That had been a pseudodemocratic process that permitted a fraudulent sequence of four military presidents, and it ended with General Romero. Since that time what we have had until the final months of the Duarte presidency has been confrontation between the FMLN revolutionary project and the counterrevolutionary project of the United States and its Salvadoran allies. This confrontation has now entered a new phase. . . . It is the FMLN and ARENA that have most transformed their tactics and even their conceptualization of the situation, and consequently, their strategies.

> United States policy in the region has failed even with the total collaboration of Duarte and the armed forces. Despite more than 60,000 deaths, despite four billion dollars worth of aid, despite increasing the size of the military five times since 1981, the FMLN has not been defeated militarily. It has gotten even stronger, and the economy is so much worse that extreme poverty has deepened and expanded—a principal cause of the war. The political design to open up a center between two extremes has become inoperative, and has finally been rejected by the Salvadoran electors themselves. . . .

> There was an attempt at an intermediate project, that of structural democratic reforms, but it was impossible for this model to suc-

ceed, fundamentally because it was artificial, brought from outside the process, and with the primary purpose of finishing off the revolutionaries and making the conservatives seem more moderate. As a result they did not achieve a middle ground nor could they count on their own efforts to bring it to completion.

Even though Ellacuría saw some hopes for moderation on all sides, pressure began to mount against the church. In an article under a pseudonym, Jon Sobrino gives a scary recital of specific events that suggest a stepping up of violence, and which eventually culminated during the insurrection and provoked further repression, including the assassination of the Jesuits. The armed forces publicly assailed the legal assistance office of the Archdiocese of San Salvador (Tutela Legal); the ARENA party bulletin accused Segundo Montes of defending what they called "FMLN terrorism." Colonel Orlando Zepeda, later identified by Congressman J. Joseph Moakley as an intellectual author of the UCA assassination, was quoted in *El Diario de Hoy*, the newspaper of the far right, as saying the UCA was training the urban guerrilla. Vice President Merino attacked Father Daniel Sánchez, a diocesan priest in a poor San Salvador slum parish where Jesuits had a community and did pastoral work, as a supposed FMLN urban commando. More bombs were placed in the UCA. "But the most recent accusations are directly against the church and are so scurrilous that they constitute real provocation."[20]

Sobrino concludes: "To bring truth into the light is always something that those in darkness fear. Whether this is done with the pastoral simplicity of Archbishop Chávez [1938 to 1977], or the bravery of Archbishop Romero, or the depth of Archbishop Rivera, the truth is not tolerated; the forces of darkness see it as a threat."

Ignacio Martín-Baró, the academic vice rector, wrote the author about these attacks but he made clear that the UCA would not change course. "As you know, once again they have put various bombs in the University Press. The damage was quite extensive, but most is reparable. Thank God, no one was hurt. But with bombs they will never stop us; instead, these bombs motivate us to intensify our service on behalf of the majority of our people."[21]

Alfredo Cristiani, the ARENA presidential victor, took office in June, and the *ECA* editorial was skeptical but reserved judgment until after the first 100 days.[22] The journal kept its promise and dedicated the whole August–September issue to the first 100 days of ARENA with an editorial, seven articles, and relevant documents. The editorial expressed "cautious optimism" and pointed out several areas in which the Cristiani moderate ARENA wing had begun to consolidate power, especially in the president's offer of dialogue with the FMLN.[23] Nevertheless, there was fear of the impact of ARENA economic measures, and continued violations of human rights by the security forces.

"There has certainly not been any appreciable, open struggle between the two factions, nor any imposition of the D'Aubuisson line." Vice President Merino, a D'Aubuisson ally, was eased out as minister of the interior, a key position with authority over police affairs in the country. The cabinet is "rather homogeneous without great or strong personalities, a group which resonates more with the style and wishes of Cristiani rather than other ARENA factions and chieftains."

Despite provocations, "the Cristiani government and the high command have not fallen into the trap, and despite pressures they have maintained a moderate approach. They have not gotten to the point of retiring their dialogue proposal, which would not have been difficult to postpone, given the gravity of the crisis [the murder of Rodríguez Porth, the minister of the presidency and a Cristiani ally]."

On the economy: "The big question is who is going to bear the costs and who will be the primary benefactors, the poorest or the richest." On a pessimistic note, the editorial mentions that "in the first 100 days of Cristiani there were already clear symptoms of economic Darwinism and only timid government steps to protect the beleaguered consumer from the law of the jungle, regulated today only by market mechanisms."

The editorial, Ellacuría's last for *ECA,* concludes: "This is the big question which catches our attention after these 100 days: Will Cristiani represent once again firmer and consolidated moderation and economic and political modernization of the right, which will work toward peace through negotiation and achieve a wide national consensus on the economy, or will he represent just a facade of new processes of oligarchization in which the war and repression will get harder, and poverty will increase, opening up even more the gap between the rich and the poor?"

Just ten days before his assassination, Ellacuría accepted the Alfonso Comín prize in Barcelona on behalf of the UCA and gave what turned out to be his final words on the nature of the UCA.[24]

> Much remains to be done. Only in a utopian and hope-filled spirit can one believe and have enough energy to join with all the poor and oppressed of the world to overturn history, to subvert it and send it in another direction. But this huge task . . . seems to indicate that this civilization is gravely ill and that in order to prevent it from ending in destruction, we must try to change it from within. Helping to stimu-

late and nourish a collective consciousness of the need for substantial change is, in itself, a great first step.

There remains a further fundamental step to take—that of creating economic, political, and cultural models that may enable a civilization of work to replace a civilization of capital. . . . Criticism and tearing apart are not enough; constructive criticism that offers a real alternative is also necessary. . . .

Our primary aim as a university is to contribute to this historic struggle. We believe we ought to play an active role in this struggle, and therefore we want to do so . . . as a university, but that does not mean we seek to do so primarily by training professionals. That is important, albeit ambiguous, but the country needs rapid economic development. Rather, we also intend to make our contribution by creating a body of thought, models, and proposals which by starting with negotiations, . . . can then attempt to bring this active negotiation into society's immediate awareness. That in turn will make it possible to move towards both immediate and structural solutions, in all realms of the national reality— political and religious, economic and technological, artistic and cultural. That task requires as much academic excellence as possible, for otherwise we would have little to contribute as intellectuals to such complex problems. It also demands a great deal of honesty, which not only relates to our calling to objectivity, but demands that we strive for the greatest independence and freedom. Finally it requires much courage in a country where the weapons of death are fired too often and in very threatening proximity. (173–44)

Striking once again a theme he had developed so often in the past, Ellacuría reminds his listeners that

it is often said that the university should be impartial. We do not agree. The university should strive to be free and objective, but objectivity and freedom may demand taking sides. We are freely on the side of the popular majority because they are unjustly oppressed and because the truth of the situation lies within them. . . . Our university as a university has an acknowledged preferential option for the poor, and it learns from them in their reality and in their many expressions which . . . draw matters together and point the way ahead. We take this stand with them in order to be able to find the truth of what is happening and the truth that all of us must be seeking and building together. . . .

Our university is of Christian inspiration when it places itself in this preferential option for the poor. . . .

From within this option, in theological terms, we favor placing faith in tension with justice. It is an indispensable, although perhaps not sufficient, condition of faith, that it be confronted with justice; the justice being sought is profoundly enlightened in turn by faith lived through the preferential option for the poor. We do not regard faith and justice as two separate realities brought together by an effort of our will, but as two interrelated realities that form or should form a single structural totality, as liberation theology and other related theological movements have said repeatedly. . . .

This is how our university works in a revolutionary fashion for the cause of liberation in El Salvador. In a university manner we want to accompany a process led primarily by the masses, although perhaps in a partial and imperfect way, and we wish to do so out of a Christian inspiration which regards a preferential option for the historic cause of the poor as obligatory. (175)

This is an important statement because it summarizes what the UCA had tried to do, and the tasks that lay ahead.

But did the UCA have the resources to do it? When the war ended, would the UCA have a critical mass of well-trained Jesuits and lay colleagues to help create solutions for El Salvador's profound problems and new opportunities?

Ignacio Ellacuría's final piece of correspondence was a fax sent to Colonel Juan Antonio Martínez Varela, minister of the presidency, in which he tentatively accepted President Alfredo Cristiani's invitation to form part of the commission to investigate the bombing of the FENASTRAS labor union building.[25] In it we see Ellacuría's willingness to help, but also his insistence on examining the local scene before a final commitment.

I am overwhelmed by this terrorist attack, and I am willing to work for the promotion of human rights. I am convinced that President Cristiani rejects this type of attack and that with good will he is proposing this mechanism to deal with the case. I would like to support any reasonable effort so that the dialogue/negotiations might proceed in the most effective way possible. Precisely for this reason, in the first place, I want to thank the president for his invitation, and secondly,

I want to make my decision in a responsible way to benefit the peace and democratization of the country.

As soon as I return to the country I will bring myself up to date on what is happening in the various sectors so as to be able to appreciate what might be the best way in which I can contribute.

It is interesting to add that Ellacuría tried to contact President Cristiani using private phone numbers from the time he arrived on Monday night, November 13, 1989, and again on Tuesday and Wednesday. His calls were not returned.[26] He was murdered on Thursday morning by the Salvadoran military, while President Cristiani was at military headquarters, less than a mile away from the UCA.

EPILOGUE

Even before the sad procession filed down from the Romero Chapel to the university auditorium for the funeral of the UCA martyrs, a hastily organized board of directors had started to put the UCA back together again. The surviving members, Francisco Javier Ibisate and Axel Soderberg, supplemented by deans and other administrators, elected three new members of the board: Jon Sobrino, the theologian; René Alberto Zelaya, academic vice rector for basic programs; and Miguel Francisco Estrada, former vice provincial and the soon-to-be rector of the Jesuit high school, Externado de San José. The new board selected Father Estrada as UCA rector for a three-year term.

Jon Sobrino had left El Salvador shortly before the assassination to give talks at Santa Clara University in California and in Thailand, where he received news of the massacre. The other member of the Jesuit community, Rodolfo Cardenal, had felt uneasy after the residence search on Monday evening, November 13, 1989, and left for the Del Carmen parish in Santa Tecla to spend a few days. Thus Sobrino and Cardenal escaped the terrible fate of their community, and lived to help usher in a new day—Sobrino continuing his writing, teaching, and speaking, and Cardenal assuming the editorship of *ECA* and later the role of vice rector for social outreach.

The Central American Jesuits and Pieter Hans Kolvenbach, the Jesuit superior general, invited a number of Jesuits to supplement the survivors and carry on the work of the UCA: Michael Czerny (Canada), Director of IDHUCA (the Human Rights Institute) and vice rector for social outreach; Fernando Azuela (Mexico), Romero Pastoral Center staff; Rafael de Sivatte (Spain), theology professor and seminary rector; J. Dean Brackley (New York), theology and philosophy professor; Juan Antonio Estrada

(Spain), theology professor; and the author as academic vice rector for research, graduate programs, and development. UCA faculty members assumed the chairmanships of the philosophy, psychology, and sociology/political science departments. Juan Lecuona took over directorship of the Fe y Alegría programs for Joaquín López y López, who had been killed with the UCA staff.

Some feared that the soul had been ripped out of the UCA when such prominent members met their deaths, and it is not difficult to understand this reaction because each martyr had held several university positions—as vice rectors, department chairs, institute directors, teachers, and board members, to mention only their main tasks. Ellacuría, Martín-Baró, and Montes had been the public presence of the UCA in the mass media, especially Ellacuría. And now they were dead.

The successors turned their attention to rebuilding the university from the inside, rather than trying to take the place of their predecessors in the public forum, though the UCA continued the tradition of speaking out publicly on relevant national issues and crises. But there were positions to fill, students to teach, books to write, and the major university publications to keep on the newsstands. In post-assassination El Salvador there was even greater need for the university's voice in the outside communities.

A very serious shadow lurked over the UCA as well: the $10 million Inter-American Development Bank (IDB) debt incurred a decade earlier. The loan had helped the university build up infrastructure, strengthen faculty, and get into a position to meet the needs of the people. But Salvadoran currency had experienced a more than 100 percent devaluation since the loan was made, and now the ten-year grace period had expired. The debt had to be paid—over half a million dollars a year, when the whole university budget did not reach $5 million. The UCA was either on the way to bankruptcy or would have to go hat in hand to often hostile governments for help with payments.

Father Estrada, the new rector, mentioned the university plight to a group of United States Jesuit college and university presidents when they visited the UCA as a sign of solidarity just months after the massacre. When they asked how they could help, Estrada suggested they look for ways that the United States funds plowed into the country for war might be changed to more positive goals like helping pay the UCA debt. The presidents took on the challenge and commissioned the Association of Jesuit Colleges and Universities (AJCU) president, Paul S. Tipton, S.J., to assume the task. Thanks to Father Tipton's extensive labors late in 1990, the United States Congress approved the designation of $10,000,000 of El Salvador's economic aid to be used over two years to pay the UCA debt. The Salvadoran government, which had already planned to spend the money on other programs, asked the UCA to make a new arrangement: the Salvadoran government would pick up the UCA debt as its own, freeing the university from this burden, if the government could use the congressional funds for already planned social and economic programs. The UCA agreed and the debt disappeared.

After the debt issue was solved, Father J. Donald Monan, then president of Boston College, took a very active role in helping strengthen UCA financial stability by hosting its fund raising activities and spearheading specific events such as a 1993 testimonial dinner in honor of Congressman J. Joseph Moakley, who had headed the special task force appointed by the Speaker of the House of Representatives to investigate the Jesuit killing. Proceeds from the dinner funded a chair and a scholarship endowment in Congressman Moakley's name at the UCA, and President Clinton attended the event as a sign of his respect for Moakley and the Jesuits.

Internal disagreements began to crop up within the first year after the assassination. Some felt the UCA was taking a lower profile, becoming "developmentalist" *(desarrollista)* instead of staying faithful to its liberationist role. These disputes threatened to accomplish what the Salvadoran armed forces had not been able to; namely, to split the UCA. But the university weathered the storm and turned its efforts toward one of its longstanding goals—helping to bring about a negotiated solution to the civil war, and more importantly, to attack the root causes of the war in an unjust society.

Rodolfo Cardenal and the editorial staff of *ECA* hammered away at the need for peace with justice; Michael Czerny expanded the role of IDHUCA, the Human Rights Institute, and played an important role in preparatory sessions for the peace process; and Miguel Francisco Estrada encouraged initiatives to start the radio station, a video program, planning for a school of public health, and raising funds in Europe for UCA projects. The Institute for Social and Economic Research was begun, planning started for a similar institute in education, and new support was given to study of the problems of women under the direction of Zoila González de Innocenti. UCA faculty members gained scholarships for graduate studies in the United States (Fulbright-LASPAU) and in Europe. A university academic, financial, and facilities master plan began to take shape, and the UCA started to receive more technical resources and other support from sources all over the world.

How successfully has the UCA risen from the ashes of the assassination debacle? We will leave that question to future historians because it is too early to say, and those of us who have played even a small role in this task are too close to the experience to evaluate it with objectivity.

At the martyrs' funeral, the provincial stated that "they have killed our brothers, but they have not killed either the UCA or the Society of Jesus in El Salvador." A major objective of the Salvadoran military on November 16, 1989, was thwarted.

The signing of the peace agreements on January 16, 1992, in Mexico was accelerated by the UCA assassination, and the ups and downs of implementation of the agreements have opened up new challenges for the UCA, perhaps more along the lines of *"anunciar"* (announce) than the *"denunciar"* (denounce) that necessarily dominated so much of the past. It will not be easy for the UCA to adjust. As Hannah Stewart-Gambino says, "It is easier to build a consensus in opposition to a regime having an underlying ideology that not only assaults the humanity of its citizens, but also attacks any individual or institution (including the church) that questions the legitimacy of the state's authority. In a democracy in which competition is phrased in terms of the best means to achieve such goals as economic growth or justice, clergy will find it more difficult to find their prophetic voice without at least appearing to endorse one political program over another."[27]

The Salvadoran government's foot dragging on implementation of the peace agreements and the recommendations of the UN Ad Hoc and Truth Commissions have given much material for *ECA* editorials and articles.[28] And the struggle goes on, now that the country faces five more years of ARENA government with the election in 1994 of Armando Calderón Sol as president to succeed Alfredo Cristiani.

It is now time to turn to an evaluation of the main elements in the UCA model, its strengths and weaknesses, and its significance beyond its own campus.

NOTES

1. *ECA* 40 (1985), 1–16.
2. *ECA* 40 (1985), 205–14. In this issue there is also an article by Segundo Montes along the same lines.
3. *ECA* 40 (1985), 325–44.
4. Ignacio Martín-Baró, "La Oferta Política de Duarte," *ECA* 40 (1985), 345–56.
5. Whitfield, 297 ff.
6. RUCA, "Participation del Rector en los canjes de prisioneros, secuestrados y lisiados," October 29, 1985.
7. Conversation with Miguel Francisco Estrada, December 1994.
8. *ECA* 41 (1986), 375–87.
9. "Towards a Liberation Psychology," trans. Adrianne Aron, in Hassett and Lacey, 319–32. Page numbers of citations are in the test. See also Ignacio Martín Baró, *Writings for a Liberation Theology*, eds. Adrianne Aron and Shawn Corne (Cambridge, MA: Harvard University Press, 1994).

10. RUCA, Ignacio Ellacuría to J. Joseph Moakley, September 4, 1986.

11. *ECA* 42 (1987), 277–81.

12. ASJCA–P87/29, Valentin Menéndez to Peter Hans Kolvenbach, September 13, 1987.

13. *ECA* 42 (1987), 665.

14. *ECA* 43 (1988), 5.

15. "From Dirty War to Psychological War: The Case of El Salvador," trans. Adrianne Aron, in Hassett and Lacey, 306–16. Page references are in the text.

16. *ECA* 43 (1988), 164–70.

17. RUCA, Ignacio Ellacuría to Dr. Waldo Chávez Velasco, July 5, 1988.

18. RUCA, Ignacio Ellacuría to Archbishop Arturo Rivera Damas, July 21, 1988. For more details on the National Debate see Whitfield, 317 ff.

19. Ignacio Ellacuría, *ECA* 44 (1989), 167–71.

20. Jon Sobrino (H.D), "Ataques a la iglesia," *ECA* 44 (1989), 361–64.

21. Correspondence with the author, August 10, 1989.

22. For a detailed analysis of the relationship between Ellacuría and Cristiani, see Whitfield, 335 ff.

23. *ECA* 44 (1989), 632–45.

24. "The Challenge of the Poor Majority," in Hassett and Lacey, 171–6. Page references are in the text.

25. RUCA, Ignacio Ellacuría to Colonel Juan Antonio Martínez Varela, November 9, 1989.

26. Interview with Miguel Francisco Estrada, August, 1992.

27. Edward L. Cleary and Hannah Stewart-Gambino, eds., *Conflict and Competition: The Latin American Church in a Changing Environment* (Boulder: Lynne Reinner, 1992), 9–10.

28. For a full explanation of the peace accords see Terry Lynn Karl, "El Salvador's Negotiated Revolution," *Foreign Affairs* 71 (1992), 147–64. The Spanish edition of the Truth Commission Report is in the March 1993 edition of *ECA*.

12 WHAT DOES IT ALL MEAN?

This book began with a grisly assassination and the question, "Why did it happen?" The basic answer is that the Jesuits were murdered because of the kind of university they sponsored: an institution that strove for academic excellence with a faith vision and a commitment to help create a just society for El Salvador. We have taken this story from the university's founding years up to the assassination aftermath, and have tried both to suggest answers to the questions raised in the introduction and also to say something about the role of any university in the developing world.

Now it is time to review the strengths and weaknesses of the model, to examine what has worked and what has still to be done, and then to stimulate discussion on the significance of the model for other universities. First, the strengths.

STRENGTHS OF THE MODEL
A Clear University Vision

The UCA switched from the developmentalist rhetoric of the 1965 inauguration day speeches to a ringing call for a university to stimulate social change when it accepted the first loan from the Inter-American Development Bank (IDB) in 1970. The university took for itself the task of serving as creative and critical conscience for the nation and reservoir of solutions for its major social, technical, and ethical problems. University colleagues honed this vision over the years so that it gained the coherence and a breadth we saw in Ellacuría's tenth anniversary article in *ECA*, "Is a Different Kind of University Possible?" and in the 1979 document "Las Funciones Fundamentales de la Universidad y su Operativización."[1]

The university's horizon was the Salvadoran people—a focus outside itself, immersed in the national reality of an unjust society. The university's "word" was to be effective: based on academic programs, motivated by

Christian inspiration, and having taken concrete form in issues facing the nation such as land reform, education, economic justice, and an end to the causes of civil war.

The UCA determined not to stand on the sidelines, sending occasional good wishes to those who struggled; the UCA put itself at the side of the poor and attempted to be their voice until the day they could speak for themselves. It took sides, but in the way on which Ignacio Ellacuría constantly insisted—in a university fashion *(universitariamente)*.

In taking these stands, the UCA contrasted with the University of El Salvador, which committed itself more fully to political opposition in what Ellacuría considered subordination of scholarship and learning to a particular political solution. This is not to suggest that the UCA stayed at the level of general principles. Through its public declarations and publications, the university took stands on specific issues. Although in general agreement with solutions of the left and the center left, the UCA tried not to identify itself with any party, movement, or social force.

ECA editorials incurred the wrath of both the left and the oligarchy when they endorsed the 1976 land reform proposals of the Molina government. UCA criticism then sparked even greater attacks from the oligarchy and the government after President Molina backtracked on his commitment to these changes.

The UCA Higher Education Council encouraged tentative steps of a 1979 reformist civilian/military political solution, and supplied government ministers to help the project succeed, but the university did not jeopardize its freedom to analyze because it did not identify itself with this "solution" uncritically.

After the debacle of the 1979 coup, the UCA looked hopefully to the FDR-FMLN political/military solution, but soon after the 1981 FMLN "final offensive," the UCA began a long campaign to urge all parties to the conference table and a negotiated solution, a goal achieved only after the UCA leaders already lay in their graves. UCA scholars looked skeptically at the Duarte and ARENA "solutions," viewed critically the plans of the opposition, pointed out problems and encouraged positive points, but did not resort to polemics in favor of or against positions.

The UCA vision also contrasted with the plethora of private universities of questionable academic quality that ignored the national reality and granted professional degrees to clients willing to pay the fees.

The UCA planned for the future, built a university campus with appropriate facilities, and insisted on academic standards within the range of limited resources. The university refused merely to prepare students professionally without a social vision, because that would perpetuate the oppressive structures that held the majority in subjugation and injustice. The UCA provided the best professional education available in the country, not just for the betterment of individual students, but to prepare committed professionals the country so desperately needed for integral development and real structural change.

The proponents of this university model were not naive; they realized the consequences of their commitment, and they were willing to pay the price, both on a day-to-day basis and in the ultimate sacrifice of their lives. They saw themselves in a class struggle but they did not foment class struggle; they recognized the national reality as they found it: a country with a privileged minority enjoying affluence at the expense of the vast majority. The UCA saw the aims of the affluent and those of the poor as diametrically opposed, and it took a stand at the side of the majority.

Taking a stand, it felt, did not require the sacrifice of academic freedom, nor adoption of a party line to which all faculty, staff, and students should conform. But with resources so limited, research would be done in those areas considered most urgent for the country. Pure research or academic programs for their own sake would take a back seat to studies in economics, engineering, communication, philosophy, and theological reflection.

Structural transformation of society was the objective of university activity, and for this reason the primary emphasis at the UCA, as we have seen, was social outreach—*proyección social*—in the widest sense of the term. Its publications, forums, research projects, and other public statements were signs of this commitment. Research and teaching were to provide the underpinnings.

This vision was clear and present to the university community and to the public at large because it was repeated, reaffirmed, and reinforced in so much that the university did: its publications, the announcements of research results or opinion polls, and the public addresses at home and abroad by its leaders, especially Ignacio Ellacuría, Luis de Sebastián, Román Mayorga, Ignacio Martín-Baró, Segundo Montes, and Jon Sobrino.

The UCA had a specific vision: to be a creative and critical conscience for the nation, and to dedicate its faith-inspired academic resources toward the emergence of a just society. It strove to have all the pieces fit together integrally, so that one activity would not contradict another, and so that the ultimate beneficiaries of its efforts would be the Salvadoran people as a whole, not just privileged students educated there. The UCA had a vision.

Effective Teamwork and Community Spirit

The founding team, especially Luis Achaerandio, Florentino Idoate, José

María Gondra, and Joaquín López y López, gathered the initial resources, put up the buildings, hired the staff, and established basic programs in business and engineering. Provincial superiors with foresight like Achaerandio identified promising young Jesuits such as Ignacio Ellacuría, Jon Sobrino, Amando López, Jon Cortina, Ricardo Falla, Luis de Sebastián, César Jerez, Xabier Gorostiaga, and Juan Hernández Pico, and sent them to graduate studies. When they returned, they helped transform the Society of Jesus itself and its institutions such as the UCA so that they had a new focus on the poor. The efforts of these change agents received mostly encouragement from the superiors in Rome such as Pedro Arrupe and Peter Hans Kolvenbach, and later provincial superiors such as Miguel Francisco Estrada and César Jerez, who in turn sent others to studies, including Ignacio Martín Baró, Segundo Montes, Nicolás Mariscal, and Rodolfo Cardenal.

Some of these Jesuits worked together; all of them were friends. Some lived in the same or nearby communities, and they all learned to work in sister institutions (UCA and CIAS): supporting each other many times, and contrasting their views on occasion. They experienced persecution; they were constantly forced to clarify their positions and motives; they had to link their theoretical vision to concrete projects, and then evaluate the results with as much objectivity as they could muster, while at the same time teaching, administering, writing, speaking out, and just staying alive.

The community had effective leadership in its presidents: the prestige of Florentino Idoate, which gave credibility to the project early on; the practicality of Luis Achaerandio; the planning skills of Román Mayorga; and the eloquent, creative brilliance of Ignacio Ellacuría. Idoate helped garner funding and resources; Achaerandio consolidated the formation process—university autonomy, the beginnings of a library and classrooms—and laid the groundwork for a community of scholars, both Jesuit and lay; Mayorga strengthened the sense of community, developed new resources such as the IDB loans, and shaped a coherent academic organization; and Ellacuría articulated the vision and applied it, especially in the pages of *ECA,* and later through Cátedra de la Realidad Nacional (University Forum on National Reality) and the media. He also devised so many instruments by which this vision would come to life: CIDAI, the documentation center; IDHUCA, the human rights institute; and IUDOP, the opinion polling center.

Especially in the 1970s there was close rapprochement between the Jesuits and their lay colleagues such as Román Mayorga, Italo López Vallecillo, Axel Soderberg, Eduardo Stein, and Guillermo Ungo. There was usually a small but solid core of other committed Jesuits and lay colleagues who shared the vision and worked together to implement and evaluate it.

They also shared the risks and they encouraged each other in tough times. They chuckled at Father Gondra's penny-pinching, but they appreciated his efforts to stretch out the meager resources of the early years. They battled each other in discussions about the new vision for the university and the Jesuit order at the famous retreat in 1969 and the development of the university organizational manual in the early 1970s, and they gathered together in 1977 at the coffin of their first martyr, Rutilio Grande. They worked closely on a variety of projects, and sometimes took refuge in exile. Especially in the 1970s, they worked together to forge seminal documents and the processes to implement their goals. They were a community.

Historical and International Links

The UCA founders and those who spearheaded its identity change did not have to rely solely on their own wits. Some were members of a religious order with a rich spiritual and academic history, and others had studied at the Jesuit high school in San Salvador. Ignatius of Loyola had formulated his religious insights in the "spiritual exercises" and founded the Society of Jesus (Jesuits) in 1540. By the time of his death in 1556, his followers had become educators in all of Europe, and soon formulated a *ratio studiorum*, an educational vision that required academic discipline and the learner's active participation in the educational process.

The UCA leadership, both Jesuit and lay, came of age in a changing Catholic church after Vatican Council II, Medellín, and Puebla, and a changing Jesuit order after Río, the sociological survey of Jesuit works, the Central American province retreat, and the Thirty-second General Congregation, with its new formulation on the service of the faith and the promotion of justice.

Two of its key members, Ignacio Ellacuría and Jon Sobrino, made internationally recognized contributions to develop a theology for Latin America and the whole Catholic church: liberation theology, a process that combined efforts with other scholars such as Gustavo Gutiérrez of Peru, Juan Luis Segundo of Uruguay, and the Boff brothers of Brazil.

Ignacio Martín-Baró attracted international interest in a "psychology of liberation," which had been discussed in scholarly congresses in the United States, Europe, and Latin America.

When death squads gave the Jesuits a month to leave the country in 1977, heads of state intervened and demanded protection from the Salvadoran government. The United States Congress heard testimony from Miguel Francisco Estrada, and international universities offered honorary degrees and a platform for UCA faculty. These international contacts not only brought protection and encouragement, they also served as sounding boards and funding sources for ideas and formulae, models and experiments.

The National Reality as a Context and Chief Object of Study

From its earliest days, the UCA plunged into the middle of urgent national problems: the 1969 war between El Salvador and Honduras, the teachers' strike, and the fraudulent election of 1972. The country's long-term problems captured its ongoing attention and became the locus of its scholarship, teaching, and social outreach: agrarian and educational reform, political models such as the military/oligarchic alliances in the 1960s and 1970s, the reformist attempt of October 15, 1979, the Duarte and ARENA approaches of the 1980s, and, above all, the urgency for a negotiated political and social solution during the final decade before the assassination.

It began academic programs such as law and communication; it published journals such as *Estudios Centroamericanos (ECA)*, Revista Latinoamericana de Teología, *Proceso, Carta a Las Iglesias,* and others in the fields of business administration, economics, and psychology so as to translate scholarship into policy in a way similar to the "scholarship" model advocated in the Ernest Boyer study explained in the chapter 2. Sometimes the journals were rushed to print with no time to edit, but a sense of urgency saw them glued for many hours to typewriters and later to computers.

UCA cooperated in applied research projects such as *vivienda mínima* (low-cost housing cooperatives), appropriate technology and energy sources, and mass education through dissemination of research in radio programs, and its scholars used their analytical abilities to sift through the myriad events that affected the country on an almost daily basis.

Ellacuría was in constant dialogue with national leaders of various stripes both at home and abroad, from FMLN leader Joaquín Villalobos to Ambassador Jeanne Kirkpatrick. Segundo Montes traveled the nation studying its basic social structures and the violation of human rights, talking to people who suffered these realities in their own flesh. Ignacio Martín-Baró conducted opinion polls, one of the few ways the people of El Salvador could make their views known, and a far more effective way than periodic elections with a narrowly limited gamut of candidates from the right and center right. His contacts in the community provided a context for his psychological research. Luis de Sebastián sketched out elements of a new economic order and Jon Sobrino reflected on all this activity from a theological point of view. Fermín Saínz (psychology), Francisco Ibisate (economics), Nicolás Mariscal (political science), and Jon Cortina (engineering) combined teaching, administration, and pastoral activity.

Segundo Montes (sociology), Ignacio Martín-Baró (psychology), Amando López (theology), and Rodolfo Cardenal (history) supplemented their scholarly activities with pastoral experience outside the university in poor parishes that enriched them personally and reminded them week after week of why they were doing scholarship, teaching, and administering in the first place. They saw poor parishes and university halls as dynamically related to each other, mutually enriching and interdependent. These Jesuits were not ivory-tower scholars out of touch; their scholarship was rooted in the national reality.

A cadre of lay colleagues formed a university community with the Jesuits and brought skills in communication, political analysis, engineering, and economics. They worked for low wages but with deep motivation to capture the national reality and prepare the next generation of professionals who might make a difference in an unjust society.

Required community service programs brought the students into contact with this national reality, and gave them opportunities to use their talents to help solve serious problems in education, engineering, housing, defense of human rights, and, now, in public health.

Christian Inspiration

Luis Achaerandio and his team built independence and autonomy into the model: a special kind of public, and not an official Catholic, university. In 1965, the Salvadoran bishops and the oligarchy wanted a Catholic haven within which their charges could be protected from noxious influences outside. If the UCA had been an official Catholic university from the beginning, it is not hard to imagine how the bishops might have intervened, even dramatically and as early as 1970, when the university began to define itself as an agent for social change, and as a creative and critical conscience for the nation.

It is hardly surprising that Vatican officials and even Jesuit superiors sometimes looked askance at this independence, especially when Ellacuría insisted that the UCA answered only to itself. Even shortly before the assassination, and later in discussions that included the new Jesuits, the relationship between the university and the Society of Jesus came under scrutiny. Should a more tangible link be forged between the two? Should there be more direct control by the provincial superior?

The UCA saw its Christian inspiration as rooted in specific commitments to the poor rather than through juridical control or religious practices. In fact, we saw Ignacio Martín-Baró report on a meeting of Latin American Jesuit universities preoccupied with more strictly religious matters, while ignoring urgent needs of the vast majority, the poor.

The Center for Theological Reflection (CRT) was an effective instrument for the UCA's realization of its mission from the 1970s, and the Archbishop Romero Pastoral Center, the theological library, journals like *Carta a Las Iglesias* and the *Revista Latinoamericana de Teología,* and academic programs all the way from pastoral institutes to master's degrees were seen by the university staff as a contribution to the country's religious life.

With more Jesuit seminarians taking classes at the UCA and serving as spiritual directors, religious reflection groups such as the Christian Life Communities sprang up to answer students' personal religious needs, and there were celebrations of the eucharist on special occasions such as the anniversaries of the martyrs. The UCA became a center for religious renewal and formation, gaining the admiration of more progressive sectors of the church and the suspicions of the more traditional. Some religious orders sent their members for studies at the pastoral center, both for the associate's and the master's programs; others forbade their members to participate.

All in all, however, the Christian inspiration of the university was clear and important.

Academic Standards

The university curriculum was revised in the 1970s to broaden its scope and improve the quality of instruction, especially in areas of social awareness. Students participated in faculty research projects through their graduation theses, tackling problems which were national priorities.

The tightly centralized academic system helped strengthen a unified vision, with all department chairs reporting to the academic vice rector rather than fortifying themselves into separate faculties that might have discouraged research and social outreach and put the most emphasis on teaching and professional preparation. This system worked more effectively when the university was small, but it did get the institution off to a good start in implementing its new vision and using resources according to priorities.

UCA academic standards contrasted with those of the national university and the many private institutions, whose students would come to the UCA library because they usually had no such resources at their own institutions, or because the armed forces had closed off the campus of the University of El Salvador.

Effective Use of Resources

UCA officials and colleagues saw from the beginning that they had to establish a real university with appropriate facilities, even though resources would be limited. They found a suitable location, carefully planned its use, took the risk of incurring debt to build classrooms, offices, laboratories, and a library, and they created a campus which was an oasis from the chaos outside, yet rooted in the national reality.

Then they went through a second stage of investment after much planning, incurred more debt, and made more ambitious plans, with a bold vision of making a national impact via research institutes in key areas such as human rights and a computer center.

Ellacuría spent a fair amount of his time gathering funds in Europe to support the social outreach programs of the UCA.

A differentiated tuition program was established so that lack of funds would not keep out qualified students. As a result, the UCA drew students from a wider socioeconomic range, though these programs did not directly help the very poor because so few of them ever got beyond early elementary school. But many students were able to enter degree programs while working to support themselves and their families.

A great boost to resource strengthening, for example, was an October 1993 grant of $335,000 from the Andrew W. Mellon Foundation to automate the UCA library, and grants for several endowed chairs.

PROBLEMS WITH THE MODEL

We have to distinguish between problems with the model itself, and those due to administrative decisions and lack of resources. Annual faculty salaries of about $7,000 are a problem for the university, and perhaps a comment on university priorities, but not necessarily a defect in the model. The same is true of rundown scientific and engineering labs. We should also distinguish between problems with the model and areas that have not yet been developed because of pressures engendered by more than a decade of civil war. Since it is difficult to distinguish between problems of implementation and those of the model itself, we will make distinctions as we go along.

Governance

The assassination pointed out a glaring problem: overdependence on a few key people rather than sustained development of a multilayered cadre of lay and Jesuit colleagues to implement the model. Take, for example, Ignacio Ellacuría: he was rector, vice rector for social outreach, president of the board of directors, editor of *ECA*, chair of the philosophy department, teacher, and principal spokesman for the UCA in the national and international communities. Ignacio Martín-Baró was academic vice rector, member of the board of directors, chair of the psychology department, director of IUDOP (the polling center), teacher and researcher, and a university spokesman, not to mention weekend pastor in Jayaque. Segundo Montes was superior of the Jesuit community, member of the board of directors, chair of the sociology/political science department, director of IDHUCA (the human rights center), teacher and researcher, and weekend pastor. These three men were the principal presence of the UCA in the public forum. One can just imagine the effect of their assassinations on the university.

The personality of Ignacio Ellacuría gave inspiration and shape to the UCA for so many years, but he did not suffer fools gladly. There was an elegance and an arrogance about him, which was sometimes a compensation for personal shyness. Still, his magnetic eloquence did not encourage challenges from within the UCA. Except for an inner circle of close friends, most colleagues found him an admired yet distant leader. He did not put people down, though his ironic comments sometimes discouraged further dialogue, and he sometimes gave the impression that he would not brook opposition. His natural brilliance made others think twice before speaking up because they stood in such awe of his contributions, and often felt they could not match him. This distance was not something that Ellacuría cultivated or encouraged; it was just the way he was. In many ways this giant was the UCA of the 1980s, and as with a giant oak, not too many trees grow in its vicinity.[2]

The correspondence between the Jesuit provincials and the superior general showed an awareness of the UCA's dependence on Ellacuría in the 1980s, and they had already determined that when he finished his term of office in 1991 someone else was going to be the rector.

The importance of Ellacuría as an individual was intensified structurally by his role as president of a five-person board of directors for a decade, and member for twelve years earlier. He served along with two other martyrs, Montes and Martín-Baró, and in earlier years, for example, with key players such as Estrada, de Sebastián, Mayorga, and longtime board member Ibisate. Every major issue and many minor ones were decided in the weekly board meetings. The circle was somewhat widened by frequent discussions with the UCA II Jesuit community. But all department chairs reported directly to the academic vice rector, which was Martín-Baró during most of the 1980s. All heads of institutes and centers reported directly to Ellacuría, either as rector or as vice rector for social outreach. Although most of the giants are gone, this highly centralized governance model is still in place at the UCA.

Theoretically the higher education council had a role in university governance, but the rector headed this group, too. Its twenty-three–person membership was unwieldy, and discussions often bogged down in reviewing either individual cases petitioning exceptions to academic regulations, or academic program details. This council served an important role as a sounding board on major issues, however, and its suggestions were incorporated into university pronouncements. Nevertheless, the main texts were usually authored by the same few people.

It is not enough to suggest that if there were more and better-prepared people the tasks would have been spread around more evenly. Perhaps they would have, but de facto, there were not many well-prepared people. Which comes first: the chicken or the egg? How do younger staff members grow and take on responsibility when the reins are in the hands of highly respected giants?

Related to this problem was distancing of the younger Jesuit generation of philosophy and theology students as a result of their formation, and communication problems with some of the UCA Jesuits. Right from the noviceship, which lays the groundwork for their spiritual preparation, these young Jesuits are deeply involved in direct pastoral work with the poor, which helps them understand the context for their work—the national realities that Ellacuría felt were so important. But these activities are also time-consuming.

Then these students went to the UCA in Managua for humanities studies and pastoral activities. Conversations with many of these young men give the impression that studies enjoyed little priority. Many aspired to return to direct pastoral work after their studies, and few were attracted to the arduous university vocation that requires lengthy formation and intellectual attitudes and customs. Isolation from the UCA Jesuits intensified this distance and at times erupted in hostility, because younger men felt that the university apostolate had little impact on the daily lives of the poor whom they were encountering in their pastoral activities.

The assassination had a remarkable effect on these attitudes, because it showed that at least the Salvadoran military thought the UCA was having an impact. In addition, as a security measure, the UCA Jesuits, the survivors and the new team members, began to live in five or six different Jesuit communities rather than in one residence by themselves. As a result, much more dialogue began to take place about the "why" of the UCA and its long-range importance for the country and the region.

It is hard to say at this point whether there will be a significant increase in younger Jesuits going to graduate studies, as their predecessors did, to take hold of such an important apostolate. There are good signs with several very talented young men currently in graduate studies, but some of the younger generation wish they had greater say in the choice of study areas. Only time will tell.

There is another, related problem, and it has to do with the attitude toward the intellectual life itself, but this will be discussed in the section on the UCA's academic life.

An extremely important governance issue is the role of the laity. In the 1970s, in the Achaerandio and Mayorga rectorates, there seemed to be a larger number of laypersons in the inner circle. In more recent years, Jesuits have held the major positions and generally kept counsel among themselves. A number of Jesuits and lay colleagues feel that some Jesuits fear that laypeople might take over the university. It should be pointed out, however, that in the early years various political groups, such as the Christian Democrats, and later, the FMLN, tried to influence UCA ideology, and the university had to struggle to maintain independence.

There was less sharing of responsibility with non-Jesuit colleagues in the 1980s as compared to the teams of the 1970s that included important players such as Román Mayorga, Italo López Vallecillo, Eduardo Stein, Guillermo Ungo, Héctor Oqueli Colindres, Axel Soderberg, Héctor Dada, Father Jesús Delgado of the Archdiocese of San Salvador, and others.

In post-assassination discussions some seemed to identify power with influence, recommending as many Jesuits as possible on the board of directors, and decisions discussed in Jesuit meetings first, and then shared with lay colleagues. The martyrs had expressed the fear that there might not be any Jesuit successors available when the time came, and that the UCA might have to rely on laypeople for positions in the future, but except for some annual retreat gatherings, there were few major efforts to share widely the *"mística"* of the UCA, and to prepare and retain lay colleagues.

It is interesting to see the list of projects for funding that Ellacuría brought to European agencies; they tended to be exclusively for social outreach projects such as the human rights institute, the polling center, and university publications. This tendency continued in the immediate aftermath of the assassination with proposals for the radio station and a video center.

Financial problems were not the only reason why the UCA had difficulty retaining lay faculty; the exodus after the 1979 coup and threats against the lives of faculty members in the 1970s and 1980s also had a devastating and cumulative effect.

The 1975–1981 planning process gave high priority to investment in specialized training for faculty and staff. A good number received this training but did not stay long at the UCA once they had fulfilled their minimal service obligation. Some even asked to be relieved of this teaching and research requirement. They said they could not live on UCA salaries; critics responded that they lacked *"mística"* and had been lured away by higher salaries. Disenchanted faculty responded that in addition to low salaries, they often felt they were not taken seriously as professionals and colleagues, and that they were seen as a threat to Jesuit hegemony.

Foundations tend not to fund basic items such as faculty and staff salaries, but, conscious of the importance of lay colleagues, the UCA might have dedicated more resources to preparation of creative proposals for funding, so that faculty could meet basic expenses and talented colleagues would not have had to choose between the UCA and much better-paying positions in the private sector

The crucial problems affecting the country partially explain the concentration on social outreach programs and the deemphasis on building university infrastructure—teaching, research, and salaries. But the gravity of this infrastructure problem became even more clear after the assassination, when major United States foundations were ready to finance UCA research and community action programs but there was a considerable shortage of qualified personnel to design and engage in these projects. One observer said that when the house is on fire, you do not have much time to plan for the future, and the house was often on fire. In fact, the whole country was on fire, and the UCA had had to address life-and-death issues of a very immediate and important nature, therefore spending less time on administrative and day-to-day academic questions.

Despite these short-term critical concerns, however, we have seen in the late 1970s and early 1980s how the UCA spent much time thinking creatively about national problems and the future: for example, the need for a negotiated settlement of the war, the importance of getting at the root causes of injustice, and the dramatic need for construction of new educational and justice systems.

The lack of a critical mass of Jesuit and lay personnel in the mid-1990s to realize the UCA mission, however, is very serious. Perhaps with progress in the peace process, however, the UCA will give more importance to these issues and strengthen its personnel so as to respond with competence and creativity to new challenges.

Academic Programs

The original fields chosen for study were the practical ones of economics, business administration, and engineering. In the Salvadoran educational system, with the few existing resources and scarce personnel needed for many fields, the curriculum focuses almost exclusively on courses appropriate to individual disciplines. At the UCA, as we have seen, there were courses on national social problems, and offerings in philosophy, theology, and some social sciences. But if the university offered courses in general education, history, and humanities, they were mainly general surveys. A pragmatic educational philosophy pervades the curriculum, and students tend to take courses linked closely with immediate career application.

In contrast with Cardinal Newman's "idea of a university," UCA vision statements give little importance to knowledge as a value in itself. The litmus test is usually the *"realidad nacional"* and the country's grave problems, and their urgency certainly helps make such an emphasis understandable. But we saw Yale's President Giamatti prizing knowledge first as a value in itself, because in and through its intrinsic value, knowledge can then go beyond itself, becoming a social value and a way of preparing students to transform knowledge into beneficial projects and policies.

One sometimes hears the phrase "beyond academic excellence" used to suggest the priority of education's moral and social implications. But the problem with this approach is that it encourages short-term decisions about the "usefulness" of learning, and gives importance to what seems immediately significant. The UCA must address this form of pragmatism and consider its implications.[3]

One strong point of the UCA approach, however, is that it recognizes the "reality" dimension of any excellent education—hands-on contact with the world as it is, rather than an isolated, textbook view. Many educational programs add community service to their curriculum, and some, like Santa Clara University in California, integrate community involvement into specific courses through programs like the East Side Project. This is a fruitful area for development.

But how does the national reality actually pervade the curriculum when, until recently, there was little review of the curriculum, when courses concentrate on the technical specifics of the professional field, and when there is little or no supervision of what actually happens in the classroom? Integrating seminars at the end of the educational process would be very helpful, but the vast majority of students do not stay in the university long enough to write a thesis.

There is also a need to reexamine the role of the thesis, which for many students is a great burden rather than a synthesis of their previous learning or the integration of ethical or national reality questions in a systematic and less rhetorical way. The University of El Salvador has already changed the thesis requirement for graduation.

Related to the problem of attitudes toward the intellectual life is that of pedagogy, or educational methodologies. So many UCA faculty members rely on lectures as the only format for learning. Students dutifully take notes during class, as teachers often read from their own notes. Because of the departure of more experienced faculty, the university has often hired recent UCA graduates and even students who have not yet completed their graduation theses. As a result, young, inexperienced teachers tend to repeat the faulty methods to which they themselves have been subjected.

The need to work long hours to cover basic living expenses leaves students little time for study outside class hours, and the lack of sufficient reading materials means that learning is often limited to what the students hear from the teachers in class.

Up until 1994, there was little teacher orientation in basic methodology and in the very philosophy of the UCA. In some departments, such as business administration and sections of engineering, there is little discussion of ethical and values questions so important in the UCA philosophy. Instead, teachers and students mainly concern themselves with the basics of their professions and do not look beyond the classroom to the community the UCA seeks to serve.

In 1993, the UCA began to look at the curriculum as a whole, and to develop more dynamic pedagogical methods with the assistance of a new education department.

Much improvisation was understandable in wartime when it was amazing that so much was accomplished with so few resources while under the pressure of threats and attacks. But the result is also a considerable gap between the rhetoric and the reality of the UCA. Many academic programs need revision and faculty members need updating in content and pedagogical methodology for the UCA model to be more functional and realize its great potential. Such weaknesses make it difficult to act "in a university fashion." And it should be no consolation that the other universities are worse.

A number of young Jesuit seminarians share this utilitarian approach to the intellectual life and, as was indicated earlier, some give studies little priority in comparison with direct pastoral work. Several talented young Jesuits have said they felt they were swimming upstream in efforts to encourage intellectual development and hopes for graduate studies.

On the other hand, some feel there is now preparation of a new generation of Jesuit scholars to tackle structural problems. While it is true that young Jesuits have begun to see the value of additional studies after ordination, when they start to work with day-to-day community problems and see their structural causes, it is difficult to start to develop intellectual attitudes and habits after the age of thirty.

The role of science and technology is another area for future growth of the UCA. With such stress on explicit social issues, little effort has been spent on the social impact of technology—health, environment, energy, and industrial and agricultural development. UCA engineering and science labs have fallen into disrepair. Some faculty have just begun to introduce computers into these technical fields.

At times the UCA has tried to begin graduate programs in areas such as political science, education, and economics without sufficient faculty prepared in these fields at the doctoral level. The UCA looked seriously at establishing a medical school even though science labs were deficient and the university had few prepared faculty in the natural sciences. Once again, the coming of peace should give more time for planning and preparation in crucial areas for the country.

It is important to realize, however, that the UCA's potential for helping create solutions to the country's problems is seriously weakened in the mid-1990s, because it lacks a critical mass of staff trained at the doctoral or other terminal degree levels. It will be very difficult to act in a university fashion if there is not a significant increase in faculty prepared for teaching and research by the beginning of the twenty-first century.

Christian Inspiration

The UCA commitment to the poor has been a very effective form of Christian witness; for example, through publications and degree programs in theology. But some feel that religious celebrations, especially the eucharist, should receive higher priority. Archbishop Romero and Jesuit superiors have urged the university to devote more resources to this more specifically religious goal. Perhaps to distinguish itself from those "Christian" universities that faithfully offered pastoral services, but left justice questions on the shelf, the UCA is only now beginning to develop these aspects of the model.

There were few personnel available for these academic and spiritual tasks when life-and-death questions called for elaborating courageous public statements. In the early 1990s, however, the UCA has accelerated the development of pastoral activities that complement academic tasks without neglecting other commitments to the community. There is now a full-time layperson on the staff, monthly masses and other religious activities and conferences, and a university parish was established in late 1994. But much remains to be done.

Besides religious practices, there are important concerns like the dialogue between religion and culture, reflection on the ethical implications of business and legal practices, and a bevy of other questions to which a university of Christian inspiration might turn in the postwar period. This is a whole field to which the UCA has not had the leisure to turn because of the civil war, the shortage of prepared staff, and other urgent issues. But these questions will be an important part of the UCA's shift to *"anunciar,"* with less emphasis on *"denunciar,"* in the 1990s and into the next century.

Students

Because of urgent concerns mentioned earlier, the UCA has sometimes seen students as a "necessary evil," sources of limited income rather than potential agents of change. The UCA must now ask itself: Who will implement the solutions and policies elaborated by the university? Because of persecution, many socially aware graduates had to flee for their lives; others decided to join the armed struggle. But now, if a really new political climate takes root in El Salvador, how can the UCA better prepare its graduates to take leadership roles in the community?

The whole gamut of student services so common in the universities of more affluent nations are largely inappropriate in the developing world, but the university must decide what types of programs are necessary for the UCA to develop so that a cadre of academically prepared women and men with deeply rooted values and commitment to bring about a just society in El Salvador can emerge.

The university must also face the dropout rate. At least one-fourth of the students never get beyond the first year of university studies, and only one-fourth ever graduate. Serious consideration must be given to developing bridge programs that link elementary and secondary schools with the university. Too often, academic failures have been attributed just to inadequate preparation of the students, without sufficient study of the socioeconomic reasons why so many students are poorly prepared. There are indications of a high correlation between socioeconomic class and academic survival. Much more time and resources must be dedicated to developing cooperative programs that join all levels of education in a common project. If the UCA sees a potential student for the first time at the entrance examination, then the battle is already lost for the vast majority of potential candidates, and much talent and time is wasted.

Regional Cooperation

With civil wars raging in El Salvador and Nicaragua, and with extermination of indigenous peoples and violation of other human rights in Guatemala, each university in the Jesuit tradition has understandably tended to focus on problems in its own country. The CIAS think-tank team has kept a more regional perspective, and now there is greater cooperation between the El Salvador and Managua campuses. But this is an area for much greater development now that the beginnings of peace are a reality, and conversations have already begun for greater cooperation between these two universities.

Xabier Gorostiaga, in his *La Nueva Generación Centroamericana: La UCA hacia el 2000,* sees a potential era of cooperation between the UCA of El Salvador and the UCA in Nicaragua, of which he is rector.[4] He stresses the importance of preparing highly competent professionals with a social vision who can make practical applications of technology to regional problems. He does not want to see developing nations relegated to being merely the source of raw materials, and surrendering technological and informational development to wealthier nations.

He asks pertinent questions, such as "what significance is there in preparing 'successful' professionals in a sea of poverty, for a civilization and a society that is every day more exclusive, unstable and less governable?" (14). He calls instead for "bridge persons who have the capacity to create forums and communication links among different local experiences, and to promote experimentation among them, to create viable national programs which take local experiments as a point of departure" (19). He sees "productive transformation with equity" as the ideal (21). There is much to be said for regional cooperation now that wars are suspended.

IMPLICATIONS OF THE MODEL

What might a university run by the Jesuits and their colleagues in Latin America's smallest country have to say to universities elsewhere? Because of its urgent situation, the UCA staff has been forced back to basics so very often, and consequently the model they developed under pressure has much to say to other universities asking fundamental questions. Strengths of the model can help put into relief the same complicated issues faced by other universities, such as *why* does the institution exist in the first place, and *whom* does it really serve?

And yet there are limitations and underdeveloped sectors in the model, which need attention if the UCA itself is going to realize its potential on behalf of the Salvadoran people. UCA dialogue with other universities can be mutually beneficial; no institution should feel pressured to adopt an outside model. With its strengths and weaknesses, the UCA suggests a number of areas for reflection.

Vision

A university must have a clear, well-articulated vision or mission statement which is reviewed regularly and shared by key personnel. It should highlight central university features; for example:

(a)   The communities the university wishes to serve, and how the university will relate to them—the "national reality" so important for the UCA.

(b)   The faith vision, tradition, and values system that motivate the institution, and an examination of ways by which these are made operational in all aspects of the institution's life.

(c)   The fields of interest which the university chooses to offer and why, and the curriculum vision that will tie the programs all together.

(d)   The pedagogy to be employed: dynamic, active learning.

So often the vision or mission statements are printed in the university catalog and forgotten, and then contradictions creep in as faculty and staff are recruited without taking this vision into consideration, or programs are adopted mainly because a market exists. For example, some departments look mainly at a faculty candidate's academic credentials without also probing in more detail the values and priorities of the prospective colleague. In no way does this goal mean that all faculty members should think alike; a variety of traditions enriches the institution and helps clarify what it is all about. But indifference or opposition to the basic mission could seriously impair the university's ability to implement its vision, and tacking on programs far from the core of the mission might produce badly needed revenue, but could lead to weakening of the institution's basic thrust.

A number of universities offer simple but attractive orientation programs in which faculty members learn more about the traditions and values of the institution and how they can contribute to the development of these traditions. When faculty share the institution's basic values, they tend to pick colleagues with these values implicitly in mind. Preservation of an institution's vision is not the sole responsibility of administrators.

Having a clear vision of what the university wants to accomplish seems a truism, but the regularly reexamined UCA vision enabled the university to make decisions based on priorities; to fend off opposition from military governments, zealous revolutionaries, and wary ecclesiastical superiors; and to resist persecution and survive even exile and assassination— they learned to distinguish the essential from the expendable.

Development of the UCA organizational manual in the early 1970s and the 1978–1979 process that produced "Las Funciones Fundamentales de la Universidad y su Operativización" involved the whole university community and clarified the university's sense of direction in times of crisis. The war interrupted follow-up and most university activity concentrated on advocacy of a negotiated settlement to the national crisis. Then there was the devastation of the assassination. The UCA of the mid-1990s can learn from its own history.

Consistency of Rhetoric and Action

A university must determine who are the ultimate beneficiaries of its labors. The UCA decided not to be a haven for the well-to-do nor to protect them from "evils" rampant at the national university. It chose to benefit the poor, but it also had to face the reality that many poor people do not even finish elementary school, never mind come to a university. Therefore, the poor would have to be the ultimate beneficiaries through the mediation of others who were fortunate enough to gain a higher place on the country's educational pyramid. But it is not hard to get caught up in the daily tasks of teaching, administering, and researching, and thus lose sight of this ultimate goal.

Another way of putting the question is: Does the university prepare agents of change or more humane oppressors? Will its graduates leave unjust structures intact or will they be prepared and motivated to make a difference? Or, more realistically, will a sufficient percentage achieve the hopes the university has for them and for the communities they should be serving? It is so easy just to concentrate on educating the people who come to classes or seminars rather than look at the potential or real outcomes of this educational activity.

Working toward consistency between rhetoric and action is a real strength of the UCA—making the poor the focus of all its activities, and doing so in a university fashion.

J. Dean Brackley, S.J., UCA faculty member, puts it this way:[5] "Today, in the face of massive and morally unnecessary poverty and death, of unspeakable suffering of the innocent, the Church and the Christian university must declare: the option for the poor is essential to the search for truth and the unmasking of lies"(10).

He adds that "the university does not fulfill its function today unless it allows its students to break out of their narrow world, to broaden their horizons and formulate the questions they really need for a university education worthy of the name. Middle-class students need the poor more than the poor need them" (13).

Such a task is not easy. "A university committed in this way to the liberation of the poor, and therefore to the humanization of the world, must be prepared to give up the debilitating and compromising lust for prestige which leaves us beholden to the government and the military and panting after reactionary board members solely because of the money they can bring in. Let us help create Christian and humanist alumni committed to the transformation of the world" (17).

Planning

It is important to identify resources needed for realization of the vision, and to determine the steps necessary to achieve it. Sometimes the UCA did this effectively, and at other times, as we have seen, it did not.

The UCA reexamined its goals in the light of its vision, and from the very beginning planned facilities, fields of study, and media by which the outcomes would be shared with the larger communities. Contracting the Inter-American Development Bank loans and laying a strong foundation for the university made a crucial difference later on: a good library, documentation services, and research/action institutes in crucial areas such as human rights.

And yet a lack of planning has weakened the university, too: concentration of responsibility on a small group of key persons who make most decisions, only sporadic financial planning for staff retention and for loan repayments, underestimating the resources needed for graduate and professional education, and neglect of scientific and technological facilities.

Planning means more than elaboration of lengthy documents with lofty rhetoric and little relationship to real needs and available resources. Planning is, to some extent, a state of mind, an attitude, a commitment to keeping the bigger picture in view, and then translating it into creative programs that are reviewed periodically. Planning is difficult when bombs are exploding in the computer center, but such occurrences have a way of forcing educators back to the basics: Why did we come here in the first place, and why do we stay? Or how can we achieve our goals and still keep the institution open? What are the consequences five years from now of the decisions made today: the opportunity costs, the latent effects?

Part of this planning process is the identification of resources. For the UCA, keeping well-trained, highly motivated staff became a problem because of persecution, failure to integrate colleagues into governance of the project, and the gap between UCA salaries and outside opportunities. There was attrition that seemed to go unperceived over time, and deterioration of the community spirit that had energized the 1970s, until their effects became blatant with the assassination. So, planning is essential for survival of the institution and for preservation and realization of its mission.

The UCA itself needs to develop a new statement of purpose, as it did in 1978–1979, and initiate a planning process like that of the mid-1970s, which prepared for the second IDB loan. Otherwise it will be handicapped in its efforts to act "in a university fashion," and to change its mode of dialogue to match changing national conditions and new opportunities.

Community Spirit Is Essential

Whether the university is a relatively small one in a developing country or a large one in an urban center in the United States, there must be a community spirit that includes a critical mass of talented and dedicated colleagues who coordinate the administration and planning of the institution. This spirit must be shared throughout the institution.

The UCA was at its most creative when it functioned as a team of Jesuits and lay colleagues who lived out a common mission and enjoyed an esprit de corps. The many social, liturgical, and educational gatherings of the 1970s fostered such a community spirit. The UCA became less effective during the 1980s when the university had different priorities because of the crisis that engulfed the nation. This lesson was even more evident after the assassination, when profound effects of the killings were not confronted realistically and there were few meetings of the survivors and the newcomers to form community.

The most recent congregation of the Jesuit order, the thirty-fourth, reaffirmed the importance of close collaboration between Jesuits and their lay colleagues and called upon Jesuits to welcome such collaboration as essential to effective institutions.[6]

Institutional size will affect the format of such a community spirit, and it will probably function in concentric circles. But the more these levels relate to and seek nourishment from each other and from a common sense of purpose as expressed in their seminal documents, the more likely it is that they will succeed in implementing their goals.

The National Reality as Context and Focus

The UCA has made a serious contribution to an understanding of how to integrate the academic life of a university and the everyday life of the community it wishes to serve, both by offering a platform for discussion of crucial national or regional issues, especially when no other forums existed, and by sending its students into the communities for service that was integral to what was happening in the classroom. The civil war put limitations on student community involvement, but this dimension of education was still seen as an integral part of the model itself.

Many UCA publications and some research centered on national problems, and the university saw itself in a dynamic relationship with the nation. Such a role can perhaps be accomplished more easily in a country like El Salvador, which is the size of Massachusetts, but size is not the most important factor—it depends on a mentality, an awareness and sharing of mission, and development of resources to accomplish the goals.

United States universities are now giving more importance to student community service, and groups such as the Jesuit Volunteer Corps, its international counterpart, and similar organizations offer opportunities for at least a year of service after graduation. Some universities give academic credit for service related to specific courses in the curriculum. But many faculty members and administrators still see such programs as "extras," or "social activism" unrelated and possibly detrimental to the real business of a university. While there will probably never be quite the same sense of urgency for an integral relationship between a United States university and its surrounding or national community, nevertheless, the UCA model suggests the potential for such relationships that can be mutually beneficial for the university and the community.

SOME FINAL REFLECTIONS

As we said in the beginning, the UCA story is fascinating in itself—thirty whirlwind years that saw changes in orientation, the high price of commitment, the development of a university model that brings to life social change and liberation, and the gaps that occur between rhetoric and reality. The starkness of both the vision and the reality forces us to pause and look critically at what we do in universities all over the world, and to examine honestly the ultimate effects of what we do: Who are the beneficiaries, and are we consistent in our goals and our outcomes?

NOTES

1. In Hassett and Lacey, eds., Philip Berryman, trans., 177–207.

2. Juan Hernández Pico says, however, that from his time as delegate for formation of the Central American region, and through his years at UCA, Ellacuría "took pride in defying people to tell him when he had been unjust to those under his authority. He said that much of what was [said] about his arrogance referred to his dealings with persons who had either religious or political power over him." Correspondence with the author, July 1993.

3. Juan Hernández Pico says that "'instrumentalism' does not do justice to the broad vision of knowledge in, say, Ellacuría, Sobrino, or Martín-Baró. I personally heard Ellacuría vindicate, just one year before he died, the urgency of attracting young Jesuits not only to social sciences, theology, or philosophy, but also to physical sciences, the law, literature, and so on." He also adds that "I do not see pragmatism. I do see the fundamental choice of having value-bound learning." Correspondence with the author, July 1993.

4. Xabier Gorostiaga, *La Nueva Generación Centroamericana: La UCA hacia*

el 2000 (Managua: Imprenta de la UCA, 1993). Page references are in the text.

5. J. Dean Brackley, *The Christian University and Liberation: The Challenge of the UCA,* (St. Louis: Institute of Jesuit Sources, 1992). Page references in the text.

6. Society of Jesus, "The Interim Documents of General Congregation 34 of the Society of Jesus," *National Jesuit News,* special section, April 1995, 28–31.

SELECT BIBLIOGRAPHY

PRIMARY SOURCES

ASJCA   Archives of the Society of Jesus, Central American Province, San Salvador, El Salvador.

AUCA   Archives of the University of Central America, José Simeón Cañas (UCA), San Salvador, El Salvador.

ECA   *Estudios Centroamericanos*

RUCA   Correspondence file of the university rector, Archives of the UCA.

SECONDARY SOURCES

Abbott, Walter, ed. *The Documents of Vatican II.* New York: Association Press and America Press, 1966.

Altbach, Philip G. *Higher Education in the Third World: Themes and Variations.* Buffalo: State University of New York, 1993.

Anderson, Thomas P. *La Matanza.* Lincoln: University of Nebraska Press, 1971.

———. *The War of the Dispossessed: Honduras and El Salvador, 1969.* Lincoln: University of Nebraska Press, 1981.

Arnson, Cynthia. *Crossroads: Congress, the President and Central America, 1976–1993.* 2nd ed. University Park: Pennsylvania State University Press, 1993.

Baloyra, Enrique A. *El Salvador in Transition.* Chapel Hill: University of North Carolina Press, 1982.

Bangert, William V. *A History of the Society of Jesus.* 2nd ed. St. Louis: Institute of Jesuit Sources, 1986.

Beirne, Charles J. "Jesuit Education for Justice: The Colegio in El Salvador, 1968–1984," *Harvard Educational Review* 55 (1985): 1–19.

———. "Latin American Bishops of the First Vatican Council, 1869–1870," *The Americas* 25 (1969): 265–80.

———. *The Problem of Americanization in the Catholic Schools of Puerto Rico.* San Juan: Editorial Universitaria, 1975.

Berryman, Philip. *The Religious Roots of Rebellion: Christians in Central American Revolutions.* New York: Orbis, 1984.

Bethell, Leslie, ed. *Central America Since Independence.* Cambridge, England: Cambridge University Press, 1991.

Bonner, Raymond. *Weakness and Deceit: U.S. Policy and El Salvador.* New York: Times Books, 1985.

Boyer, Ernest L. *Scholarship Reconsidered.* Princeton: Carnegie Foundation for the Advancement of Teaching, 1990.

Brackley, J. Dean. *The Christian University and Liberation.* St. Louis: Institute of Jesuit Sources, 1992.

Brockett, Charles D. *Land, Power and Poverty: Agrarian Transformation and Political Conflict in Central America.* Boston: Unwin Hyman, 1990.

Brockman, James E. *Romero: A Life.* Rev. ed. New York: Orbis, 1989.

Bulmer-Thomas, Victor. *The Political Economy of Central America Since 1920.* Cambridge, England: Cambridge University Press, 1987.

Cabarrús, Carlos. *Génesis de una Revolución: Análisis de la organización campesina en El Salvador.* Mexico City: Ediciones De Casa Chata, 1983.

Cardenal, Rodolfo. *Historia de una Esperanza: Vida de Rutilio Grande.* San Salvador: UCA Editores, 1986.

―――. "The Martyrdom of the Salvadoran Church." In *Church and Politics in Latin America,* edited by Dermot Keogh. Hampshire, England: Macmillan, 1990. 225–46.

―――. *El Poder Eclesiástico en El Salvador (1871–1931).* San Salvador: UCA Editores, 1980.

CELAM (Conferencia Episcopal Latinoamericana). *The Church in the Present Day Transformation of Latin America in the Light of the Council.* 2 vols. Bogotá: CELAM, 1970.

Cleary, Edward L., and Hannah Stewart-Gambino, eds. *Conflict and Competition: The Latin American Church in a Changing Environment.* Boulder: Lynne Reinner, 1992.

Doggett, Martha. *A Death Foretold: The Jesuit Murders in El Salvador.* Washington: Georgetown University Press, 1993.

Donohue, John W. *Jesuit Education: An Essay on the Foundation of Its Idea.* New York: Fordham University Press, 1963.

Duarte, José Napoleón. *Duarte: My Story.* New York: Putnam, 1986.

Dulles, Avery. *Models of the Church.* Garden City, NY: Doubleday, 1974.

Eagleson, John, and Philip Scharper, eds. *Puebla and Beyond.* New York: Orbis, 1979.

Ellacuría, Ignacio. *Freedom Made Flesh.* New York: Orbis, 1976.

―――. *Veinte Años de Historia en El Salvador 1969–1989: Escritos Políticos.* 3 vols. San Salvador: UCA Editores, 1991.

Freire, Paulo. *Education for a Critical Consciousness.* New York: Seabury, 1974.

―――. *Pedagogy of the Oppressed.* New York: Seabury, 1971.

Ganss, George E. *Saint Ignatius' Idea of a Jesuit University: A Study in the History of Catholic Education.* 2nd ed. Milwaukee: Marquette University Press, 1956.

Giamatti, A. Bartlett. *A Free and Ordered Space.* New York: Norton, 1988.

Gutiérrez, Gustavo. *A Theology of Liberation: History, Politics, and Salvation.* Rev. ed. New York: Orbis, 1988.

Hassett, John, and Hugh Lacey. *Towards a Society That Serves Its People: The Intellectual Contribution of El Salvador's Murdered Jesuits.* Washington: Georgetown University Press, 1991.

Hebblethwaite, Peter. *The Runaway Church: Post-Conciliar Growth or Decline.* New York: Seabury, 1970.

Hennelly, Alfred T. *Liberation Theology: A Documentary History.* New York: Orbis, 1990.

Hennelly, Alfred T., and John Langan. *Human Rights in the Americas: The Struggle for Consensus.* Washington: Georgetown University Press, 1982.

Hennesey, James. *American Catholics.* Oxford: Oxford University Press, 1981.

―――. *The First Council of the Vatican: The American Experience.* New York: Herder and Herder, 1963.

Hernández Pico, Juan, César Jerez, et al. *El Salvador: Año Político, 1971–72.* San Salvador: UCA Editores, 1973.

Hesburgh, Theodore. *The Challenge and Promise of a Catholic University*. Notre Dame, IN: University of Notre Dame Press, 1994.

Ignatius of Loyola. *The Constitutions of the Society of Jesus*. Translated with an introduction and a commentary by George E. Ganss. St. Louis: Institute of Jesuit Sources, 1970.

———. *The Spiritual Exercises*. Trans. David L. Fleming. St. Louis: Institute of Jesuit Sources, 1975.

John Paul II. "The Apostolic Constitution on Catholic Universities." *Origins* 20 (1990): 265–76.

Keogh, Dermot, ed. *Church and Politics in Latin America*. Hampshire, England: Macmillan, 1990.

Ker, Ian. *The Achievement of John Henry Newman*. Notre Dame, IN: University of Notre Dame Press, 1990.

———. *John Henry Newman: A Biography*. Oxford: Clarendon Press, 1988.

Langan, John P., ed. *Catholic Universities in Church and Society: A Dialogue on "Ex Corde Ecclesia."* Washington: Georgetown University Press, 1993.

Leahy, William P. *Adapting to America: Catholics, Jesuits and Higher Education in the Twentieth Century*. Washington: Georgetown University Press, 1991.

Lernoux, Penny. *The Cry of the People*. New York: Doubleday, 1980.

———. *People of God: The Struggle for World Catholicism*. New York: Viking, 1989.

Levine, Daniel H., ed. *Churches and Politics in Latin America*. Beverly Hills: Sage, 1980.

———, ed. *Religion and Political Conflict in Latin America*. Chapel Hill: University of North Carolina Press, 1986.

Levy, Daniel C. *Higher Education and the State in Latin America: Private Challenges to Public Dominance*. Chicago: University of Chicago Press, 1986.

Lindo-Fuentes, Hector. *Weak Foundations: The Economy of El Salvador in the Nineteenth Century, 1821–1898*. Berkeley: University of California Press, 1990.

López Trujillo, Alfonso. "Análisis marxista y liberación cristiana." *Tierra Nueva* 4 (1973): 5–43.

Lourié, Sylvain. *Education and Development: Strategies and Decisions in Central America*. Stoke-on-Trent, England: Trentham Books, UNESCO, 1989.

MacLeod, Munro J. *Spanish Central America: A Socioeconomic History, 1520–1720*. Berkeley: University of California Press, 1973.

Maier, Joseph, and Richard W. Weatherhead, eds. *The Latin American University*. Albuquerque: University of New Mexico Press, 1977.

Martín-Baró, Ignacio. *Acción e Ideología: Psicología Social desde Centroamerica*. San Salvador: UCA Editores, 1983.

———. *Writings for a Liberation Psychology*. Eds. Adrianne Aron and Shawn Corne. Cambridge, MA: Harvard University Press, 1994.

Mayorga, Román. *La Universidad para el Cambio Social*. 3rd ed. San Salvador: UCA Editores, 1976.

McGinn, Noel. "Autonomía, dependéncia y la misión de la universidad." *Estudios Sociales* 25, 3 (1980): 121–34.

McGovern, Arthur. *Marxism: An American Christian Perspective*. New York: Orbis, 1981.

Mecham, J. Lloyd. *Church and State in Latin America*. Rev. ed. Chapel Hill: University of North Carolina Press, 1966.

Moncada-Davidson, Lillian. *Education and Social Change: The Case of El Salvador*. Unpublished dissertation. Teachers College, Columbia University, 1990.

Montgomery, Tommie Sue. *Revolution in El Salvador: Origins and Evolution*. Rev. ed. Boulder, CO: Westview, 1982, revised 1994.

Newman, John Henry. *The Idea of a University*. Ed. Martin J. Svaglic. New York: Holt, Rinehart and Winston, 1960.

O'Malley, John W. *The First Jesuits*. Cambridge, MA: Harvard University Press, 1993.

Pelikan, Jaroslav. *The Idea of the University: A Reexamination.* New Haven: Yale University Press, 1992.

Reimers, Fernando, ed. *La Educacíon en El Salvador De Cara Al Siglo XXI: Disafios y Oportunidades.* San Salvador: UCA Editores, 1995.

Romero, Oscar. *Voice of the Voiceless: The Four Pastoral Letters and Other Statements.* New York: Orbis, 1985.

Salmi, Jamil, et al. *Higher Education: The Lessons of Experience.* Washington: World Bank, 1994.

Sanks, T. Howland. *Salt, Leaven, and Light: The Community Called Church.* New York: Crossroad, 1992.

Smith, Brian H. *The Church and Politics in Chile: Challenges to Modern Catholicism.* Princeton: Princeton University Press, 1982.

Sobrino, Jon. *Christology at the Crossroads.* Trans. John Drury. New York: Orbis, 1978.

Sobrino, Jon, et al. *Companions of Jesus: The Jesuit Martyrs of El Salvador.* Trans. Sally Hanlon. New York: Orbis, 1990.

Society of Jesus. *Documents of the 31st and 32nd General Congregations of the Society of Jesus.* Ed. John W. Padberg. St. Louis: Institute of Jesuit Sources, 1977.

Stein, Stanley, and Barbara Stein. *The Colonial Heritage of Latin America.* New York: Oxford University Press, 1970.

Torres, Carlos Alberto. *The Church, Society, and Hegemony: A Critical Sociology of Religion in Latin America.* Trans. Richard A. Young. Westport, CT: Praeger, 1992.

Torres, Carlos Alberto, and Daniel A. Morales-Gómez, eds. *Education, Policy and Social Change: Experiences from Latin America.* Westport, CT: Praeger, 1992.

Torres Rivas, Edelberto. *Central America.* New York: Monthly Review Press, 1989.

Universidad Centroamericana (UCA). *Plan Quinquenal, 1977–81.* San Salvador: UCA Editores, 1976.

———. *Planteamiento Universitario, 1989.* San Salvador: UCA Editores, 1989.

Whitfield, Teresa. *Paying the Price: Ignacio Ellacuría and the Murdered Jesuits of El Salvador.* Philadelphia: Temple University Press, 1995.

Woodward, Ralph Lee, Jr. *Central America: A Nation Divided.* 2nd ed. New York: Oxford University Press, 1985.

Wortman, Miles L. *Government and Society in Central America, 1680–1840.* New York: Columbia University Press, 1982.

Index

Page numbers in boldface indicate primary discussion.